EARLY NUTRITION
AND
LATER DEVELOPMENT

EARLY NUTRITION
AND
LATER DEVELOPMENT

Edited by
A W Wilkinson

A PITMAN MEDICAL PUBLICATION
Distributed by
YEAR BOOK MEDICAL PUBLISHERS, INC.
35 E. Wacker Drive, Chicago

First published 1976

© Pitman Medical Publishing Co Ltd, 1976

Distributed in Continental North, South and Central America, Hawaii, Puerto Rico and The Philippines by YEAR BOOK MEDICAL PUBLISHERS, INC.

(ISBN 0–8151–9320–3)

(Library of Congress Catalog Card No: 76–4620)

by arrangement with PITMAN MEDICAL PUBLISHING CO LTD

Reproduced and printed by photolithography and bound in Great Britain at The Pitman Press, Bath

Foreword

The provision of enough food for the increasing population of the world is the greatest material problem which faces mankind today. Improvements in the control of what were formerly endemic diseases like smallpox, plague and malaria without control of the birth rate means the nutritional problem can only increase. The future well being and mental and physical development of a child may be greatly influenced by the way in which it is fed and the quality of the food it receives in the days soon after birth and in this way paediatricians have a lasting responsibility far beyond their immediate interest in the baby. In this book eighteen authors of widely different backgrounds review various aspects of the effects of nutrition in early life in a number of species other than man on later development. Although the emphasis in it is on human nutrition there is much interesting information about early nutrition in other mammals which contributes to our knowledge and understanding of early nutrition during pregnancy and soon after birth.

All mammals suckle their young, whether they are harvest mice or 90 ton blue whales, but there are enormous differences in the number of young born of one pregnancy, their individual and collective weights at birth and the rate at which they grow soon after birth. It is not surprising, therefore, that there are very big differences in the composition of the milk produced by the mammary glands of different species.

There are considerable morphological species differences in the structure and function of the placenta but there is still too little information about the relationship between placental function and fetal growth and well being in man.

The factors which affect fetal growth and determine size at birth are discussed as well as the nutritional endowments at birth and the development and use of glycogen stores and glucose homeostasis soon after birth and the storage, supply and utilisation of fatty acids. Even the baby born at full term is in some respects biochemically immature and drug kinetics in the neonate are much different to those in the older child or adult, but there are at any age important relationships between nutrition and some drugs.

Recently there has been renewed interest in breast feeding and the physiological, immunological and psychological aspects are discussed together with the choice of an artificial milk and its possible effects on the composition of the body of the baby. There are often difficult clinical problems in the nutrition of the very small premature infant and these are accentuated when the baby is born also with an anomaly of the intestinal tract which requires emergency surgical treatment just after birth. The effects of such operations in human neonates and in piglets may be very severe.

Too much food may be almost as bad for the baby and young child as too little and may have adverse effects in early life or in old age but these are difficult to study in man except for short periods. Food intake may also be markedly affected by variations in appetite and family habits. Much important information has been derived from the study of the effects of the treatment of infants with severe malnutrition associated with marasmus and Kwashiorkor. There appears to be an important connection between breast feeding and resistance to infection, and 'weaning diarrhoea' in some countries may be largely due to the substitution of an artificial milk for breast feeding with the consequent greater risk of contamination of poorer quality milk. This book describes many nutritional problems and shows where even more may lie and for some it proposes possible answers.

A W WILKINSON

Contents

List of Contributors

Mr G Chamberlain
MD, FRCS, MRCOG

Queen Charlotte's Hospital, Goldhawk Road, London, W6, England

Dr J S Garrow
MB, ChB, MD, MRCPE, PhD

Clinical Research Centre, Watford Road, Harrow, Middlesex, England

Dr M Gunther
MB, BChir, MA, MD

77 Ember Lane, Esher, Surrey, England

Professor D Hull
BSc, MB, ChB, FRCP

Department of Child Health, University Hospital Medical School, Clifton Boulevard, Nottingham, England

Professor J H P Jonxis
MD

Department of Paediatrics, State University, Groningen, The Netherlands

Dr D Lister

ARC Meat Research Institute, Langford, Bristol, England

Professor R A McCance
CBE, FRS, MA, PhD, MD, FRCP, HonFRCOG, HonDSc

Sidney Sussex College, University of Cambridge, Cambridge, England

Dr W A Marshall
BSc, MB, PhD, FIBiol

Department of Growth and Development, Institute of Child Health, University of London, England

Dr L E Mount

Institute of Animal Physiology, Agricultural Research Council, Cambridge, England

Dr E M E Poskitt
MB, BChir, MRCP

The Children's Hospital, Birmingham, England

Professor F Sereni
MD

Istituto di Puericultura, Dell'Universita di Milano, Milan, Italy

Mr D H Steven	Department of Veterinary Anatomy, Downing Site, University of Cambridge, Cambridge, England
Dr A M Thomson MB, ChB, DPH, FRCOG	MRC Reproduction and Growth Unit, Princess Mary Maternity Hospital, Newcastle-upon-Tyne, England
Professor A S Truswell MB, ChB, MD, MRCP, MFCM	Department of Nutrition and Food Science, Queen Elizabeth College, London, England
Professor J C Waterlow CMG, MD, ScD, FRCP	Department of Human Nutrition, London School of Hygiene and Tropical Medicine, London, England
Dr B A Wharton MD, FRCPE, MRCP, DCH	Child Nutrition Section, Infant Development Unit, Queen Elizabeth Medical Centre, Birmingham, England
Dr E M Widdowson DSc, PhD, FRS	Department of Medicine, Addenbrooke's Hospital, University of Cambridge, Cambridge, England
Professor A W Wilkinson ChM, FRCSEd, FRCS, FAAP(Hon)	Department of Paediatric Surgery, Institute of Child Health, University of London, England

Pregnancy and Lactation: The Comparative Point of View

ELSIE M WIDDOWSON
University of Cambridge, Cambridge, England

PREGNANCY

In 1940 a collection of essays by JBS Haldane was published and among them was one entitled 'On being the right size'. This essay begins "The most obvious differences between animals are differences of size, but for some reason the zoologists have paid singularly little attention to them. In a large textbook of zoology before me I find no indication that the eagle is larger than the sparrow, or the hippopotamus bigger than the hare, though some grudging admissions are made in the case of the mouse and the whale. But yet it is easy to show that a hare could not be as large as a hippopotamus, or a whale as small as a herring. For every type of animal there is a most convenient size, and a large change in size inevitably carries with it a change of form". Haldane was writing about adult animals, but what he says in this essay applies with just as much force to the newborn. It is obvious that the mother has to deliver her young while they are still smaller than herself, but the amount by which they are smaller is not the same in all species. Leitch et al (1959), who also complained that zoologists rarely record weights of mothers and newborn young, did manage to find information about the weights of mothers and newborn of over 100 species of mammals. Weights for some small and large mammals are shown in Table I. The smallest mother was the lesser horseshoe bat which weighs 6 gram and the largest was the blue whale which weighs 79,000 kilograms, a difference in weight of over 10 million times. Both produce one young and both, incidentally, deliver their young in a remarkable way — the bat produces her offspring hanging upside down, and the whale delivers her young into the sea. The bat's young weighs 2 gram, over 30% of her own weight, the whale's 2000 kg, which is 2.5% of the weight of

1

TABLE I. Relation Between the Weights of the Mother and that of her Offspring at Term

Species	Mother's weight	Weight as per cent mother's weight	
		Whole litter	One Young
Lesser horseshoe bat	6.1 g	34	34
Mouse	25 g	40	5
Rat	200 g	25	2.5
Guinea pig	560 g	68	17
Rabbit	1,175 g	19	3.8
Dog	9 kg	12	2.4
Sheep	50 kg	10	10
Woman	56 kg	6	6
Pig	200 kg	6	0.6
Cow	600 kg	7	7
Horse	800 kg	9	9
Elephant	2,590 kg	3.6	3.6
Blue whale	79,000 kg	2.5	2.5

the mother. This illustrates the general principle set out by Leitch et al, that, although the weight of offspring increases as the size of the mother increases, it does not increase in proportion and, generally speaking, the total weight of offspring at birth forms a much larger percentage of the mother's weight in small species than in large ones. The lesser horseshoe bat is rather exceptional among small mammals in only having one young and she must have something rather special in the way of a birth canal. Most small mammals have large litters, so that the total weight is divided among a number of young. The mouse's litter for example, which is 40% of the mother's weight, is divided among 8 individuals; the guinea pig, which produces a greater weight of young in relation to her own weight than any other species, over 60%, has an average litter of 4.

So far we have taken no account of length of gestation, which must clearly be included in any consideration of the demands of pregnancy on mothers of different species. Payne and Wheeler (1968) related maternal weight to gain in weight of total litter in unit time, averaged over the whole of gestation. Table II shows that the total offspring of small mammals are not only heavy in proportion to the weight of the mother at birth but, because their periods of gestation are short, their growth rate before birth related to the mother's weight is even more different from that of large species. For example the litter of the mouse gains nearly 2% of the mother's weight each day of gestation, whereas the fetus of the whale gains only 0.077% of her weight daily, in spite of its great weight of two thousand kilograms at term.

Growth in the early stages of gestation is brought about entirely by cell division

TABLE II. Relation Between the Daily Gain in Fetal Weight, Averaged over the Whole of
Gestation, and the Weight of the Mother

Species	Mother's weight	Length of gestation (days)	Weight litter at birth (g)	Gain in weight of litter per day as per cent of mother's weight
Mouse	25 g	21	10	1.90
Rat	200 g	21	50	1.19
Guinea pig	560 g	67	380	1.01
Rabbit	1,175 g	28	225	0.68
Dog	9,000 g	63	1100	0.19
Sheep	50 kg	150	5	0.07
Woman	56 kg	280	3.5	0.02
Pig	200 kg	115	12	0.05
Cow	600 kg	280	42	0.03
Horse	800 kg	340	71	0.03
Elephant	2,590 kg	600	93	0.006
Blue whale	79,000	330	2000	0.0077

without any increase in cell size, so the fetus can only grow as fast as its cells
divide. Cell division goes on much more rapidly in the fetuses of small animals
than in those of large ones. The rat, for example, increases from a single cell to
two to three thousand million during the three weeks of gestation, whereas the
human fetus only achieves about a third of this number of cells in its first eight
weeks. I know nothing about cell division in the fetal whale. It is true the human
fetus and the fetal whale ultimately grow much larger than the rat, but this is
because they stay in the uterus so much longer, so the cells have much more time

TABLE III. Relation Between Basal Metabolism and Body Weight of Adult Mammals

Species	Body weight (kg)	Basal metabolism (kCal/kg/day)
Mouse	0.025	182
Rat	0.200	88
Guinea pig	0.560	63
Rabbit	1.175	46
Dog	9.0	36
Sheep	50	23
Woman	56	26
Pig	200	14
Cow	600	15

to double and redouble their number. To bring the rat fetus to 5 gram the complete cell population has got to divide and redivide 30 times. If growth of the human fetus through the whole of gestation were entirely by cell division, then division of all the cells of the body 10 times over would take it from 5 gram, the weight of the newborn rat to 3.5 kg, the weight of the full term baby. Growth of the human fetus is not entirely by cell division, however, but also by growth in size of cells (Widdowson et al, 1972), so the cell population does not have to divide even 10 times over, but something considerably less than this during the last 7 months of gestation.

The problem is, how does all this come about? We can put it all down to genetics, but this rather begs the question as to how the young of small mammals are able to grow so much faster than those of large mammals before they are born.

Another characteristic of small and large species of mammals concerns their basal metabolism. The amount of heat they produce and oxygen they consume each day increase with increasing body weight, though they do not increase in proportion to it but at a much slower rate. In other words small animals have a higher rate of metabolism per kilogram than large ones. Table III shows some of the values given by Voit (1901) and others for the heat production of various species of mammals. A mouse, for example, produces heat at the rate of 212 kCal per kg body weight per day, and a horse 11 kCal per kg per day. Man comes in between with a basal heat production of 32 kCal per kg per day. If these are expressed per square metre of surface area they all come to about 1000 kCal per day.

We do not know for certain how closely the metabolic rate of the fetus in the uterus corresponds to that of its mother. Clearly surface area does not have much meaning for this comparison, and indeed it seems that the placental circulation has the capacity for dissipating all or nearly all the heat produced by the human fetus in its metabolism (Adamsons & Towell, 1965), though there is evidence in man and other species that at term the body temperature is higher in the fetus than in the mother (Wood & Beard, 1964; Adamsons & Towell, 1965; Mann, 1968; Abrams et al, 1969a,b). Earlier investigators (Bohr, 1900; Murlin, 1910), working with animals, concluded that the metabolic rate of the fetus was the same as that of its mother per kilogram of weight, so that it behaved in this respect as if it were part of the mother's body. However, more recent studies have suggested that in the sheep at any rate fetal metabolic rate may be a little higher than maternal per kilogram of weight (Meschia et al, 1967), and indeed one would expect it to be so in view of the cellular activity that is going on. The figure obtained by Romney et al (1955) for the oxygen consumption of the human fetus of 5 ml per min suggests that in our species too fetal metabolism may be a little higher than maternal. Even if this is so I think we can safely assume that there is a close relationship between maternal and fetal rates of metabolism per unit weight. It follows from this that the metabolic rates per unit weight of the fetus of small mammals like the mouse and rat are much higher than those of fetuses of larger species, for example man or the pig, horse or elephant. Even between man and the pig there

4

is a difference and the fetal pig at term probably has a lower heat production than the human fetus. Yet it only weighs one-third as much, so that when it is born the pig needs to increase heat production far more than the human baby to maintain its body temperature. The high rate of metabolism in small adult mammals is made possible by their rapid heart rate and circulation and hence a greater blood supply to the tissues, in fact blood supply is proportional to metabolic intensity as this varies with body size. Small mammals have wide tracheas and aortas for their size, and the number of capillaries per square millimetre cross section of muscle is much greater for small mammals than for large ones. Oxygenation of the fetus and circulation of blood within it are outside my province, but I think we can assume that the placental and fetal circulations of the small mammal shares in the general rapid turnover, so that the fetus of the small mammal is supplied with the oxygen and nutrients required for the high rate of metabolism and high rate of growth.

Pregnancy, therefore, makes far greater demands on the mothers of small mammalian species than on those of large ones and they have to eat correspondingly more food to provide for the requirements of their unborn young. Not only so, but all species so far studied deposit considerable amounts of fat in their own bodies during pregnancy. The amount of fat laid down may be considerable. Hytten and Leitch (1971) suggest that the average amount is about 4 kg during a full human pregnancy, which is quite a lot of fat. It weighs more than the average baby and may well add a third to the amount of fat the mother had in her body before she became pregnant. The fat seems to be deposited at specific sites, over the abdomen, the back and the upper thighs, but not over the arms (Taggart, 1961). Pregnant rats and mice deposit fat too. Spray (1950) found the fat in the bodies of rats to increase from 51 to 72 gram during pregnancy and in mice from 1.2 to 2.8 gram.

LACTATION

In many species lactation makes a far more exacting test than pregnancy. Table IV shows for eleven species the weight, expressed as a percentage of the mother's weight, of the young at birth and at the end of the time when they depend entirely on milk for their sustenance, and the difference between the two, which gives the gain during suckling. First on the list I have placed the small rodents, the mouse and rat, and then rather surprisingly, a carnivore, the cat. Their young are born in an immature state, but grow extremely rapidly after birth and soon become quite fat. The rabbit, sheep and pig follow the cat, and in all these species the demands on the mother for nutrition of the young after birth are far greater than those for nutrition of the fetus before birth. On the other hand the guinea pig, which has a long gestation period and is born large and mature, makes considerably more demands on the mother before birth than after. It depends on mother's milk for a very short time, and in fact begins to nibble other food very

TABLE IV. Weight of Young as per cent of Mother's Weight

Species	At birth	At end of full suckling	Gain during suckling
Mouse	40	170	130
Rat	25	120	95
Cat	12	100	88
Rabbit	19	50	31
Sheep	10	40	30
Man	6	12	6
Pig	6	40	34
Calf	7	14	7
Elephant	3.6	23	19.4
Blue whale	2.5	20	17.5
Guinea pig	68	–	–

soon after it is born.

For the human species pregnancy and lactation appear from this table to make equal demands, but this is not true for several reasons. In the first place time must be taken into account, and this applies also to the other mammals. The human baby takes twice as long to grow to 3.5 kg before birth as it does nowadays to double this weight after birth. Moreover, to provide milk for the growth of the young after birth is a less efficient process than to supply the fetus in the uterus with what it needs. Neither the production of milk by the mammary gland nor the digestion and absorption of the nutrients in the milk by the young animal or baby are carried out with 100% efficiency. The cost of lactation to the mother includes not only the nutrients in the milk and their energy value, but also the energy required to synthesise the lactose, protein and fat. It used to be thought that the energy efficiency of milk production was no more than 60%, but Thomson et al (1971) have been steadily raising their estimate and their latest figure is about 90% efficiency. So far as the utilisation of nutrients by the infant for growth are concerned, this is more efficient than at any other time of life but, even so, the infant retains only about half the nitrogen in breast milk for the synthesis of protein for growth (Fomon, 1974). The rabbit, that grows much more rapidly than the human baby retains about 70% of the nitrogen in its milk for growth (Davies et al, 1964).

A far more important reason why nutrition after birth is a less efficient process than nutrition before birth is because a great deal of the energy taken in in the milk, at any rate in some species, must be used for maintenance in an environment that is almost certainly cooler than the uterus. The more slowly the young animal grows the greater is the proportion of its energy intake which is used for maintenance, and the smaller is the proportion which is used for the deposition of new body tissue. The human baby is a particularly slow grower and Table V

TABLE V. Percentage of Energy Intake Used by Infants for Maintenance and for Growth
(kCal/kg/day)

| Age months | Intake | Expenditure | |
		Maintenance	Increment in body i.e. growth
0-2	126	93	33
2-4	111	93	18
4-6	100	93	7

shows the average energy intake of the infant at three ages, and the amount of this that is expended on maintenance, and on increments of protein and fat in the body, that is, on growth. Even during the first two months after birth only 26% of the total is used for growth and by 4–6 months the percentage has fallen to 7.

Women who breast-feed their babies probably lose most of the fat they acquired during pregnancy, and the 36000 kCal of energy stored in this way should provide a third to a half of the energy required for the production of breast milk. Rats too lose the fat deposited in their bodies during pregnancy and far more as well. The rats that had increased their fat from 51 to 72 gram during pregnancy lost all but 9 gram of it during lactation.

Other mammals do this too, and an extreme example is the grey seal. The female lays down a great deal of fat during the latter part of pregnancy in July and August. She has her young on shore in September, and the weight of the newborn is about 15 kg. The mother suckles her pup for about two weeks, during which time it puts on 20 kg in weight or 1.5 kg a day (Amoroso & Matthews, 1951; Amoroso et al, 1951). It becomes very fat indeed – seal milk contains 53% of fat. Meantime the mother takes no food at all and she loses twice the weight gained by her pup. All that the pup needs for maintenance and rapid growth comes from within the mother's body.

Most mammals, however, increase their food intakes during lactation, and a small mammal like the mouse or rat with a weight of young at the end of lactation greater than her own weight, must eat a great deal more food during lactation to provide for the rapidly growing young. In fact more food is eaten by rats in full lactation than after lesions have been made in the hypothalamus (Kennedy, 1952–53). Kennedy (1952–53) and Anderson and Turner (1963) found that the food consumption of rats in full lactation was more than double that of non-pregnant non-lactating females. The digestive tract enlarges in response to all this extra food, the stomach by some 60%, the small intestine by over 100% and the caecum by 65% (Fell et al, 1963). The increase in weight of the intestine was found to be brought about by dilation of the wall (Boyne et al, 1966) so that the surface area of the mucosa almost doubled. The liver, too, increases greatly in size in response to all this extra food, and Kennedy et al (1958) found that the enlargement was greater the more young were being suckled. When there were 8–11 young in the litter the liver doubled in size. Growth of the liver was brought about by an increase both in number and size of its cells. After lactation was over and the rats were eating less food the size of the liver returned to what it was before. There was loss of protein from it, but no loss of DNA, so the livers of parous rats have more cells in their livers than rats that have not lactated. Similar changes have been shown to occur in the livers of lactating sheep (Campbell & Fell, 1970).

Enlargement of the gastrointestinal tracts and livers of women during lactation has not been reported. There seems no reason why it should not occur, but if it does its magnitude is likely to be considerably less than that observed in the animals that have been studied.

TABLE VI. Composition of Milks of Various Species (per 100 ml)

Species	Protein (g)	Fat (g)	Carbohydrate (g)	Energy (kCal)
Rat	9	9	3	129
Guinea pig	8	6	3	98
Rabbit	13	15	2	195
Cat	11	11	3	155
Dog	8	9	4	129
Sheep	6	8	4	128
Cow	3	4	5	68
Horse	2	2	6	50
Ass	2	2	6	50
Rhinoceros	2	0.5	6	37
Elephant	8	9	4	129
Pig	6	9	5	125
Hippopotamus	7	18	2	198
Man	1	4	7	68
Monkey	2	4	6	68
Seal	11	53	3	533
Whale	12	40	1	412

The milk of rodents and carnivores that have young that are immature and helpless at birth but that grow very rapidly after birth are characterised by a low percentage of carbohydrate, a high percentage of protein and fat and a high energy value (Table VI). The milk of ruminants, cow's milk for example, has less protein than the milk of rodents and carnivores, a little less fat and more carbohydrate. The milk of ruminants differs from all other milks in containing appreciable amounts of short chain saturated fatty acids, notably butyric acid.

8

These are synthesised in the mammary gland from acetic acid and other volatile fatty acids which are produced in the rumen by the fermentation of celluloses.

The milks of the horse, ass and rhinoceros are similar to each other in containing little fat, and less protein and more carbohydrate than the milk of rodents, carnivores, or ruminant ungulates. They approximate more closely to human milk than any other animal milk apart from that of other primates.

The milk of the elephant, another non-ruminant herbivore, is quite different. It contains more protein and fat and less carbohydrate than the milk of the horse, ass or rhinoceros, but its main peculiarity is its high percentage of capric acid (C10:0) in the fat. More than 60% of the total fat is present as this unusual fatty acid. Rabbits' milk contains this fatty acid too, and it is thought to be synthesised from precursors supplied by the bacteria in the caecum of these animals.

Colostrum is extremely important to newborn piglets, as it is to other ungulates. There is no transmission of passive immunity before birth, and for 36 hours after birth they absorb their antibodies from the colostrum through the intestinal wall. Pig's milk has higher concentrations of protein, fat and carbohydrate and a higher energy value than cow's milk, and piglets grow far more rapidly than calves. The hippopotamus is zoologically similar to the pig. Its milk has the same percentage of protein as pig's milk, but it has much more fat and it has a considerably high calorific value. This may be related to the fact that the baby hippopotamus feeds under water so it has to get its calories quickly and then come up for air.

The milk of whales and of other marine mammals like the porpoise and seal contains 40–50% of fat and correspondingly little water. It has 11% protein, and only traces of carbohydrate. It is highly calorific. Whales live in the sea — they are too large to live anywhere else. They deliver their young into the sea and they suckle them under water. This may seem a strange sort of existence to us, but to finish as I began, with another of Haldane's (1940) essays entitled 'Man as a sea beast', "We pass our first nine months as aquatic animals, suspended in and protected by a salty fluid medium. We begin life as salt water animals".

References

Abrams, RM, Caton, D, Clapp, V and Barron, DH (1969a) *Physiologist, 12,* 155

Abrams, R, Caton, D, Curet, LB, Crenshaw, C, Mann, L and Barron, DH (1969b) *American Journal of Physiology, 217,* 1619

Adamsons, K Jr and Towell, ME (1965) *Anaesthesiology, 26,* 531

Amoroso, EC, Goffin, A, Halley, G, Matthews, LH and Matthews, DJ (1951) *Journal of Physiology, London, 113,* 4P

Amoroso, EC and Matthews, JH (1951) *Journal of Anatomy, 85,* 427

Anderson, RR and Turner, CW (1963) *Proceedings of the Society for Experimental Biology and Medicine, 113,* 334

Bohr, C (1900) *Skandinavisches Archiv für Physiologie, 10,* 413

Boyne, AW, Fell, BF and Roff, I (1966) *Journal of Physiology, London, 183,* 570

Campbell, RM and Fell, BF (1970) *Research in Veterinary Science, 11,* 540
Davies, JS, Widdowson, EM and McCance, RA (1964) *British Journal of Nutrition, 18,* 385
Fell, BF, Smith, KA and Campbell, RM (1963) *Journal of Pathology and Bacteriology, 85,* 179
Fomon, SJ (1974) *Infant Nutrition, 2nd Edition.* WB Saunders, Philadelphia
Haldane, JBS (1940) On being the right size. In *Possible Worlds.* Evergreen Books, London. Page 27
Hart, FM and Faber, JJ (1965) *Journal of Applied Physiology, 20,* 737
Hytten, FE and Leitch, I (1971) *The Physiology of Human Pregnancy, 2nd Edition.* Blackwell, Oxford
Kennedy, GC (1952–53) *Proceedings of the Royal Society, B, 140,* 578
Kennedy, GC, Pearce, WM and Parrott, DMV (1958) *Journal of Endocrinology, 17,* 158
Leitch, I, Hytten, FE and Billewicz, WZ (1959) *Proceedings of the Zoological Society, London, 133,* 11
Mann, TP (1968) *Journal of Obstetrics and Gynaecology of the British Commonwealth, 75,* 316
Meschia, G, Cotter, JR, Makowski, EL and Barron, DH (1967) *Quarterly Journal of Experimental Physiology, 52,* 1
Murlin, JR (1910) *American Journal of Physiology, 26,* 134
Payne, PR and Wheeler, EF (1968) *Proceedings of the Nutrition Society, 27,* 129
Romney, SL, Reid, DE, Metcalfe, J and Burwell, CS (1955) *American Journal of Obstetrics and Gynecology, 70,* 791
Spray, CM (1950) *British Journal of Nutrition, 4,* 384
Taggart, N (1961) *Proceedings of the Nutrition Society, 20,* XXX
Thomson, AM, Hytten, FE and Billewicz, WZ (1971) *British Journal of Nutrition, 24,* 565
Voit, E (1901) *Zeitschrift für Biologie, 41,* 113
Widdowson, EM, Crabb, DE and Milner, RDG (1972) *Archives of Disease in Childhood, 47,* 652
Wood, C and Beard, RW (1964) *Journal of Obstetrics and Gynaecology of the British Commonwealth, 71,* 768

Nutritional Physiology During Pregnancy

A M THOMSON

Princess Mary Maternity Hospital, Newcastle-upon-Tyne, England

Populations are increasing so rapidly in countries where malnutrition is prevalent that the human fetus must be protected with remarkable efficiency. From the point of view of physiology, the question is how this protection is conferred.

We know that pregnancy is accompanied by changes which, when they occur in non-pregnant individuals, suggest the presence of serious illness. For example, pregnant women gain weight rapidly, may behave sluggishly and often complain of digestive upsets, oedema is common, body temperature is slightly raised, and pulse, respiration and basal metabolic rates are also increased, often in association with some enlargement of the thyroid gland. Some changes in the blood constituents suggest malnutrition, while others indicate over-nutrition, the erythrocyte sedimentation rate is characteristic of chronic infection, and plasma osmolality falls to levels that would ordinarily be expected to provoke signs of diabetes insipidus. Glycosuria is common, giving rise to a suspicion of diabetes mellitus, but recent studies suggest that it may really reflect alterations of renal function (Davison, 1975). The diagnostic challenges offered by such phenomena are considerable (Hytten and Lind, 1973). Are such changes to be regarded as undesirable deviations from physiological forms and to be prevented if possible, or as adaptations which help to protect the fetus? If the latter, do they imply any disadvantages to the mother?

CHANGES IN THE CONCENTRATIONS OF NUTRIENTS IN MATERNAL BLOOD

In general the concentrations of lipids and lipid derivatives rise while those of water-soluble substances fall during pregnancy. Falling concentrations of nutrients have often been interpreted as indications of nutritional depletion, but

11

in the absence of seriously defective diets this is unlikely for the following reasons.

1. Such changes take place in well-nourished, healthy, clinically normal pregnant women.

2. Some changes begin during the first trimester, when the product of conception is far too small to exercise an appreciable drain on the maternal reserves. Similar changes can be induced in non-pregnant women by means of steroid sex hormones.

3. The changes are highly specific. For example concentration of plasma albumin falls, while those of other protein fractions exhibit a wide variety of patterns of change. Such adjustments cannot be explained in any simple manner, for example as the result of 'haemodilution' and, where they cannot be attributed directly to the product of conception, presumably connote changes in function.

4. Changes in the composition and properties of maternal blood are not confined to nutrients and their metabolites. For example, osmolality and pCO_2 fall to levels that would be regarded as clearly unphysiological in non-pregnant individuals. In fact, pH is about the only major property that remains practically unchanged. At present, we can do little more than speculate about the nature of such changes, but they are certainly not random and are unlikely to be without functional consequences.

CHANGES IN HAEMOGLOBIN CONCENTRATION AND THE EFFECT OF TREATMENT

The haematological changes in maternal blood have been widely studied, but their meaning remains controversial. In healthy pregnant women, the haemoglobin concentration falls on average by about 2g/100ml., the lowest level usually being reached about the seventh month. This is commonly interpreted as signifying anaemia, so that many obstetricians prescribe iron to be taken routinely in therapeutic doses during pregnancy. We may agree that true anaemia occurs more commonly during pregnancy, and that prophylactic therapy is justifiable in places where the risk is high, for example, where loss of blood is caused by disease or the diet is obviously deficient in iron or folate. But what is the physiological significance of a decline in haemoglobin concentration in an apparently healthy, well-fed pregnant woman, and what will be the effect of the consumption of additional iron in much larger quantities than are found in normal food?

Paintin et al (1966) investigated these problems by studying three groups of comparable primigravidae, all having haemoglobin concentrations higher than 10g/100ml at the first visit to the antenatal clinic before mid-pregnancy. The first group received 105mg iron daily, the usual dose given in routine prophylactic therapy, and much more than the amount present in food. The second group received a supplement of 12mg iron daily, estimated to double the supply already contained in food, and thus to eliminate any real risk of nutritional insufficiency. The third group received pills containing no iron. All the pills looked identical, and their nature was not revealed to either the patients or the obstetricians until the trial was over.

The following mean haemoglobin concentrations (g/100ml) were observed:

Gestation	Group 1 (High iron)	Group 2 (Supplementary iron)	Group 3 (no extra iron)
20	11.6	11.5	11.7
30	11.3	10.5	10.4
36	12.0	10.8	10.7
6–13 weeks post-partum	12.6	12.1	11.9

Thus, doubling the amount of iron supplied (Group 2 compared with Group 3) made practically no difference to the behaviour of haemoglobin concentrations. Giving iron in larger amounts (Group 1) did not prevent some fall in the average haemoglobin concentration between 20 and 30 weeks of gestation, but resulted in a higher level in late pregnancy and post-partum.

The physiological background to these findings seems to be as follows. During pregnancy, with a sufficient but not excessive iron intake, total blood volume rises by about 30%. This is an average, attributable mainly to a rise in plasma volume of about 40% and a rise in red cell volume of 10–20%. The disproportionate rise in plasma volume, which is sometimes incorrectly called 'haemodilution', results in a fall of haemoglobin concentration per unit volume of blood, which takes place in the presence of an increased amount of circulating haemoglobin and hence of capacity for transporting oxygen. Despite an increase in oxygen consumption during pregnancy, the maternal arteriovenous p O_2 apparently decreases (Stenger et al, 1965). Ability to supply oxygen to the maternal tissues and the product of conception thus increases, despite the fall in haemoglobin concentration.

Plasma volume probably increases under the influence of oestrogens, and may be considered to help the dissipation of heat from the skin, as well as increasing renal plasma flow. The increased red cell volume, which normally seems to be due to a rise in the number of circulating red cells, probably represents a response of the bone marrow to stimuli which are at present uncertain. There is no evidence that hypoxia is involved, and at present the only clue we have is from animal experiments which indicate that human placental lactogen has a potentiating effect on erythropoietin (Jepson & Friesen, 1968). It should be noted that there is evidence of increased absorption of food iron from the gut during pregnancy (Heinrich et al, 1968).

Unpublished data from this Unit suggest that the effect of giving large doses of extra iron is to increase mean red cell volume, as well as to increase still further the number of circulating red cells. Whether such a change is entirely harmless is at least worth questioning. Our own practice is not to give pregnant women large doses of iron and folate unless there is evidence that clinical anaemia is developing, with a haemoglobin concentration below 10g/100ml blood with a tendency to fall more rapidly than can be accounted for by physiological changes.

Increase in plasma volume is directly correlated with fetal growth (Hytten & Paintin, 1963), from which it follows that, under physiological conditions, birth weights tend to be inversely correlated with the fall in maternal haemoglobin concentration, as indicated by the data of Gibson (1973).

MATERNAL AND FETAL BALANCE

The concentration of nutrients and other substances in fetal blood may be higher than, lower than, or approximately equal to the levels in maternal blood (Dancis & Schneider, 1975). Not only does the fetus develop its own mechanisms for homeostatic control, but transfers through the placenta are by no means simple. Some nutrients may be converted in the fetus to forms which cannot pass back readily into the maternal circulation. Thus, according to Räihä (1959), ascorbic acid passes easily from the mother to the fetus as dehydroascorbic acid, but is converted on the fetal side to L-ascorbic acid, which does not readily pass back to the mother. Hensleigh & Krantz (1966), however, considered that active transport by the placenta is involved, and doubted Räihä's idea of a 'biochemical valve'. Whatever the reason, there is almost certainly a similar 'one-way traffic' in folate (Landon, 1975). Such mechanisms would favour the fetus under conditions where the mother is malnourished, but they may not be entirely harmless with substances, nutrients or drugs which may be given to the mother in high dosage. The mother can get rid of excess by metabolism and excretion. The fetus excretes into the amniotic fluid, which it then swallows, and thus undesirably high levels may build up in the fetal circulation. This supposition is at present hypothetical, but deserves study.

What is the significance of the relatively low concentrations of many nutrients in maternal blood? It seems reasonable to suggest that they may facilitate uptake by the placenta in competition with the needs of maternal tissues, and to this extent what is good for the fetus may not be beneficial to the mother. Hytten & Leitch (1971) have pointed out that, in the healthy non-pregnant state, 'the body maintains in its fluid environment the amounts and concentrations of the substance it needs for maximum efficiency of function; that is the purpose of homeostasis. If that is so, then the greatly altered amounts and concentrations which are characteristic of pregnancy cannot reasonably be assumed to be equally advantageous to the mother's metabolism'.

ENERGY METABOLISM

More than 30 years ago, Hammond (1944) suggested that nutrients in the maternal blood stream are partitioned in accordance with the metabolic rate of tissues, and that on this basis the product of conception receives a priority which is second only to the maternal brain. However, recent estimates and calculations suggest that the metabolic rate of the product of conception is not greatly different from that of maternal tissues (Hytten & Leitch, 1971). Although it is growing rapidly, it does not have to maintain body heat against an adverse gradient, nor a high level of muscle tone.

Yet the energy needs of the fetus seem to be well protected; thus, average birth weights fell only about 9% in the most severely affected regions of Holland during the famine of 1944/45 (Stein et al, 1975). The explanation may be that the fetus can draw on the maternal tissues, and that under normal conditions a considerable energy reserve, in the form of depot fat, is laid down before fetal requirements become large.

Hytten & Leitch (1971) have summarised the evidence. In primigravidae who were able to eat as much as they wanted, the average total weight gain during pregnancy was 12.5 kg, of which only about 7.5 kg could be accounted for by the product of conception, enlargement of the organs of reproduction and increase in maternal blood volume. Serial measurements of total body water showed that, in the absence of generalised oedema, the excess weight not accounted for up to about 30 weeks of gestation was water-free and hence must consist entirely or mainly of fat. At term, there was about 2.5 litres of excess body water, presumably oedema fluid, so that approximately 4 kg of 'dry weight' remained, representing body fat. Skinfold measurements confirmed that extensive depots of superficial fat were being laid down, especially around the lower trunk and hips, mainly during the second trimester. Such an accumulation of fat represents a large energy reserve, which is available to the growing fetus during the final weeks of pregnancy, especially if, as is usual, the mother reduces the amount of physical work she undertakes. Thus, in conformity with clinical experience, maternal needs for extra energy may be signalled by an increase of appetite early in the second trimester, and are sustained at a fairly steady level thereafter without any further increase near term, when the fetus is growing most rapidly.

Progesterone is probably responsible for the deposition of extra fat during pregnancy. Under ordinary conditions, all or most of this fat remains available to subsidise lactation. It is, however, an interesting and unexpected fact that, even in the absence of lactation, the average woman loses the fat gained within a year or two of parturition. Billewicz & Thomson (1970) have shown that average weight does not increase with parity, independently of age. We therefore presume that when the progesterone effect is switched off at the end of pregnancy, fat deposits revert to their usual level, and that lactation merely accelerates this.

Summary

We can specify, with reasonable accuracy, the amounts of additional energy and of nutrients which are necessary to support the mother and the product of conception during the course of gestation. It is of interest that the rather generous allowances that were originally made for pregnancy have been gradually reduced over the years, as physiological evidence became available. But the physiological reductions of certain nutrient levels in maternal blood, and the accelerated clearances which may be observed after test doses, are often interpreted as signifying borderline malnutrition and as justifying special supplements, sometimes in large dosage. In reasonably well-nourished communities, such supplementation may not be obviously harmful, but it is doubtful if they are beneficial; and the possibility exists that they may impair the mechanisms which the fetus has for safeguarding its own growth and development.

These considerations do not apply in populations where nutritional conditions are chronically and generally unsatisfactory, and where disease may be an important factor. Though human reproduction seems to be well-protected even under such conditions, there is a good case for paying special attention to the feeding of pregnant women, and for supplementing their diets. But it is not sufficient to concentrate on pregnancy itself. The anatomical and physiological efficiency of women may have been permanently impaired by unsatisfactory nutrition during growth and adolescence. For the best results, it is important to feed children well, in order that they may be well-grown and healthy when mature enough to reproduce.

References

Billewicz, W Z and Thomson, A M (1970) *British Journal of Preventive and Social Medicine, 24,* 97

Dancis, J and Schneider, H (1975). In *The Placenta and its Maternal Supply Line.* (Ed) P Gruenwald. Lancaster, Medical and Technical Publishing Co.

Davison, J M (1975). *Clinics in obstetrics and gynaecology, 2,* 365

Gibson, H M (1973). *Journal of Obstetrics and Gynaecology of the British Commonwealth, 80,* 1067

Hammond, J (1944). *Proceedings of the Nutrition Society, 2,* 8

Heinrich, H C, Bartels, H, Heinisch, B, Hausmann, K, Kuse, R and Mauss, H J (1968). *Klinische Wochenschrift 46,* 199

Hensleigh, P A and Krantz, K E (1966). *American Journal of Obstetrics and Gynaecology, 96,* 5

Hytten, F E and Leitch, I (1971). *The Physiology of Human Pregnancy.* Oxford: Blackwell Scientific Publications

Hytten, F E and Lind, T (1973). *Diagnostic Indices in Pregnancy.* Basle, Ciba-Geigy Ltd.

Hytten, F E and Paintin, D B (1963). *Journal of Obstetrics and Gynaecology of the British Commonwealth, 70,* 402

16

Jepson, J H and Friesen, H G (1968). *British Journal of Haematology, 15,* 465

Landon, M (1975). *Clinics in Obstetrics and Gynaecology, 2,* 413

Paintin, D B, Thomson, A M and Hytten, F E (1966). *Journal of Obstetrics and Gynaecology of the British Commonwealth, 73,* 181

Räihä, N (1959). *Acta Physiologica Scandinavica, 45, Supple. 115,* 1

Stein, Z, Susser, M, Saenger, G and Marolla, F (1975). *Famine and Human Development.* New York: Oxford University Press

Stenger, V, Eitzman, D, Anderson, T, Cotter, J and Prystowsky, H (1965). *American Journal of Obstetrics and Gynaecology, 93,* 376

Morphological Basis of Placental Transport

D H STEVEN and CAROLE A SAMUEL
University of Cambridge, Cambridge, England

Over the broad spectrum of eutherian mammals there appears to be a division of labour between different regions of the fetal-maternal interface, so that routes of placental transport may differ widely according to the nature of the substance transferred. In the rabbit for example, and to a lesser extent in rats, mice and guinea pigs antibodies pass from mother to fetus across the inverted yolk sac placenta; in carnivores maternal erythrocytes are ingested and broken down in specialised regions of the paraplacental chorion, whilst in all species gases and small molecules are believed to cross the placental barrier primarily in those areas where fetal and maternal bloodstreams are in most intimate apposition. Furthermore in some domestic ungulates the activity of the uterine glands appears to be of major importance in the economy of fetus and placenta, for glandular secretion and absorption of secretory products continues throughout the course of pregnancy (Samuel & Steven, 1976).

Against this general background the capacity of the human placenta to transmit not only antibodies but also a wide variety of other substances is one of its most intriguing characteristics, especially as the yolk sac plays no part in placentation (Hemmings & Brambell, 1961) and there is little structural evidence of regional specialisation within the trophoblast. Opportunities for in vivo placental studies in man are limited, and thus the temptation to transpose to the human situation information derived from experimental animals can often be extreme. Since in the field of comparative placentation structural and functional similarities between species is the exception rather than the rule, such interspecific transposition should always be regarded with healthy scepticism. On the other hand it is only from comparative studies that the fundamental principles of placentation are likely to emerge. In this communication we review the structural basis of placental transport in a number of mammals, and comment on the possible functional significance of certain morphological features.

CHORIOVITELLINE PATHWAYS

In the domestic ungulates (pig, sheep, cow, goat and horse) antibodies are absorbed from the first milk or colostrum through the endodermal epithelium of the small intestine: in these mammals intrauterine transfer of passive immunity does not take place. In man, the rhesus monkey, rabbit and guinea pig the reverse is true, for not only are maternally-derived antibodies transmitted to the fetus before the time of birth, but there is little or no post-natal supplementation by the alimentary route. In the rat and mouse, probably also in the dog, pre-natal passive immunity is reinforced by alimentary absorption of γ globulins in the first 10—20 days after birth (Brambell, 1958; Clarke & Hardy, 1969; Morris & Morris, 1976).

Yolk sac placentation is by no means universal amongst mammals, but when present it may take one of two main forms. A simple choriovitelline placenta is formed when the outer vascular surface of the yolk sac makes contact with the inner surface of the chorion. Simple choriovitelline placentation is found in marsupials (see Amoroso, 1952; Morriss, 1975) and in the early stages of development in the mare, the dog, the cat and various mustelids. Little is known of the functional attributes of these placentas, but they are generally assumed to provide temporary support for the embryo between the stage of histiotrophic nutrition of the blastocyst and the time at which the allantois makes contact with the chorion to form the chorioallantoic placenta. No antibodies cross the choriovitelline placenta of the mare, and it seems unlikely that the yolk sac is involved in the transmission of the small amounts of antibody found in the sera of puppies born to immunised bitches (Brambell, 1958). This may be due to the fact that in simple choriovitelline placentation the yolk sac vesicle remains intact: its endodermal lining therefore makes no direct contact with fluids derived from the maternal organism.

The choriovitelline placenta of rodents and lagomorphs is basically a modification of the simple type, but is much more complex in function. Confusingly known as the 'inverted yolk sac placenta' it is formed by the degeneration and breakdown of the avascular abembryonic segment of the yolk sac, together with that part of the overlying chorion with which it is in contact (for explanatory diagrams see Steven, 1975a). The inner endodermal surface of the yolk sac is thereby directly exposed to fluids secreted into the uterine lumen, and it is by this route that the selective transfer of antibodies from mother to fetus takes place (Figure 1). Materials such as amino acids, vitamin B_{12}, exogenous proteins and colloidal substances are also absorbed (for references see King & Enders, 1970), but proteins other than antibodies are probably degraded by lysosomal activity (Beck et al, 1967). Furthermore only a small proportion of gamma

19

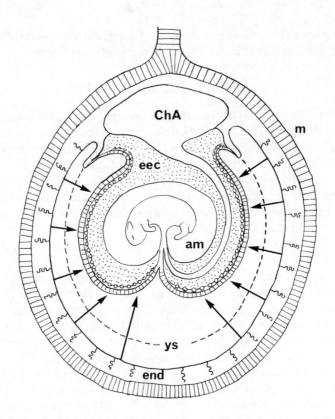

Figure 1. Diagram to show the pathway of transfer of antibodies from mother to fetus in inverted (visceral) yolk sac placentation (arrows).
am = amniotic cavity; ChA = chorioallantoic placenta; eec = extraembryonic coelom; end = endometrium; m = myometrium of uterine wall. The dotted line ys marks the position in which the abembryonic segment of the yolk sac would lie if present. In the absence of this segment the endodermal epithelium of the yolk sac cavity is directly exposed to uterine secretions

globulins injected into the uterine cavity of the pregnant rabbit are transported unchanged across the yolk sac endoderm (Hemmings, 1958). The pathways followed by colloidal thorium dioxide and two exogenous proteins (ferritin and horseradish peroxidase) across the inverted yolk sac placenta of the guinea pig were studied by King and Enders (1970) at ultrastructural level. All three tracer molecules were rapidly absorbed by the yolk sac endoderm after injection into the uterine lumen. Although all of the thorium dioxide and most of the protein was retained within the yolk sac endoderm, some of the protein was transmitted across the epithelium. It then followed one of three pathways, (a) across the basement membrane of the yolk sac endoderm and into the capillaries of the vitelline circulation; (b) across the yolk sac mesoderm and into the extraembryonic coelom, or (c) into the yolk sac mesoderm, where it was taken up by macrophages.

If these are indeed the pathways taken by antibodies it appears that the first is probably the most important route. The second may well account for the presence of antibodies in guinea pig exocoelomic fluid after day 35 of gestation (Leissring & Anderson, 1961).

CHORIOALLANTOIC PATHWAYS

Although a respiratory function for the placenta was suggested by Mayow as long ago as 1674, the concept of placental transfer of gases awaited experimental confirmation until the early years of the 20th century (Huggett, 1927). Today it is generally accepted that gases and small molecules cross the chorioallantoic placenta primarily in those areas where fetal and maternal bloodstreams are in most intimate apposition, yet even now the bulk of supporting evidence is indirect or circumstantial in nature. The principal obstacle to conclusive proof lies in the complexity of the vasculature on both fetal and maternal sides, for the blood which leaves the placenta represents the common outflow from tissues which differ widely in structural and functional characteristics. On the maternal side this is of particular importance for uterine venous blood is a mixture of placental, endometrial and myometrial contributions. Blood-flow experiments with isotope-labelled microspheres have shown that these relative proportions may vary from species to species (Makowski et al, 1968; Duncan, 1969) and also from time to time over the course of pregnancy (for further references see Carter, 1975). Nevertheless the evidence which emerges from microsphere studies in the sheep, the rabbit and the mare confirms beyond reasonable doubt that those regions which on histological grounds were previously designated 'placental exchange areas' do in fact receive by far the greatest proportion of placental arterial blood.

The atructure of the chorioallantoic placental barrier differs considerably from species to species (Enders, 1965; Steven, 1975b), but the pathways available for placental transport appear to fall into two principal categories. A *transcellular* route is almost certainly taken by gases and lipid-soluble substances which diffuse with great rapidity across the placental barrier (Faber, 1973). By contrast most water-soluble substances, with the exception of those with specific transport mechanisms or molecules of very large dimensions, probably cross by a *paracellular* route (Figure 2).

The contribution of descriptive electron microscopy to the functional interpretation of the *transcellular* pathway is necessarily indirect in nature, for functional properties can be determined only by direct experimental methods. Nevertheless a knowledge of ultrastructure can sometimes elucidate experimental results. Campbell et al (1966) showed that the oxygen consumption of the placenta of the ewe in the last one-third of pregnancy accounts for a significant proportion of the supply to the feto-placental unit. Electron micrographs of the placental barrier at this stage of gestation show that mitochondria are concentrated principally within the chorionic epithelium near the fetal-maternal interface. It thus

21

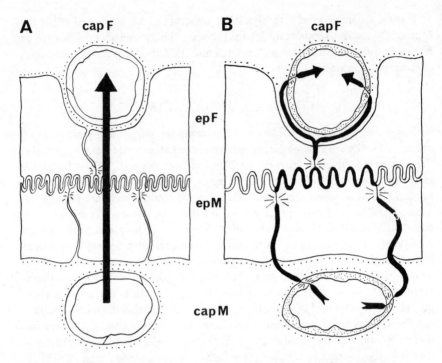

Figure 2A. Diagram to illustrate the transcellular pathway in a typical epitheliochorial placenta.

Figure 2B. Diagram to illustrate the paracellular pathway in a typical epitheliochorial placenta. The constrictions in the pathway indicate the sites of intercellular connections. capF = fetal capillary; capM = maternal capillary; epF = chorionic epithelium; epM = uterine epithelium

seems reasonable to assume that the chorionic epithelium is the component of the barrier with the highest metabolic rate. If this is in fact the case, and if the results of Campbell et al (1966) can for the sake of argument be extended on ultrastructural evidence to other species, there emerges a possible explanation for the development of 'intra-epithelial' capillaries over the course of gestation. Intra-epithelial capillaries were first described by Goldstein (1926) in the placenta of the pig, but a progressive indentation of the trophoblast by fetal capillaries appears to be a constant characteristic of the fetal side of the placenta in all species so far studied (for references see Steven, 1975b). Amoroso (1954) was the first to point out that the development of intra-epithelial capillaries must necessarily reduce the effective length of the diffusion pathway, but as the permeability of the barrier to blood gases is now thought unlikely to limit their transfer under normal circumstances (Meschia et al, 1967; Longo et al, 1972) it would seem logical to look further for a satisfactory explanation. The answer may lie in the conflicting but interdependent requirements of fetus and placenta in the last third of gestation. In early pregnancy, when fetal utilisation of oxygen is relatively small, the placenta is effectively in series with the fetus within the diffusion pathway (Figure 3). Later, as the fetus outstrips the placenta in its metabolic requirements, the diffusion pathways begin to diverge, becoming less

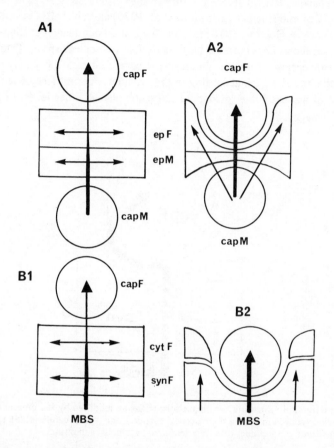

Figure 3. Diagrams to illustrate the possible sequences of the intra-epithelial position of fetal capillaries. A1: early epitheliochorial placentation; B1: early human placentation. At this stage the diffusion pathway to placental tissue tends to be in series with that to the fetal circulation. A2: late epitheliochorial placentation; B2: late human placentation. The diffusion pathways to placental tissue are now much more in parallel with those to the fetal circulation.

cap F = fetal capillary; capM = maternal capillary; cytF = cytotrophoblast; epF = chorionic epithelium; epM = uterine epithelium; MBS = maternal blood space; synF = syncytiotrophoblast

in series and more in parallel as gestation proceeds (Figure 3). Such arguments would appear to apply with equal force to all types of chorioallantoic placenta, from the human haemochorial condition to the epitheliochorial arrangement in ungulates. It would be interesting to test this hypothesis by direct experiment, or to examine abnormal placentas with these ideas in mind.

The concept of *paracellular* transport appears to be acceptable on structural grounds in all placentas which do not have a syncytial component within the placental barrier. Recent freeze-fracture studies of intercellular 'tight junctions' in a variety of endothelia (Yamamoto et al, 1976) and epithelia (Friend & Gilula, 1972; Larsson & Horster, 1976) suggest that not all pentalamellar 'tight junctions' can be regarded as impenetrable barriers to the intercellular space. Thus the intercellular connections along the course of the paracellular pathway may well be the sites of the 'pores' which according to their diameter permit free or restricted diffusion of water-soluble substances across the placental barrier (see Faber, 1973).

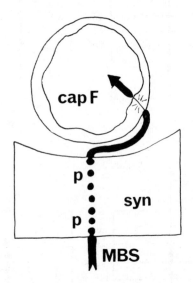

Figure 4. Diagram to illustrate the paracellular pathway modified by the presence of an epithelial syncytium within the placental barrier. CapF = fetal capillary; MBS = maternal blood space; p,p = pinocytotic vesicles; syn = epithelial syncytium

The interposition of a syncytium, whether fetal (as in man, rodents, lagomorphs and certain other species) or maternal (which is partially true of the sheep) within the transport pathway poses a very different problem, for by its nature a syncytium presents a continuous surface of cell membrane uninterrupted by intercellular connections or intercellular pathways (Figure 4). In such placentas a continuous route of paracellular transport would seem to be improbable, unless, as in the rabbit, the syncytial component is perforated by fenestrations of relatively large dimensions (Enders, 1965). A transcellular (or transsyncytial) component may possibly be provided by micropinocytosis, which is particularly evident in the syncytiotrophoblast of man (Wynn & Davies, 1965; Boyd & Hamilton, 1970).

24

For other haemochorial placentas however the situation is less well defined. Micropinocytotic vesicles have been reported in the syncytial layers of the haemotrichorial placenta of the rat (Jollie, 1976), and Tillack (1966) has shown that ferritin is transported in both directions across the placenta of the same species. The latter observation has led Faber (1973) to postulate (a) that a paracellular pathway is present in the rat placenta, and (b) that in order to permit the passage of ferritin the channels of this pathway must be more than 120 Å wide. There is however no evidence to suggest that any such channels penetrate the middle syncytial layer (Enders, 1965; Forsmann et al, 1975; Jollie, 1976): indeed Tillack's micrographs appear to show that ferritin is transported across the syncytium within numerous membrane-bound vacuoles. Furthermore if a system of continuous channels was present it would be difficult to explain on purely physical grounds why transport from fetus to mother is more rapid than transfer in the reverse direction.

This example serves to illustrate some of the drawbacks of the 'pore theory' or paracellular placental transport. The placenta may be shown to be permeable to water-soluble substances of known molecular size (Faber, 1973; Boyd et al, 1976), but unless a transcellular component can definitely be excluded it does not necessarily follow that such substances are invariably transmitted through 'pores' in the paracellular pathway.

ACCESSORY CHORIOALLANTOIC PATHWAYS

Accessory chorioallantoic pathways may be defined as pathways from the uterus to those regions of the chorion which are not normally in intimate contact with maternal tissues. A simple example is found in the sow, where specialised areas of the chorion known as areolas are situated opposite the openings of the uterine glands (Amoroso, 1952).

Uterine gland secretions, which in the sow are produced throughout pregnancy (Crombie, 1972) are phagocytosed by the cells of the chorion which form the areola.

A similar but more complex arrangement is found in the mare, where the mouths of the uterine glands open between the microcotyledons (Steven & Samuel, 1975). In the mare, as in the sow, the uterine glands continue secretory activity throughout pregnancy, and the intermicrocotyledonary chorion (which corresponds to the more localised areolas of the sow) engulfs the secretory products (Samuel & Steven, 1976) [Figure 5].

Areolas have been described in the intercotyledonary chorion of the sheep (Wimsatt, 1950), but in comparison with those of the sow they are small and insignificant. In the sheep, however, there is another and more dramatic accessory chorioallantoic pathway which becomes fully functional during the last third of gestation. At the central depression of the cotyledon maternal erythrocytes escape from degenerate blood vessels through fenestrations in the uterine epithelial

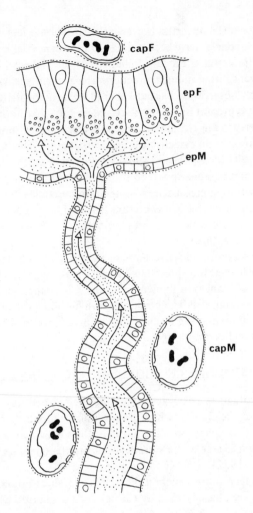

Figure 5. Diagram to show the route of maternal-fetal tranfer from uterine glands to fetal chorion. capF = fetal capillary; capM = maternal capillary; epF = chorionic epithelium; epM = uterine epithelium

syncytium to enter the space between the stems of the fetal villi and the extremities of the maternal crypts. In this space they form a stagnant mass of uncoagulated blood which is clearly visible to the naked eye. Once freed from the confines of maternal tissues many of these erythrocytes are ingested and broken down by the cells of the chorion with which they come into contact (Burton et al, 1976) [Figure 6].

Haemophagous regions of the placenta are uncommon amongst ungulates, but are a prominent feature of the placenta in almost all carnivora. In the dog and cat they form a pigmented margin to the zonary placenta, while in Mustelidae the

26

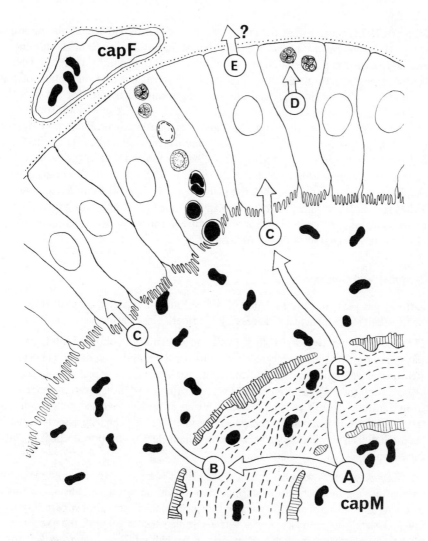

Figure 6. Highly diagrammatic representation of the absorption and degradation of maternal erythrocytes by the chorionic epithelium of the sheep in the last third of pregnancy. Maternal erythrocytes escape from degenerate capillaries (A) and pass through fenestrations in the uterine epithelial syncytium (B). They are then ingested by the chorionic epithelium at the bases of the fetal villi (C). Membranous debris is ultimately deposited in the basal region of the cytoplasm (D). The fate of the red cell contents is not yet clear. capF = fetal capillary; capM = maternal capillary

haemophagous region of the placenta is a distended blood-filled pouch (Sinha & Mossman, 1966; Gulamhusein & Beck, 1975). Wislocki and Dempsey (1946) who studied the uptake of maternal erythrocytes in the haemophagous region of the placenta in the cat, suggested that this might be an important pathway for the transfer of iron from mother to fetus. The elegant experiments of Baker and

Morgan (1973) showed that the rate of passage of transferrin-bound plasma iron across the feline placenta from the 53rd day of gestation until term is quite inadequate to account for the rate of accumulation of iron within the fetus. There is thus strong structural and functional evidence to suggest that the uptake of erythrocytes by the chorion may represent an important mechanism for the transfer of iron from mother to fetus where plasma transfer and the uptake of iron-rich uterine gland secretions do not provide an efficient alternative. Baker and Morgan (1973) suggest that the maternal capillary endothelium (the placenta of the cat is endotheliochorial in structure) may be the barrier which restricts the access of plasma transferrin-bound iron to the chorionic epithelium. With this concept in mind it is interesting to note that the placenta of the hyena (Wynn & Amoroso, 1964) is unusual amongst the carnivora in two respects: it does not have a haemophagous region, and its haemochorial structure permits free access of maternal blood to the surface of the trophoblast.

Summary and Conclusions

Pathways of placental transfer may be divided into choriovitelline pathways, chorioallantoic pathways and accessory chorioallantoic pathways.

Choriovitelline pathways. In simple yolk sac placentation, choriovitelline pathways provide a temporary means of support for the embryo before the chorioallantoic placenta becomes fully functional. In 'inverted' or 'visceral' yolk sac placentation maternal antibodies and certain other substances are transmitted from mother to fetus over the course of intrauterine life. Inverted yolk sac placentation is not found in man or the rhesus monkey, but is primarily associated with haemodichorial and haemotrichorial chorioallantoic placentation in rodents and lagomorphs.

Chorioallantoic pathways are found within the placenta where fetal and maternal circulations are in most intimate apposition. Gases, lipid-soluble substances and water-soluble substances with specific transport mechanisms almost certainly follow a *transcellular* pathway. Other water-soluble substances, with the exception of those of very large molecular dimensions, probably follow a *paracellular* route. However if a syncytial membrane forms part of the placental barrier, the paracellular pathway is necessarily interrupted. Under these circumstances the transport of substances which do not normally pass through the cell membrane is probably undertaken by a pinocytotic mechanism.

Accessory chorioallantoic pathways are found where the chorion is not normally in intimate contact with maternal tissues. They include (a) the uptake of uterine gland secretions by the trophoblast, and (b) the ingestion of extravasated maternal blood by specialised regions of the paraplacental chorion. These routes of transfer appear to increase in importance where maternal endothelium forms part of the placental barrier.

The human placenta. No accessory pathways, whether chorio-vitelline or chorio-allantoic, have been shown to be of any importance in the human placenta. All placental transport (including the transfer of antibodies from mother to fetus) would therefore appear to take place across the villous syncytiotrophoblast which is bathed by maternal blood within the intervillous space.

Other mammals. Because of the wide variation in placental structure and function even between closely related species, and because of the existence of choriovitelline and accessory chorioallantoic pathways in many experimental animals, extreme caution must be exercised in the interspecific transposition of experimental data. This caution is of particular importance in the transposition of data to the human situation, where experimental opportunities are necessarily limited and the pressures to adopt an uncritical approach are sometimes very great.

Acknowledgment

This work was supported by the Agricultural Research Council and the Wellcome Trust.

References

Amoroso, EC (1952) In *Marshall's Physiology of Reproduction, Volume 2.* (Ed) AS Parkes. Longmans Green, London. Page 127

Amoroso, EC (1954) In *Gestation, Transactions of the First Conference.* (Ed) LB Flexner. Josiah Macy Jr Foundation, New York

Baker, EH and Morgan, EH (1973) *Journal of Physiology, 232,* 485

Beck, F, Lloyd, JB and Griffiths, A (1967) *Journal of Anatomy, 101,* 461

Boyd, JD and Hamilton, WJ (1970) *The Human Placenta.* Heffer, Cambridge

Boyd, RDH, Haworth, R, Stacey, TE and Ward, RHT (1976) *Journal of Physiology, 254,* 16P

Brambell, FWR (1958) *Biological Reviews, 33,* 488

Burton, GJ, Samuel, CA and Steven, DH (1976) *Quarterly Journal of Experimental Physiology* (In press)

Campbell, AGM, Dawes, GS, Fishman, AP, Hyman, AI and James, GB (1966) *Journal of Physiology, 182,* 439

Carter, AM (1975) In *Comparative Placentation.* (Ed) DH Steven. Academic Press, London. Page 108

Clarke, RM and Hardy, RN (1969) *Journal of Anatomy, 108,* 63

Crombie, PR (1972) PhD Thesis, University of Cambridge

Duncan, SLB (1969) *Journal of Physiology, 204,* 421

Enders, AC (1965) *American Journal of Anatomy, 116,* 29

Faber, JJ (1973) In *Foetal and Neonatal Physiology.* (Ed) RS Comline, KW Cross, GS Dawes and PW Nathanielsz. Cambridge University Press, Cambridge. Page 306

Forsmann, WG, Metz, J and Heinrich, D (1975) *Journal of Ultrastructure Research, 53,* 374

Friend, DS and Gilula, NB (1972) *Journal of Cell Biology, 53,* 758

Goldstein, SR (1926) *Anatomical Record, 34,* 25

Gulamhusein, AP and Beck, F (1975) *Journal of Anatomy, 120,* 349
Hemmings, WA (1958) *Proceedings of the Royal Society Series B, 148,* 76
Hemmings, WA and Brambell, FWR (1961) *British Medical Bulletin, 17,* 96
Huggett, A StG (1927) *Journal of Physiology, 62,* 373
Jollie, WP (1976) *Anatomical Record, 184,* 73
King, BF and Enders, AC (1970) *American Journal of Anatomy, 129,* 261
Larsson, L and Horster, M (1976) *Journal of Ultrastructure Research, 54,* 27
Leissring, JC and Anderson, JW (1961) *American Journal of Anatomy, 109,* 149
Longo, LD, Hill, EP and Power, GG (1972) *American Journal of Physiology, 222,* 730
Makowski, EL, Meschia, G, Droegmueller, W and Battaglia, FC (1968) *Circulation Research, 23,* 623
Mayow, J (1674) *Medico-Physical Works.* The Alembic Club, Edinburgh, 1907
Meschia, G, Battaglia, FC and Bruns, PD (1967) *Journal of Applied Physiology, 22,* 1171
Morris, B and Morris, R (1976) *Journal of Physiology, 254,* 389
Morriss, GM (1975) In *Comparative Placentation.* (Ed) DH Steven. Academic Press, London. Page 87
Samuel, CA and Steven, DH (1976) *Proceedings of the Anatomical Society, April 1976. Journal of Anatomy* (In press)
Sinha, AA and Mossman, HW (1966) *American Journal of Anatomy, 119,* 521
Steven, DH (1975a) In *Comparative Placentation.* (Ed) DH Steven. Academic Press, London. Page 26
Steven, DH (1975b) In *Comparative Placentation.* (Ed) DH Steven. Academic Press, London. Page 25
Steven, DH and Samuel, CA (1975) *Journal of Reproduction and Fertility, Supplement 23,* 579
Tillack, TW (1966) *Laboratory Investigation, 15,* 896
Wimsatt, WA (1960) *American Journal of Anatomy, 87,* 391
Wislocki, GB and Dempsey, EW (1946) *American Journal of Anatomy, 78,* 1
Wynn, RM and Amoroso, EC (1964) *American Journal of Anatomy, 115,* 327
Wynn, RM and Davies, J (1965) *American Journal of Obstetrics and Gynecology, 91,* 533
Yamamoto, K, Fujimoto, S and Takeshige, Y (1976) *Journal of Ultrastructure Research, 54,* 22

Fetal Growth: Favourable and Unfavourable Factors

A M THOMSON
Princess Mary Maternity Hospital, Newcastle-upon-Tyne, England

AVERAGE FETAL GROWTH RATES
AND THEIR DETERMINATION

Before discussing factors which favour or hinder fetal growth, something needs to be said about the nature of the evidence. Some serial measurements can be made by X-rays or sonar, but most of our information comes from cross-sectional data, each fetus being measured only once, as soon as possible after delivery. Fortunately, the averages obtained by plotting size at birth against gestational age do seem to give a reliable idea of the average patterns of rates of growth, though not necessarily of the growth of individual fetuses. Most of the data are in terms of weight, and in this paper only birth weights will be discussed. On this basis, the average fetal growth curve is S-shaped. Average weight increments per week are greatest around the end of the second trimester and the beginning of the third trimester; thereafter growth slows down until term. This will be discussed later.

Growth rates are estimated by plotting size against against age, but it is almost impossible to determine gestational age exactly. Obstetricians use the convention that gestation starts on the first day of the last menstrual period (LMP). This date is often unknown, imprecisely known, or grossly inaccurate. Furthermore, it is questionable whether the first day of withdrawal bleeding in women who have been using a hormonal contraceptive really corresponds to that of a menstrual bleed. Fetal growth does not, of course, really start at menstruation, but after an ensuing ovulation, conventionally assumed to occur 14 days after the last menstruation. In fact, the interval between menstruation and ovulation varies by a week or more around an average of about 14 days. Even if the date of ovulation could be precisely determined, there are still

31

unknown but undoubtedly variable intervals between ovulation, fertilisation and implantation. Sources of error in timing, which are practically unavoidable, have important implications for the interpretation of fetal growth curves, because during most of gestation the fetus is growing very rapidly. For example, the *average* fetus gains nearly 20mm in crown-heel length and 26g in weight between 100 and 107 days of gestational age, estimated from the last menstrual bleeding. Such considerable differences in length and weight could be found in two fetuses of the same gestational age, merely as a result of unavoidable errors in estimating true fetal age (Birkbeck et al, 1975).

VARIATIONS IN AVERAGE FETAL GROWTH

At any given stage of gestation, one fetus may be twice as heavy as another. For the reasons given above, it is difficult to decide whether growth becomes more variable during the final weeks of gestation, as a result of 'placental insufficiency' or other factors. Nevertheless, it is commonly assumed that fetal growth rates are fairly constant during the earlier months, and that impairment of growth rates becomes obvious only during the final weeks.

Gruenwald (1966, 1975) has illustrated that assumption by diagrams which suggest that in different groups fetuses depart from ideal straight-line growth at varying stages, under the influence of socio-economic, nutritional and other factors; the greater the 'handicap' the earlier the onset of faltering growth. For example, under nearly-ideal conditions in Sweden, the fetus is thought to grow almost uninterruptedly until term, whereas under less favourable conditions growth slows down or ceases during the final weeks. There are two difficulties about Gruenwald's concept. First, the original data on which the concept is based do not fit the theory very well. Second, one would expect multiple pregnancies, which place unusually large demands on the placenta and its supply line, to show unusually early and exceptionally severe impairment of late fetal growth. This is true if the birth weights of individual babies from twin pairs or triplets are considered. But the combined average weight of the twins or triplets increases with gestation in parallel with the weight of singletons, but at a higher level (McKeown and Record, 1952; Daw and Walker, 1975). This casts doubt on the idea that the capacity of the placenta and its supply line is reached or exceeded near term sufficiently commonly to account for differences in average birth weights at term or in their distributions at specific gestational ages. The explanation for faltering fetal growth near term may have little to do with the ability of the placenta to pass nutrients to the fetus.

MATERNAL SIZE

Leitch et al (1959) showed that over a wide range of animal species, from bats weighing a few grammes to whales weighing 10,000 kg, the litter weights of newborns are proportional to maternal size. In human beings, tall mothers tend to have bigger babies than short mothers; and at any given height there is an independent association between birth weight and maternal weight (Thomson et al, 1968). It is interesting that paternal size has no effect on birth weight; the effect is purely maternal (Morton, 1955). Ounsted and Ounsted (1973) have proposed a theory of 'maternal constraint', according to which the greater the antigenic difference between mother and fetus, the faster the rate of fetal growth. If such an effect exists it does not appear to be related to maternal size. The weight of the baby at birth is also related to the amount of weight gained by the mother during pregnancy, as would be expected since fetal weight forms part of the weight being gained. The extent to which maternal gain in weight is related to fetal weight is more doubtful; the relationship may depend to some extent on the composition of the weight gained by the mother.

ETHNIC DIFFERENCES

Reports of extreme birth weights in certain ethnic groups have to be treated with caution; thus, the data of Adams and Niswander (1968) showing unusually high birth weights in American Indians were explained by a computing error, and Meredith's (1970) claim that the highest average birth weights in the world were found in Anguilla proved to be due to a misinterpretation of the original report.

Roberts (1976) reviewed published reports and has presented average birth weights which range from 3341g in Europe to 2808g in Melanesia, New Guinea and Australia. He points out that we do not know the extent to which such variations are due to climate, food supply, poverty, disease, physique, genetic constitution, or other factors. There is a general correlation of birth weight and standard of living, from which it seems reasonable to suppose that ethnic differences in birth weights are considerably influenced by nutritional and other environmental influences. Gruenwald et al (1967) claim that fetal growth (i.e. birth weight for gestation) has risen considerably in Japan since the end of World War II.

DIETARY DIFFERENCES

The main effect of starvation is to reduce fertility; when pregnancy does occur, there is impairment of fetal growth. The effect, however, is not as dramatic as might be expected; thus, during the undoubtedly severe Dutch famine of 1944/45, average birth weights fell by only about 9 per cent (Stein et al, 1975). Under less extreme conditions, Read et al, (1975) found that birth weights in a poor rural community in Guatemala increased in parallel with the calorie value of supplements given to pregnant women: this is probably the most direct proof so far available that improving the diets of pregnant women who are undernourished can result in an increase of fetal growth rate. Whether this is so where dietary conditions are not obviously defective and where pregnant women can get enough to eat is more doubtful. Thomson (1959) found a small correlation between the food intakes of women in Aberdeen, Scotland and the birth weights of their babies, but this disappeared when differences of maternal height and weight were taken into account.

As mentioned already, the weight gained by the mother during pregnancy, which includes the weight of the fetus, is an important intermediate variable. The average gain of the Aberdeen women was about 12.5kg, that of the Guatemalan mothers about 7kg, while during the Dutch famine mothers were reported to have gained little weight if any during pregnancy. Where the calorie supply is insufficient, and the total weight gain is low, mothers may be unable to store a significant amount of extra depot fat, and thus have little or no physiological reserve during late pregnancy when the fetal demands are largest.

OTHER FACTORS

Some other factors influence fetal growth. Female babies have a slightly lower average birth weight than male babies, and this difference seems to appear during the final weeks of pregnancy (Thomson et al, 1968). The difference is probably hormonal in origin, but Ounsted and Ounsted (1973) attributed it to a difference of maternal-fetal antigenicity. First babies are slightly lighter than subsequent babies, possibly due to an increase in maternal vascular capacity following a first pregnancy.

Some disorders of pregnancy affect fetal growth; severe pre-eclampsia may result in the birth of a light-for-dates baby, whereas in diabetes mellitus the baby may be unusually heavy, though functionally immature. Birth weight decreases with increasing altitude above sea-level. Hytten and Leitch (1971) calculated from published data that an increase of 1000m in altitude results in a decrease of about 100g in birth weight. This may be a direct result of hypoxia. Of immediate concern, because the obstetrician may be able to do something about it, is the relationship between cigarette smoking and birth weight. For example, Butler and Alberman (1969) found the average birth weight at all late gestational ages to be about 100g lighter in mothers who smoked than in those who did not smoke. The decrease in birth weight was accompanied by a rise in perinatal mortality. Persuading mothers to stop smoking during pregnancy is therefore likely to increase birth weights and to reduce death rates.

References

Adams, M S and Niswander, J D (1968) *Human Biology, 40,* 226
Birkbeck, J A, Billewicz, W Z and Thomson, A M (1975). *Annals of Human Biology, 2,* 319

Butler, N R and Alberman, E D (1969). *Perinatal Problems: the Second Report of the 1958 British Perinatal Mortality Survey.* Edinburgh: E & S Livingstone Ltd.

Daw, E and Walker, J (1975). *British Journal of Obstetrics and Gynaecology, 82,* 29

Gruenwald, P (1966). *American Journal of Obstetrics and Gynaecology, 94,* 1112

Gruenwald, P (1975). *The Placenta and its Maternal Supply Line,* p.1. Lancaster, Medical & Technical Publishing Co.

Gruenwald, P, Funukawa, H, Mitani, S, Nishimura, T and Takenchi, S (1967). *Lancet, i,* 1026

Hytten, F E and Leitch, I (1971). *The Physiology of Human Pregnancy.* Oxford: Blackwell Scientific Publications.

Leitch, I, Hytten, F E and Billewicz, W Z (1959). *Proceedings of the Zoological Society of London, 133,* 11

McKeown, T and Record, R G (1952). *Journal of Endocrinology, 8,* 386

Meredith, H V (1970). *Human Biology, 42,* 217

Morton, N E (1955). *Annals of Human Genetics, 20,* 125

Ounsted, M and Ounsted, C (1973). *On Fetal Growth Rate* Clinics in Developmental Medicine, No.46

Read, M S, Habicht, J-P, Lechtig, A, and Klein, R E (1975). *Modern Problems in Paediatrics, 14,* 203

Roberts, D F (1976). In: *The Biology of Human Fetal Growth* London: Taylor and Francis. (In press)

Stein, Z, Susser, M, Saenger, G and Marolla, F (1975). *Famine and Human Development.* New York: Oxford University Press

Thomson, A M (1959). *British Journal of Nutrition, 13,* 509

Thomson, A M, Billewicz, W Z and Hytten, F E (1968). *Journal of Obstetrics and Gynaecology of the British Commonwealth, 75,* 903

The Measurement of Fetal Growth and Diagnosis of Well-being

G CHAMBERLAIN
Queen Charlotte's Hospital, London, England

The first thirty-eight weeks of human life are spent in the uterus where the fetus grows, dependent upon placental exchange. The make-up of fetal tissues are kept within the biological range of normal by the transfer functions of the placenta for while fetal homeostatic mechanisms do exist, it is only the placenta which com-

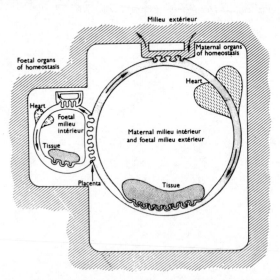

Figure 1. Although the fetus has homeostatic organs, exchange takes place through the placenta to the maternal blood. Thus the fetal milieu exterieu is the mother.
(Taken from Chamberlain, G (1973) In 'Integrated Obstetrics and Gynaecology for Postgraduates'. (Ed) CJ Dewhurst. Blackwell, Oxford)

municates with the environment (Figure 1); at the placenta, the fetal and maternal circulations are close but separate. An alteration in the capacity of the placenta to handle the exchange of nutrients would lead to deprivation of the fetus; this placental insufficiency is a clinical concept and many attempts are made to try to quantify it.

It must be remembered that the placenta is an organ which has two functions. As well as exchange regulation between the mother and the fetus, the placenta is an organ producing hormones. These two activities are independent of each other and although there may be a relationship between them, it is a complex and maybe an altering one. There is no justification to extrapolate automatically from one to the other yet this is often done. Tests of placental function are usually concerned with the hormone activity of the placenta but a measure of the capacity of exchange is lacking.

MEASURING FETAL GROWTH

The commonest method of assessing fetal growth is to examine the patient at regular intervals at an ante-natal clinic. While this is often thought to be fairly accurate in the hands of one experienced observer, even such people can be wrong (Figure 2). It is remarkable how inaccurate the examiner can be if he

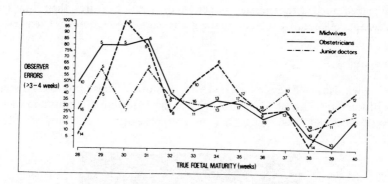

Figure 2. Percentage of opinions about fetal maturity expressed by groups of health care attendants. The numbers represent the examinations performed by each group at any gestation. (Taken from Beazley, JM and Kurjak, A (1973) 'Nursing Times', 69, 124)

knows neither the patient's history nor what the last observer found at the previous clinic visit. When these errors are multiplied by compounding several observers, as so often occurs in the ante-natal clinics in the Western World, the clinical assessment of rate of growth may be less exact than is usually considered.

In the earlier visits, hypertrophy of myometrium is assessed, and only after 24 weeks can the fetus and its amniotic fluid become a major component in the clinical assessment of the increase in size of the uterus.

Clinical assessment of growth in the early pregnancy can probably be a useful guide to dating a pregnancy, particularly if a bimanual examination is performed in the first 12 weeks when the increments of growth are greatest. This short account of the clinical assessment of fetal growth should not be taken as an indication of its lack of importance. In many parts of the world it is the only method of assessment.

X-Rays

Radiological demonstrations of the fetus in the uterus were the earliest investigations in this field. The stage of gestation can be determined at different points in pregnancy by the size of the fetus, the thickness of the subcutaneous fat layer and by the presence of certain ossification centres in the long bones. The most useful are those of the lower femur appearing at 36—38 weeks and of the upper tibia appearing at 38—40 weeks. The appearance of calcification in the placenta is of little use; so rarely is the fetal head in the correct antero-posterior position in relation to the X-ray plate, that biparietal diameters cannot often be measured. Fetal growth is a dynamic situation and, therefore, usually needs more than one point upon a graph to be fully assessed. X-rays are dangerous and are rarely repeated in pregnancy and their value is limited; however, if certain milestones have been passed, such as the presence of certain ossification centres, then X-rays may be a useful collaborative method that a given stage of gestation has been reached.

Ultrasound

The known risks of X-rays stimulated efforts in other fields of physical investigation of the fetus. One of the best of these is the reflection of ultrasound waves from tissue planes. Whenever there is an interphase of solid and fluid or of two

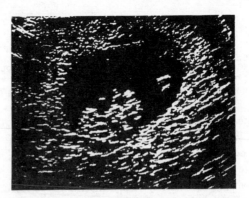

Figure 3. A gestation sac and fetus at 8 weeks outlined by ultrasound (loaned by S Campbell)

solids of different acoustic density, ultrasound can be echoed off this. Measurements of the gestation sac can be made in the first few weeks of pregnancy (Figure 3) and allow the length of gestation to be measured.

Ultrasound estimations are probably of more practical use, however, in later pregnancy when serial readings can be taken as often as weekly to assess the growth weight pattern.

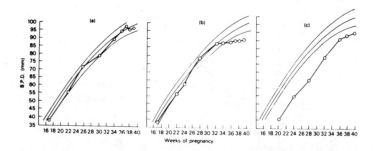

Figure 4. Growth of fetal head as measured by serial biparietal diameter measurements. The lines on the graph represent the mean $\pm$ SD from the mean. (a) normal pregnancy; (b) growth retardation with chronic placental malperfusion; (c) a patient who was incorrect in the dating of her period of gestation. The fetus grows at a normal rate. (Taken from Chamberlain, G (1975) In 'Lecture Notes in Obstetrics'. Blackwell, Oxford)

In Figure 4 it should be noted that the mean line of this population and those of the two standard deviations on either side of the mean are very close to each other, indicating a test with a narrow range of variation.

Fetal head measurements have been used for years to assess growth. The biparietal diameter can be measured by looking at the mid-line echo where the cerebral hemispheres are separated thus ensuring that the scan is at right angles to the transverse axis. Campbell and Dewhurst (1971) showed this method to be accurate with a mean error in early pregnancy of less than 1 mm. When a series of readings is taken with the first being before 24 weeks, the rate of growth can be shown to flatten off in later pregnancy so that it is possible to predict the expected date of confinement to within nine days in 80% of cases. This assumes that the ultrasound estimations are performed by an accurate worker. The method causes the patient little inconvenience and no danger. Readings can be performed weekly to show that fetal growth is within normal limits and at present is the most reliable method of measuring fetal growth.

In intrauterine fetal malnutrition, the head is the last part of the body to reflect deprivation and a reduction in its growth rate is a late sign that the fetus is affected other easily measured regions of the fetus such as the circumference of the abdomen are better indications. The abdominal circumference is measured at the level of the umbilical vein, and gives a fairly precise assessment of fetal weight, particu-

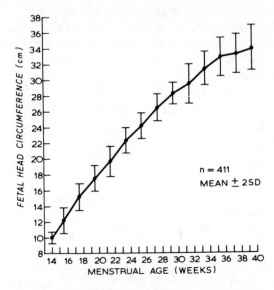

Figure 5a. Fetal head circumferences throughout pregnancy

FETAL ABDOMEN CIRCUMFERENCE MEASUREMENTS
AND MENSTRUAL AGE

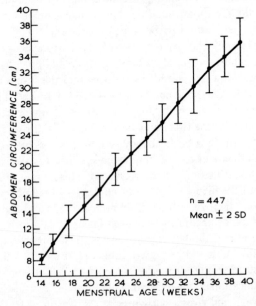

Figure 5b. Fetal abdominal circumference throughout pregnancy

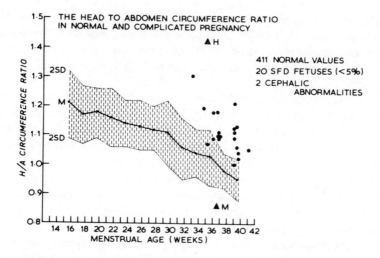

Figure 5c. Head/abdomen ratios showing the small for dates fetus mostly having a higher ratio at delivery (loaned by S Campbell)

larly in the smaller fetus (Campbell & Wilkins, 1975). This also allows a comparison of the sizes of the head and abdomen and the ratio between them may be a better indication of retardation of growth; while the head circumferences tail off at the end of pregnancy, the abdominal circumferences goes on increasing and in the normal fetus the head/abdomen ratio falls and those who will be small for dates have higher ratios (Figure 5).

MEASURING FETAL WELL-BEING

Measurement is a physical reading and a series of these can show a trend, as in fetal growth. When considering well-being, opinion is added to fact and correlation with outcome becomes less precise.

Clinical Measures

The concept of high risk has evolved over the last decade. The correct phrase should be 'higher risk' for even when the risk is considered to be low there are still some hazards. The concept of higher risk is however useful and may be determined by events in the past history or those happening early in the current pregnancy. Campbell et al (1976) are currently investigating the total population in Aberdeen having determined the characteristics of women who produce small-for-dates babies below the tenth percentile of birthweight.They are devising a simple screening based upon easily obtained measures of weight, weight gain and height of the mother. This has been used in an attempt to select women prospectively for intensive obstetrical care or for dietary supplements. If two or more of

41

the characteristics of low birthweight were taken, then 45% of the women destined to produce a baby on the tenth percentile can be identified. Some mathematical rearrangement of the cut-off points of the characteristics might improve this choice, but such simple tests as this may well allow us to identify those at higher risk.

Others have examined socio-economic factors and influences related to past pregnancies. For example infants under 2.5 kg occur in 4.8% of pregnancies from social classes I and II but in 8.4% of those of social classes IV and V (Chamberlain et al, 1975). Such influences are particularly important when added to other affecting factors such as smoking or pre-eclampsia.

As pregnancy progresses clinical guides to fetal well-being may be garnered. Lack of growth has already been discussed; lack of weight gain and increase of the girth of the mother's abdomen may be associated with an affected fetus, particularly in hypertensive states (Elder et al, 1970).

The mother usually feels fetal movements first in mid-pregnancy and is commonly aware of some movements each day until the last weeks when reduction of amniotic fluid may restrict the fetus whose movements are no longer felt so acutely. Until recently there has been no quantification of fetal movement in relation to well-being beyond the general thought that violent fetal movements were associated with extreme hypoxia. Sardrosky and Yaffe (1973) have recorded fetal movements as observed by the mother. They considered that each fetus had its own rhythm but there was no significance in the number of movements a day, unless there was a reduction below a certain level of daily movement which was a cheap and easy warning system of impending hypoxia. Practical use has been made of this by Pearson (1976) in Cardiff who found that a drop in the daily fetal movement rate below 11 per 12 hours was significantly related to hypoxia; he combines observations of fetal heart rate with those of fetal movement.

Hormone Measurements

Hormones regulate fetal growth acting at first directly in the fluid in which the fertilised ovum is suspended and later through chorionic control of the utero-placental circulation. Hormone assays therefore are only coarse estimates of fetal well-being and often reflect the bulk of trophoblastic tissue that is present or is damaged rather than the state of the fetus. Only currently is the sequential measurement of total production of oestrogens over 24 hour periods seen to be of real value.

Oestrogens are present in all body fluids and about 10—20% of each day's production is excreted in the urine. Since excretion varies throughout the day and the night a 24-hour collection of urine must be made. In late pregnancy about 85% of the total excreted oestrogens is oestriol. Hydrolysis of the specimen liberates conjugated steroids and a Kobler reaction is used. This has been improved and modified (Brown et al, 1957) and with semi-automatic techniques one technician can deal with over forty samples a day.

Whilst oestriol and oestrone can both be synthesised by the placenta, their excretion in pregnancy is very small compared with that of oestriol. This is a product of both placental and fetal metabolism and cannot be made in the absence of the fetus. Pregnenalone is converted in the fetal adrenal gland to dehydroepiandrosterone sulphate (DHAS) for fetal tissues are rich in sulphatases. DHAS is then hydroxylated in the fetal liver to 16 α hydroxydehydroepiandrosterone sulphate. This passes back to the placenta where it is hydrolysed to the free steroid which is then aramatised to oestriol. In pregnancy therefore the developing fetus is responsible for the production of large quantities of neutral precursors which are converted to oestriol. These constitute the major portion of the total oestrogens excreted from the maternal urine and so measuring the total oestrogen levels in pregnancy is an assessment of fetal adrenal and liver metabolism as well as that of the placenta.

Twenty-four hour collections of urine present problems for they depend upon the passage of urine through another organ — the kidney. This may be the seat of disease and commonly in conditions when the fetus is put at risk, glomerular filtration is affected. Further, certain drugs can affect oestrogen secretion whilst low fluid intakes can also alter the output. There are errors produced by forgetting to put urine samples into the collecting pot and compounding this, particularly in outpatients, when other members of the family have contributed in a helpful way to bring up the volume of urine collected. There are great day-to-day variations in excretion of steroids. Klopper and Diczfalusky (1969) pointed out that

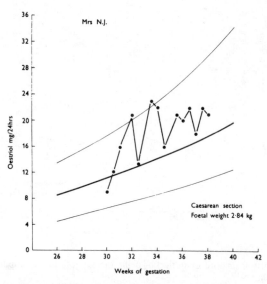

Figure 6a. Twenty-four hour excretion of urine in the normal patient

43

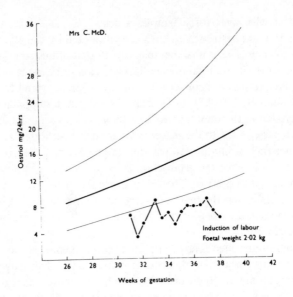

Figure 6b. Twenty-four hour excretion of urine in growth retardation with chronic placental malperfusion

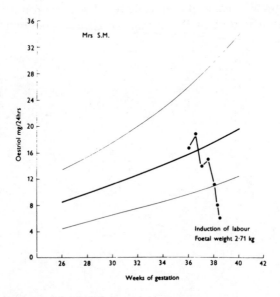

Figure 6c. Twenty-four hour excretion of urine in acute placental malperfusion as occlusion pre-eclampsia.
(Taken from Chamberlain, G (1973) In 'Integrated Obstetrics and Gynaecology for Postgraduates'. (Ed) CJ Dewhurst. Blackwell, Oxford)

44

since the daily coefficient of variation of excretion is about 30%, values had to be at least 60% above or below the mean before alterations became significant. Single values are not very useful but a series of readings can show a trend; this of course is true of any chronic alteration where serial observations are required to show significant results. Conversely, estimations of oestrogens in the urine are not very useful for detecting acute changes in the fetus.

The test is of most use in intrauterine growth retardation, in some slower evolving cases of pre-eclampsia and in post-maturity. With fetal intrauterine growth retardation, a falling series of readings show poor feto-placental function; if this is not improved, the fetus is not going to survive for long inside the uterus and should be delivered (Figure 6b). In pre-eclampsia the placental exchange is altered acutely in the last weeks of pregnancy (Figure 6c). If the fetal oestriol levels stay in the normal range, this is reassuring and is a sign of continuing well-being so that it staves off the need for induction of labour. In essential hypertension the test is not quite so useful unless there is also pre-eclampsia.

In post-maturity the fetus outgrows the capacity of placental exchange. However, so long as the oestrogen secretion is normal, the fetus is probably not at high risk and induction of labour is not indicated. However oestrogen levels may fall very suddenly from the normal and if reliance is to be placed on them they should be measured on alternate days if the pregnancy goes past 41 weeks; most obstetricians will have acted before then if they are sure of dates.

It might perhaps be better to screen patients and so predict the high risk states. Beischer and Brown (1972) have shown that if the urinary oestriol levels are subnormal in the ante-natal clinic, perinatal mortality rates and the incidence of

TABLE I. Outcome of Pregnancy of 698 Women Broken Down by their 24-hour Oestrogen Excretion Performed at 30 and 36 weeks Gestation. A Subnormal Excretion was one of 6 mg, or Less in 24 hours

Excretion Pattern	Still births (% of group)	Neonatal Deaths (% of group)	Birthweight below tenth percentile (% of group)
Normal (n=628)	0.3	1.3	9.5
Subnormal (n=70)	15.7	8.6	37.1

intrauterine growth retardation are increased (Table I). They assayed 24-hour oestrogen excretions at 30 and 36 weeks' gestation and using this as a screening test, showed a difference between women with high rates of stillbirth and neonatal death compared with those who had living children. Oestrogen excretion was reduced also in women who bore babies who were small for dates or had congenital abnormalities. More work is required to eliminate the false positives and, perhaps more important, the false negatives from this test.

To avoid the difficulties and errors of 24-hour collections of urine, measurements have been made on single samples of blood or amniotic fluid. Since the production of oestrogens fluctuates in the 24 hours these samples must be taken at the same time of day and compared in a serial fashion. Masson (1973) and Chamberlain and Kitchen (1976) have not shown any strong correlation between plasma levels of the three principal oestrogens and the incidence of small-for-dates babies (under 2.5 kg). Mather et al (1973) found in their patients that in the last weeks of pregnancy if the plasma level is below 10 micrograms per cent the fetus is at high risk and if below 4 micrograms per cent fetal death is imminent.

The placenta produces many hormones and these have from time to time been used in an attempt to assay fetal well-being; mostly however they assess the mass of active trophoblastic tissue rather than its endocrine or exchange function. For some years progesterone excretion was estimated by the measurement of its major catabolite pregnegalone in 24-hour urine samples. In early pregnancy this may be useful in the management of recurrent or threatened abortion. In later gestation serial progesterone levels are low in the presence of very poor placental function and correlations with fetal outcome are not good.

Human placental lactogen is produced in the syncytotrophoblast and levels rise progressively until the last weeks of pregnancy when the curve flattens. Blood samples are taken and the hormone is measured by radioimmune assay. There are variations from one laboratory to the other but absolute standards are now being established and evaluated. There is a good correlation between human placental lactogen levels and fetal outcome (Letchworth & Chard, 1972) and a fetal high risk zone below the line of 4 micrograms per millilitre after 35 weeks of gestation is useful in prognosis.

PHYSIOLOGICAL MEASUREMENTS OF THE FETUS

Fetal Breathing Movements

Until recently it was considered that the fetus made respiratory movements in the uterus only under hypoxic stress. It was considered reasonable that a mammal could move into efficient respiratory action within a few minutes of birth without any previous practice. Boddy and Dawes (1975) using ultrasound have been able to measure respiratory movements in the human fetus. They are identifiable at 14 weeks but are irregular until 20 weeks. Their frequency is 30 to 70 per minute and there is an individual variation. There is some loose correlation with behaviour in labour and this is being investigated further at the moment.

Evocative Stimulation of the Fetus

A series of tests have been used to measure the transfer rate of specific chemicals across the placenta. Atropine, adrenalin and isoxsuprin in appropriate dosage all cause alterations to the fetal heart rate. Pajutav (1968) has shown a loose relationship between slowed fetal cardiac response and diminution of placental function, particularly in serial studies.

Hypoxia can be induced when the mother breathes 12 per cent oxygen. Ballie (1974) has shown that the resulting fetal tachycardia should return to a normal rate within four minutes; if it takes more than eight minutes the fetus is at high risk.

Boyd et al (1974) described the use of oxytocin to stimulate the uterus to contract under controlled conditions to test the ability of the feto-placental unit to withstand labour. The results were very variable and the test is of doubtful value because the contractions of labour may be different than those produced by a small dose of oxytocin.

The fetal response to maternal exercise such as step-testing and static bicycling is a bradycardia which has a loose correlation with fetal hypoxia and subsequent labour, but these tests are crude and need much further evaluation.

Conclusions

There is no single absolute test of fetal well-being. Some in every day use have been discussed; others, such as the correlation of maternal plasma volume and birth size, are still experimental. All, however, tend to measure one facet only of fetal development (Table II).

TABLE II. Some Fetal Tests and the Data Derived from Them

Test	What is measured	What is inferred
Clinical history	Menstrual age	Fetal age
Clinical examination	Uterine and fetal size	Fetal age
Oestrogen excretion	Steroid synthesis of feto-placental unit	Fetal well-being
Placental lactogen secretion	Protein synthesis of placenta	Fetal well-being
Ultrasound		
Cephalic	Biparietal diameter of head	Fetal growth
Abdominal	Circumference of abdomen	Fetal growth
Amniocentesis		
for fetal cells	Skin maturity	Fetal maturity
for lecalthin-syphingo-myelin ratio	Lung maturity	Fetal maturity

47

The implications of what these tests mean is not always substantiated and it should be remembered that the second column of Table II is fact while the third column is implication.

References

Ballie, P (1974) *Fetal Medicine.* Saunders, London

Bescher, NA and Brown, JB (1972) *Obstetrical and Gynecological Surgey, 27,* 336

Boddy, K and Dawes, GS (1975) *British Medical Bulletin, 31,* 3

Boyd, I, Chamberlain, G and Fergusson, I (1974) *Journal of Obstetrics and Gynaecology of the British Commonwealth, 81,* 120

Brown, JB, Bulbrook, RD and Greenwood, FC (1957) *Journal of Endocrinology, 16,* 49

Campbell, DM, Campbell Brown, FD, Johnstone, I, MacGilivray, I and Wilson, AW (1976) Personal communication

Campbell, S and Dewhurst, CJ (1971) *Lancet, ii,* 1002

Campbell, S and Wilkins, D (1975) *British Journal of Obstetrics and Gynaecology, 82,* 9

Chamberlain, G and Kitchen, Y (1976) *Postgraduate Medical Journal* (In press)

Chamberlain, R, Chamberlain, G, Howlett, B, Claireaux, AE (1975) *British Births 1970.* Heinemann Medical Books, London

Elder, MG, Burton, ER, Gordon, H, Hawkins, DF and Browne, JC McC (1970) *Journal of Obstetrics and Gynaecology of the British Commonwealth, 77,* 481

Klopper, A and Diczfalusky, F (1969) *Fetus and Placenta.* Blackwell Scientific, Oxford

Letchworth, AT and Chard, T (1972) *Lancet, i,* 704

Massom, GM (1973) *Journal of Obstetrics and Gynaecology of the British Commonwealth, 80,* 423

Mathur, RS, Chestnut, SK, Leaming, AB and Wilkinson, HO (1973) *American Journal of Obstetrics and Gynaecology, 117,* 210

Pajutav, M and Lavric, M (1968) *Obstetrics and Gynecology, 32,* 520

Pearson, JF (1976) *Prevention of Handicap Through Ante-natal Care.* (Ed) AC Turnbull and FP Woodford. Excerpta Medica, Amsterdam. Page 177

Nutritional Endowments at Birth

D HULL
University Hospital Medical School, Nottingham, England

In their development, as in the final shape, mammals show striking species variations. They demonstrate many ways of solving the biological problems set by intrauterine development, birth and post-natal growth. A thorough consideration of the nutritional endowments at birth should include some statement on such widely differing topics as the wide disparity between the weight of the newborn and the mother, the rates of growth of various organs at birth, the motor skills

	Birth Weight (g)	Lipid Stores (g. kg. body wt.$^{-1}$)	Carbohydrate Stores Liver and Muscle (g. kg. body wt.$^{-1}$)	Oxygen Consumption Minimal (ml. kg.$^{-1}$ min.$^{-1}$)	Oxygen Consumption Maximal (ml. kg.$^{-1}$ min.$^{-1}$)	Very Approximate Theoretical Survival (days)
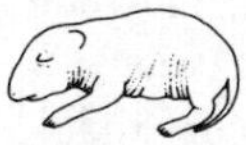	5	11	8	25	50	0.8
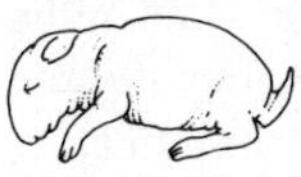	50	58	5	20	60	4
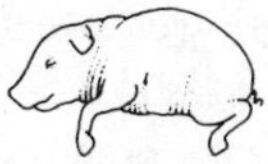	500	11	23	12	36	2.2
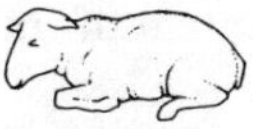	5000	30	11	5→10	30	6
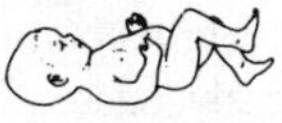	3500	160	11	6	16	35

Figure 1

of the newborn and their capacity to seek their own food. I shall discuss only storage and mobilisation of carbohydrates and fat.

The capacity of newborn mammals to survive starvation varies from a few hours in some to many days in others. The difference largely depends on the size of the fat stores, but it is also greatly influenced by the metabolic demands (Figure 1). In this respect the smaller mammals with their large metabolic rates in relation to their body weights are at a disadvantage and cold exposure presents a much greater threat. Most newborn mammals more than treble their metabolic rates on cold exposure so their theoretical survival time shown in Figure 1 would be reduced by over a third. Carbohydrate stores make a small but significant contribution to the newborn's chances of surviving if they are temporarily separated from the mother, particularly in those species with limited fat reserves. In all species glycogen stores are critically important during the periods of hypoxia which might accompany birth.

FETAL DEPOSITION OF CARBOHYDRATE

Glucose crosses the placenta by facilitated transport and it is generally considered to be the main energy source of the fetus. Whether the fetus receives *excess* glucose begs a question, but fetal tissues certainly take up glucose and store it as glycogen and fat. The capacity of fetal tissues to store glycogen appears to develop at different stages in gestation for different tissues in the same species and for the same tissue in different species and it is clearly related to the development of enzyme systems (Shelley, 1961; 1964; Shelley & Milner, 1975). Notwithstanding it is a fair generalisation that glycogen stores in the liver reach very high levels towards term in most newborn mammals and fall rapidly after birth to meet the early demands for glucose. Skeletal muscle also has sizeable deposits of glycogen at birth, but these appear to be available only for local consumption. The fetal heart muscle works actively from an early stage in development and likewise develops large deposits of glycogen early. It would be wrong to consider that all these depositions are preparations for birth. The initial deposition may reflect only the development of the appropriate enzyme systems and subsequently the function of the glycogen stores in the fetus may be the same as in the adult. Certainly fetal liver glycogen stores fall with maternal starvation and lower levels are found in 'light for dates' infants. In the fetus, anoxia rapidly depletes glycogen in the heart and brain and partially mobilises the liver stores. In experimental animals there is a fair correlation between the initial carbohydrate content of the cardiac muscle and the ability of the newborn animal to survive acute total hypoxia (Mott, 1961). So there is evidence to suggest that the fetus makes some attempt to maintain its own blood sugar concentrations and under certain conditions to use its own local glycogen reserves. Although there are large glycogen deposits in the placenta in mid-gestation, there is little support for the early suggestion by Bernard (1859) that these reserves are liberated to the fetus at times

50

of crisis. The deposition of glycogen is dependent on the fetal pituitary-adrenal axis and as this system has been demonstrated to have a critical role in precipitating birth (Challis & Thorburn, 1975); it might likewise tune the development systems and stores in preparation for it. The unexpected, unprepared pre-term infant has comparatively low glycogen stores.

The fetal liver and adipose tissues have a considerable capacity to form fatty acids by lipogenesis from glucose and other substrates (Jones, 1973). These activities fall rapidly after birth (Iliffe et al, 1973). Judging by the distribution of the fatty acids in the fetal stores when the mother is well nourished and unstressed the fetal lipid may be largely formed by lipogenesis from glucose.

FETAL DEPOSITION OF FAT

The fetus stores fat in the liver and adipose tissue. Phylogenetically and ontogenetically adipose tissue is one of the last major body tissues to appear. In most mammals it develops in the last third of gestation; in some very little triglyceride may be laid down before birth. Many newborn mammals have two distinct forms of adipose tissue, one of which, brown adipose tissue, has an important role of thermoregulatory heat production in the newborn (Hull, 1974; Alexander, 1975). These two forms of adipose tissue have different growth patterns. Brown adipose tissue appears earlier, deposits fat sooner and reaches a peak growth velocity about the time of birth (Hudson & Hull, 1975). White adipose tissue develops later and in most species with the notable exception of man, does not deposit sizeable amounts of fat until after birth. Its growth rate is accelerating at the time of birth.

The fetal triglyceride stores may have a high percentage of palmitate ($C_{16}:0$)

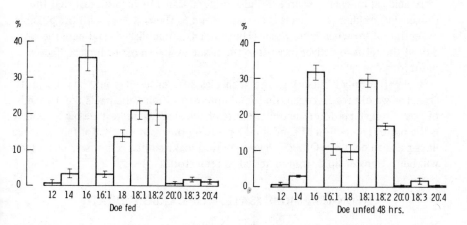

Figure 2. Percentage distribution of fatty acids in rabbit fetal white adipose tissue (Mean$^+$SD)

51

suggesting that they are derived from glucose by lipogenesis, but this varies. For example, if a pregnant rabbit is not fed for 48 hours prior to delivery, the fetal lipid stores, reflecting a net flux of fatty acids to the fetus, have a higher percentage of fatty acids $C_{16}:1$ and $C_{18}:1$ (Figure 2) [Edson, JL & Hull, D, unpublished]. There is now abundant evidence that fatty acids easily cross the placenta in most mammalian species tested (Hull, 1975) and in man and rabbits at least the net flux is directly related to maternal concentrations of free fatty acids (FFA) (Elphick et al, 1974, 1976). Maternal concentrations of FFA rise towards the end of pregnancy, during labour, during anaesthesia and surgical operations, and during acute maternal starvation. If the doe rabbit is given fluids but calories are withheld for 48 hours towards term, the content of stored fat in fetal tissues increases on average by 80% (Edson et al, 1975). Thus, one factor determining the lipid stores in the fetus is the state of nutrition in the mother. In starvation the mother's own homeostatic mechanisms by maintaining her own blood sugar and mobilising her lipid reserves are of considerable advantage to the fetus which may not be maintained as the mother adjusts to prolonged starvation.

The fetal liver rapidly takes up free fatty acids which it may store as triglyceride and release into the circulation as endogenous triglyceride. The fetal liver appears to have only a limited capacity to produce ketones. The endogenous triglyceride will be cleared by the action of lipoprotein lipase in the capillaries of peripheral tissues. Equally, and in contrast to the situation after birth, adipose tissue also rapidly clears free fatty acids from the circulation. Fetal adipose tissues also release their fat stores possibly either for fetal use or for transfer back to the mother. A variable percentage of fetal circulating FFA, depending on the net flux from the mother is derived from fetal adipose tissues. Rabbit fetal adipose tissue in vitro responds in a similar way to lipolytic agents as tissue from the newborn (Hudson, DG, unpublished). It is uncertain to what degree the fetus can use fatty acids as an energy source. Studies on fetal tissue in vitro suggest that the capacity to oxidise fatty acids is limited (Roux & Myers, 1974) with the possible exception of brown adipose tissue (Hudson, DG, unpublished) and here the capacity of the fetus to deliver oxygen to the tissue may be a major limiting factor in utero.

Even after only a cursory glance at species differences, it would be difficult to argue, as we did for glycogen, that fetal lipid deposition anticipates the demands of post-natal starvation. The only feature of teleological interest we have noticed is the natural reduction of food intake made by pregnant rabbits for two or three days prior to delivery. Other species may well make similar responses. The effect will be to transfer lipid from maternal to fetal stores.

NEONATAL MOBILISATION OF CARBOHYDRATE

Many articles have been written on the circulating concentrations of glucose, free fatty acids, ketones, etc after birth in animal and man, and extensive comparisons have been made between infants born early and late, or born heavy or light. This, if nothing else, reflects the clinical importance of detecting those infants who might run out of glucose because of the effects hypoglycaemia has on the developing brain. However, individual measures of circulating concentrations give very little indication of the biochemical situation. A series of concentrations which show a rise indicates a *net* input that exceeds a *net* output or consumption but all may be either rising or falling. It tells us very little of what is happening in a single tissue, for example, the brain. The correlation between clinical hypoglycaemia in the human newborn and the blood metabolite concentrations, illustrate this point. Infants of diabetic mothers appear to withstand periods when their blood sugar concentrations are exceedingly low without harmful effects and certainly without obvious signs of disturbance. On the other hand, recent evidence, based on temperature differences, indicating that a major fraction – possibly as much as 70% – of the resting of oxygen consumption of the human infant takes place in the brain, emphasises the infant's dependence on a large alternative supply of glucose following placental interruption (Cross & Stratton, 1974). However, the developing brain may use other fuels, e.g. ketone bodies (Williamson & Buckley, 1973).

In asphyxia, the blood glucose and the FFA concentrations rise rapidly and liver glycogen stores are depleted. Muscle glycogen is broken down to lactic acid, which on return to the liver may be reformed into glucose.

Pre-term infants, undernourished term infants and infants experiencing asphyxia during birth are all born with depleted glycogen stores and this is reflected by the observation that their blood glucose concentrations drop to lower levels than usual over the first 48 hours of life (Payne, 1974) and it is these infants which are more at risk of developing clinical hypoglycaemia. The fetus appears to use glucose as its major source of energy. The newborn may for a period continue to do so, but most mammals including man have only sufficient glycogen stores to last for 12 or so hours. The peripheral tissues must switch to fatty acids and delay in doing so will increase the risk of hypoglycaemia. Exposure to cold greatly increases the metabolic rate and also increases the demand for glucose. Initially cold exposure stimulates a rise in blood glucose concentrations. Severe cold exposure leading to hypothermia increases the risk of hypoglycaemia, particularly during the recovery or rewarming period. Gluconeogenesis develops rapidly after birth, but its quantitative contribution in the first critical hours and days is uncertain (Walker & Snell, 1973).

NEONATAL MOBILISATION OF FAT

During and after birth, inevitably the infant is handled and stimulated and is exposed to cold for the first time. The blood concentrations of FFA rise rapidly which suggests that fetal adipose tissue has the capacity to release FFA, and it is interesting to note that in 'small for dates' infants higher levels than normal occur,

53

whereas in infants of diabetic mothers lower levels are found which might indicate a different setting towards supply before birth. This possibility is supported by the observation that 2 hours after birth rabbits which were born from does who had not been fed for 48 hours before delivery had a higher resting FFA concentration and the FFA concentrations after exposure to cold rose higher than in newborn rabbits from does who were fed normally. There was also a smaller increment in blood sugar concentrations.

It has been known for many years that the respiratory quotient falls after birth, suggesting a move from carbohydrate to fat oxidation. The activity of enzyme systems concerned with fatty acid oxidation increase rapidly after birth (Wolf et al, 1974) although there may be some delay. That fatty acid mobilisation exceeds peripheral utilisation is reflected by the increased deposition of lipid in the liver and peripheral tissues, a phenomenon which may be very marked in 'light for dates' infants (Aherne, 1956). An excess of fatty acids going to the liver may accelerate the rate of ketone production and ketones may well be metabolised by the developing brain (Dahlquist et al, 1972; Kraus et al, 1974).

Once the peripheral tissues are orientated to fatty acid oxidation then the human infant, given adequate fluids, can mobilise his lipid reserves and use them effectively during critical periods of starvation, when, for example, oral feeding is impossible before the surgical correction of anomalies of the alimentary tract (Elphick & Wilkinson, 1974).

From clinical experience alone it is clear that the amounts of lipid stored at birth differ greatly from one apparently healthy infant to another, and we are only beginning to appreciate the possible physiological and pathological factors concerned. Accurate clinical measurement of fat stores at birth is difficult. However, Whitelaw (1976) has shown that a fair estimate is given by the sum of 8 skinfold measurements (4 on both sides) and this might prove to be a convenient way of identifying those 'light for dates' infants who require special attention, as well as a valuable research tool.

Summary

The dramatic changes associated with the onset of breathing have tended to overshadow equally impressive events at the other end of the sequence of respiration, cellular oxidation. Before birth the fetal tissues appear to use glucose as the main source of energy, after birth survival of the newborn infant depends on the early onset of oxidation of fatty acids. All newborn mammals appear to have adequate carbohydrate stores to support life over the first few hours until milk feeding is established. Some have adequate fat reserves to meet emergencies which might arise due to hazards which interrupt the early establishment of feeding. In this respect, the full term infant is singularly fortunate.

References

Aherne, W (1965) *Archives of Disease in Childhood, 40,* 406
Alexander, G (1975) *British Medical Bulletin, 31,* 62
Bernard, C (1859) *Comptes rendus hebdomadaires des sèances l'Académie des sciences (Paris), 48,* 77
Challis, JRG and Thorburn, GD (1975) *British Medical Bulletin, 31,* 57
Cross, KW and Stratton, D (1974) *Lancet, ii,* 1179
Dahlquist, G, Persson, U and Persson, B (1972) *Biology of the Neonate, 20,* 40
Edson, JL, Hudson, DG and Hull, D (1975) *Biology of the Neonate, 27,* 50
Elphick, MC and Wilkinson, AW (1973) *Proceedings of the Neonatal Society Meeting held in London on 15 November 1973*
Elphick, MC, Hull, D and Sanders, RR (1976) *British Journal of Obstetrics and Gynaecology* (In press)
Elphick, MC, Hudson, DG and Hull, D (1975) *Journal of Physiology, 252,* 29
Hudson, DG and Hull, D (1975) *Biology of the Neonate, 27,* 71
Hull, D (1974) *Comparative Physiology of Thermoregulation, 3,* 167
Hull, D (1975) *British Medical Bulletin, 31,* 32
Iliffe, J, Knight, BL and Myant, NB (1973) *Biochemical Journal, 134,* 341
Jones, CT (1973) In *Fetal and Neonatal Physiology. Proceedings of Sir Joseph Barcroft Centenary Symposium.* Cambridge University Press, Cambridge. Page 403
Kraus, H, Schlenker, S and Schwedesky, D (1974) *Hoppe-Seylers Zeitschrift für pathologie Chemie, 355,* 164
Mott, JC (1961) *British Medical Bulletin, 17,* 144
Payne, WW (1974) In *Scientific Foundations of Paediatrics.* (Ed) JA Davis and J Dobbing. Page 86
Roux, JF and Myers, RE (1974)*American Journal of Obstetrics and Gynecology, 118,* 385
Shelley, HJ (1961) *British Medical Bulletin, 17,* 137
Shelley, HJ (1964) *British Medical Journal, 1,* 273
Shelley, HJ and Milner, RDG (1975) *British Medical Bulletin, 31,* 37
Walker, DG and Snell, K (1973) In *Inborn Errors of Metabolism.* (Ed) FA Hommes and CJ Van Den Berg. Academic Press, London. Page 93
Whitelaw, AGL (1976) *Proceedings of the 47th Annual Meeting of the British Paediatric Association, York, April 1976*
Williamson, DH and Bulkley, BM (1973) In *Inborn Errors of Metabolism.* (Ed) FA Hommes and CJ Van Den Berg. Academic Press, London. Page 81
Wolf, H, Stave, U, Novak, M and Monkus, EF (1974) *Journal of Perinatal Medicine, 2,* 75

Biochemical Immaturity and Drug Kinetics

F SERENI and ANN V GISALBERTI
Dell'Universita di Milano, Milan, Italy

During the last decade many problems concerning developmental pharmacology have been investigated, both by paediatricians and clinical pharmacologists. Most of the original contributions concerned only single or a few aspects of drug kinetics, such as the determination of apparent plasma half-life and plasma protein binding; a comprehensive approach was seldom adopted.

Moreover, the attention of the majority of authors was often focused on the immediate post-natal period and on premature infants, while other developmental stages were neglected. Few studies were longitudinal, and little is known about the age at which the adult level for different processes is reached.

Since several excellent, comprehensive reviews of developmental pharmacology have appeared recently (Weber & Cohen, 1975; Morselli, 1976; Rane & Wilson, 1976) the main purpose of this article is to discuss critically selected information, and to interpret peculiarities of drug kinetics in infancy and childhood on the basis of what is already known about the physiology and biochemistry of human subjects during development.

The Physiology of the Gastrointestinal Tract in Neonates and Infants and the Absorption of Drugs Given by Mouth

The following peculiarities of the gastrointestinal tract of neonates and infants may cause great variation both in the rate and in the total amount of drug which is absorbed after oral administration:

1. The relative gastric achlorhydria
2. The slow emptying time of the stomach
3. The delayed gastrointestinal transit time
4. The relatively greater mucosal surface area

Some of these characteristics will influence the absorption of almost all drugs similarly, whereas in other cases the chemical structure of the drug is important in determining the difference between newborn and older subjects.

Gastric pH is almost neutral at birth, falls to between 1 and 3 during the first post-natal days, but then until the age of about three years the gastric acidity is lower than in adults (Weber & Cohen, 1975). This relative gastric achlorhydria probably accounts for the increased absorption in the newborn of penicillin G (Huang & High, 1953) and the semisynthetic penicillins (Grossman & Ticknor, 1965) all of which are acid-labile.

Most drugs are absorbed, after oral administration, by a pH-dependent process of passive diffusion in the small intestine (Schanker, 1971). Thus the slower rate of gastric emptying in the neonate (Davidson, 1968) should result in a slower rate of drug absorption. The delayed peak of plasma drug concentration, often observed in the neonate (Boothman et al, 1973; Silverio & Poole, 1973; Cohen et al, 1975) may be related to this delay.

The lower gastrointestinal motility, and hence the increased intestinal transit time in the neonate (Smith, 1951) should increase the total amount of drug absorbed due to longer exposure. The same effect would be expected as a consequence of the relatively larger mucosal surface area (Koldovsky, 1969). There is also the possibility that the permeability of different segments of gut changes with age and that this affects absorption (Smith, 1951; Davidson, 1968). Changes in enteric blood flow with age and the pH at the neonatal mucosal surface have not been measured but pH in the adult has been calculated at about 5.3 when compared with a pH of about 7 for the duodenal contents (Klumpp & Neale, 1930).

So many vital factors are unknown in the newborn that it is not surprising that little is known about drug absorption from the intestinal mucosa at this time. It is also impossible to collect enough samples of blood to determine the rate constant of absorption with a reasonable degree of accuracy. Apart from the penicillins it is believed that drug absorption in the neonate is either the same or slightly reduced when compared with the adult (Morselli, 1976) but few valid comparisons have been made by measuring the relevant kinetic parameters.

The practical conclusion to be drawn is that it is essential to measure drug levels in neonates and infants whenever the difference between the therapeutic and toxic threshold is narrow and the possibility of ineffective or dangerous levels is high.

Variations in Body Compositions with Age and their Implications in Drug Distribution

The problem of plasma drug binding. Quantitative or qualitative differences in serum albumin, or interfering factors?

There is not much variation in either relative plasma volume (Friis-Hansen, 1961) or plasma protein (American Association Clinical Chemistry, 1974) from birth to puberty. Since drugs are bound mainly to albumin in plasma changes in albumin concentration with age may affect binding. However its level in cord or neonatal blood at term is very similar to that in the adult (Erhnebo et al, 1971; Pruitt & Dayton, 1971; Short et al, 1975) and low plasma albumin is found only in very premature infants (Gitlin & Boesman, 1966).

Despite these similarities it is well accepted that the plasma binding capacity for most drugs is lower in the neonate than in the adult. Care must be taken when comparing binding at different drug concentrations but nevertheless strictly controlled studies (for example Ganshorn & Kurz, 1968) do demonstrate a significant decrease in drug binding in neonatal plasma. Consequently the percentage of free or active drug is higher in younger subjects.

Since the lower binding cannot be explained by decreased albumin levels, two other alternatives are possible, either that neonatal albumin is intrinsically different from adult albumin and has a lower avidity for drugs, or that some endogenous plasma factors compete with the drugs for protein binding sites.

Miyoshi et al (1966) reported that albumin isolated from human cord blood showed some different physicochemical properties from adult albumin, but it is not known whether these differences affect drug binding. It is probable that they do not, since Chignell et al (1971) demonstrated that, despite a lower association constant for sulphaphenazole in the newborn, the number of drug binding sites on purified albumin was the same at all ages. In addition charcoal treatment of cord albumin (Chignell et al, 1971) or extensive dialysis of cord blood (Krasner & Yaffe, 1975) yield albumin with identical binding constants for sulphaphenazole and salicylate as in the adult. These observations suggest that, rather than any structural difference in cord albumin, there are in neonatal plasma some dialysable charcoal removable factors which inhibit drug binding.

The presence of interfering factors has also been postulated on the basis of the decreased plasma binding of bilirubin in the newborn (Kaputilnik et al, 1975) although Krasner & Yaffe (1971) reported increased binding at this time. Valaes and Hyte (unpublished observations) have recently demonstrated that even after exchange transfusion of the newborn, where the neonatal albumin is replaced by adult albumin, the bilirubin binding remains at the low pre-transfusion level. This suggests that the newborn continues to produce some compounds which bind to adult albumin and decrease bilirubin binding.

What these inhibitory factors are is a matter of controversy, and hydrogen ions, free fatty acids (FFA) and bilirubin (for drug binding) may all be involved. In order to determine which, if any, of these factors are important it is essential to establish a temporal correlation. At birth plasma pH is low whereas bilirubin and FFA concentrations are high, so all may be involved in the low drug binding in the neonate. However, plasma pH and bilirubin rise to the normal range within a few days or weeks of birth when sulphaphenazole binding, at least, is still low (Chignell et al, 1971). In contrast, plasma FFA are elevated for many months

58

and so may continue to affect albumin binding in both neonates and infants. Several authors (Starinsky & Shafrir, 1970; Thiessen et al, 1972) have stated that in most normal or pathological conditions the FFA : albumin ratio is never high enough to displace bilirubin from albumin. The small for dates newborn may be an exception to this, since albumin levels at term are lower than in normal babies (Bergstrand et al, 1972) while plasma FFA concentrations, during the first eight days of life at least, are much higher than normal (Anagnostakis & Lardinois, 1071). Furthermore, most drugs bind to albumin with an association constant of about 10^5 M^{-1} which is at least an order of magnitude less than for bilirubin (Starinsky & Shafrir, 1970; Krasner & Yaffe, 1971). Consequently, they will be displaced from albumin by circulating FFA more easily than is bilirubin. The paediatrician must measure the levels of free, as well as total, drug in plasma if he is to avoid toxicity in the neonate due to an increase in the percentage of unbound drug.

Other relevant aspects of the influence of changing tissue composition during growth

Drug distribution is affected by both plasma protein binding and by other changes in tissue composition during the last part of intrauterine life and the first years after birth.

Body water (and its partition into extra- and intra-cellular compartments), the amount of fat which accumulates in different areas, and the differing capacities according to age of certain tissues to concentrate specific drugs are the main factors to be considered. Total body water as a percentage of body weight is high in the full term neonate (about 80%) and is even higher in the premature infant (Friis-Hansen, 1961; Widdowson, 1974 and others). Only when the infant weighs 7—8 kg does its body appear to have reached the water-solid relationship characteristic of the adult (about 60% water). Changes in the extracellular volume are even more pronounced than for total body water. At birth, in full term infants, extracellular fluids account for about 45% of body weight. This falls sharply during the first few months of life but is still well above the adult value (about 15%) when the child weighs 25—30 kg (Friis-Hansen, 1961).

It is reasonable to conclude that the larger volume of distribution observed for most drugs in premature or full term infants is due to variations in body water content (Morselli, 1976). This however is not the rule for all drugs tested. For example, the volume of distribution of diazepam is significantly smaller in the premature neonate than in the older child (Morselli et al, 1973). This is probably due to the fact that the benzodiazepines are extremely lipid soluble and the premature neonate has very little body fat. Lipids accumulate in body tissues only during the last trimester of gestation and contribute about 1% of body weight when the fetus weighs 1 kg (26 weeks). This increases to about 16% at term (3.5 kg, 40 weeks gestation), which is close to the average found during childhood.

59

Other substances which have a smaller volume of distribution in the neonate than in older subjects are digoxin (Morselli et al, 1975) and a tetracycline derivative (Sereni et al, 1965). In both cases this is probably due to a lower drug concentration in peripheral tissues. This hypothesis is substantiated by the following observations:

1   In both cases the apparent volume of distribution is much higher than for other drugs, indicating entry into tissues from the extracellular fluid.

2   For the tetracycline it has been demonstrated that the ratio of tissue : plasma drug concentration is much lower in the newborn than in the adult rabbit (Sereni et al, 1965).

3   Digoxin accumulates in muscle and fat depots in much higher concentrations than in plasma. Gorodischer et al (1975) demonstrated that although digoxin accumulates to a greater extent in the heart of the newborn than in the adult the ratio of skeletal muscle : serum drug concentration was similar in young infants and adults. Cardiac muscle contributes little to body weight but skeletal muscle accounts for about 25% of body weight in the newborn compared with an average of 40% in the adult (Widdowson, 1974) so the volume of distribution for digoxin should be smaller in the younger subjects.

Liver Microsomal Enzyme Activities and Drug Metabolism During Development

The activities of many hepatic enzyme systems which metabolise exogenous or endogenous substrates are low in newborn animals of different species (Sereni & Principi, 1965, 1968). In newborn infants initial investigations concerned bilirubin metabolism in relation to the pathogenesis of neonatal jaundice. Use of sensitive analytical techniques has yielded more information on hepatic drug metabolism in human infants, but many problems are still open for discussion.

Firstly, it appears that the hepatocytes of the human fetus or neonate are structurally adequate for drug metabolism. Using the electron microscope Zamboni (1965) showed that the liver of the human fetus is almost completely differentiated after the third month and has all the cellular components necessary for performing the functions of the adult organ. In addition the fetal microsomes contain both cytochrome P-450 and NADPH-cytochrome C reductase which are necessary for drug metabolism (Yaffe et al, 1970). Thus it would seem that the fetal liver is well equipped to metabolise both endogenous substrates and drugs.

Despite these observations there are numerous in vitro studies demonstrating that fetal liver exhibits low activities of mixed function oxidases, compared with adult liver if exogenous compounds are used (Rane & Sjökvist, 1972; Sereni et al, 1973). This reduced capacity is also present for some time after birth. These results correlate with the prolonged half-life observed for many drugs which are metabolised before excretion (tolbutamide, Nitowsky et al, 1966; phenylbutazone,

Gladtke, 1968; amidopyrine, Reinicke et al, 1970; diphenylhydantoin, Mirkin, 1971; ethanol, Idänpään-Heikkilä et al, 1972; nortriptyline, Sjökvist et al, 1972; amobarbital, Krauer et al, 1973; diazepam, Morselli et al, 1973; salicylate, Levy & Garrettson, 1974; antipyrine, Murdock et al, 1975).

This decreased ability to metabolise drugs is in sharp contrast to the efficiency with which fetal and neonatal liver can metabolise endogenous substrates such as laurate and testosterone (Yaffe et al, 1970).

To explain these discrepancies two main hypotheses may be put forward:

1   The enzyme systems which metabolise endogenous substrates are different from those which metabolise administered drugs, and may therefore show a different developmental pattern. This hypothesis is not substantiated by any sound experimental evidence.

2   Another more likely suggestion is that some endogenous compounds may bind with high affinity to the oxidases and so compete for the metabolism of the administered drug. Laurate and testosterone both bind strongly (Yaffe et al, 1970) so it has been postulated that fatty acids or steroid hormones may be inhibitors. It is well known that fatty acid concentrations are high in the neonatal period, and progesterone, reaching the baby via the placenta and later the milk, may also be involved (Feuer & Liscio, 1969). Growth hormone can also inhibit drug metabolism, probably by increasing plasma FFA (Wilson, 1970). This hypothesis is further supported by observations on experimental animals made by many authors (see Sereni et al, 1973) where induction of microsomal enzyme activity is much more easily obtained after birth than in the fetus.

The low activity of liver microsomal enzyme systems in fetuses and newborn infants may be considered another example of how characteristics peculiar to the early stages of development may influence drug disposition and therefore drug tolerance in these subjects.

Renal Function in Neonates and Infants and their Capacity for Drug Excretion

This aspect of pharmacokinetics was the first to be considered. About thirty years ago Barnett et al (1949) reported that penicillin clearance was much reduced in premature infants and emphasised the great practical importance of this in terms of dosage. Glomerular filtration rate (GFR) is low in newborn infants compared with the adult both in terms of body weight and surface area. In premature infants this rate is even lower depending on the degree of prematurity. Proximal tubular function is even less well developed than glomerular function when related to surface area adult values of these renal functions are not reached before 6–12 months of age (see review by Edelmann & Spitzer, 1969). Most drugs are excreted via the kidneys (as is the case for almost all antibiotics) either by glomerular filtration or also by tubular secretion. It is therefore not surprising that the half-lives of these compounds are considerably longer in neonates and infants than in children (Morselli, 1976).

GFR increases sharply after birth in newborn infants as well as in other mammals, and consequently a significant fall in drug plasma half-life is observed after about the first fifteen days of life in the human neonate (Sereni et al, 1968). From the practical point of view, this means that there should be a longer period of time between drug doses, especially in newborn infants to a minimum plasma concentration (e.g. sulphonamides, Sereni et al, 1968) or to avoid toxic accumulation (e.g. aminoglycoside antibiotics, McCracken & Jones, 1970). Few complete studies or direct measurements of drug excretion have been made in neonates or infants (for a tetracycline derivative see Sereni et al, 1965 and for digoxin, Wettrell, 1976) and more relevant data is needed.

Conclusions

Our knowledge of developmental pharmacology is still very far from satisfactory, in contrast to the comprehensive information we have about human body growth and tissue maturation. The reasons for this discrepancy are numerous. Reliable data on developmental pharmacology have been accumulated only during the last few years. Moreover drug disposition depends on many factors which change greatly during infancy and childhood. From a practical point of view it is usually impossible to make simultaneous determinations of the kinetics of a certain drug and body composition and tissue function. Thus possible correlations which explain the mechanism of developmental changes in drug kinetics are in most instances only hypothetical. This limitation also prevents the prediction of drug kinetic variations which may occur when pathological conditions significantly interfere with body composition and (or) function.

The main conclusion which may be drawn from these considerations is that there is an obvious need to collect very careful drug kinetic data. Together with recording physiological and physical measurements in infants and children of various ages, this should establish more rational paediatric therapy.

Acknowledgments

AVG was the recipients of a Nestlé paediatric travelling scholarship awarded by the Australian Paediatric Association.

This work was supported by CNR Grant No 75.00709.04.

References

American Association of Clinical Chemistry (1974) *Normal values for pediatric clinical chemistry*
Anagnostakis, DE and Lardinois, R (1971) *Pediatrics, 47,* 1000

Barnett, HL, McNamara, H, Shultz, S and Tompsett, R (1949) *Pediatrics, 3,* 418
Bergstrand, CG, Karlsson, BW, Lindberg, T and Ekelund, H (1972) *Acta Paediatrica Scandinavica, 61,* 128
Boothman, R, Kerr, MM, Marshall, MJ and Burland, WL (1973) *Archives of Disease in Childhood, 48,* 147
Chignell, CF, Vesell, ES, Starkweather, DK and Berlin, CM (1971) *Clinical Pharmacology and Therapeutics, 12,* 897
Cohen, MD, Raeburn, JA, Devine, J, Kirkwood, J, Elliot, B, Cockburn, F and Forfar, JO (1975) *Archives of Disease in Childhood, 50,* 230
Davidson, M (1968) In *Biologic Basis of Pediatric Practice.* (Ed) RE Cook. McGraw Hill, New York. Page 812
Edelmann, CM and Spitzer, A (1969) *Journal of Pediatrics, 75,* 509
Ehrnebo, M, Agurell, S, Jalling, B and Boréus, L-O (1971) *European Journal of Clinical Pharmacology, 3,* 189
Feuer, G and Liscio, A (1969) *Nature, 223,* 68
Friis-Hansen, B (1961) *Pediatrics, 28,* 169
Ganshorn, A and Kurz, H (1968) *Archiv für Pharmakologie und Experimentelle Pathologie, 260,* 117
Gitlin, D and Boesman, M (1966) *Journal of Clinical Investigation, 45,* 1826
Gladtke, E (1968) *Il Farmaco (Sci. Ed), 23,* 897
Gorodischer, R, Jusko, WJ and Yaffe, SJ (1975) *Pediatric Research, 9,* 283
Grossman, M and Ticknor, W (1965) *Antimicrobial Agents and Chemotherapy,* 214
Huang, NN and High, RH (1953) *Journal of Pediatrics, 42,* 657
Idänpään-Heikkila, Jouppila, P, Akerblom, HK, Isoheo, R, Kauppila, E and Koivisto, M (1972) *American Journal of Obstetrics and Gynecology, 112,* 387
Jalling, B, Boréus, L-O, Kollberg, N and Agurell, S (1973) *European Journal of Clinical Pharmacology, 6,* 234
Kapitulnik, J, Horner-Mibasham, R, Blondheim, SH, Kaufmann, NA and Russel, A (1975) *Journal of Pediatrics, 86,* 442
Klump, TG and Neale, AV (1930) *American Journal of Diseases of Children, 40,* 1215
Koldovsky, O (1969) In *Development of the Functions of the Small Intestine in Mammals and Man.* S Karger, Basel. Page 140
Krasner, J and Yaffe, SJ (1971) *International Congress of Pediatrics, 13,* 317
Krasner, J and Yaffe, SJ (1975) In *Basic and Therapeutic Aspects of Perinatal Pharmacology.* (Ed) Morselli, Garattini and Sereni. Raven Press, New York. Page 357
Krauer, B, Draffan, GH, Williams, FM, Clare, RA, Dollery, CT and Hawkins, DF (1973) *Clinical Pharmacology and Therapeutics, 14,* 442
Levy, G and Garrettson, LK (1974) *Pediatrics, 53,* 201
McCracken, GH and Jones, LG (1970) *American Journal of Diseases of Children, 120,* 524
Mirkin, BL (1971) *American Journal of Obstetrics and Gynecology, 109,* 930
Miyoshi, K, Saijo, K, Kotani, Y, Kashiwagi, T and Kawai, H (1966) *Tokushima Journal of Experimental Medicine, 13,* 121
Morselli, PL (1976) *Clinical Pharmacokinetics, 1,* 81
Morselli, PL, Principi, N, Tognoni,) (Reali, E, Belvedere, G, Standen, SM and Sereni, F (1973) *Journal of Perinatal Medicine, 1,* 133
Morselli, PL, Assael, BM, Gomeni, R, Mandelli, M, Marini, A, Reali, E, Visconti, U and Sereni, F (1975) In *Basic and Therapeutic Aspects of Perinatal Pharma-*

cology. (Ed) Morselli, Garattini and Sereni. Raven Press, New York. Page 377
Murdock, AI, Thogeirson, SS, Rossiger, H and Davies, DS (1975) *Biology of the Neonate, 27,* 289
Nitowsky, HM, Matz, L and Berzofsky, JA (1966) *Journal of Pediatrics, 69,* 1139
Pruitt, AW and Dayton, PG (1971) *European Journal of Clinical Pharmacology, 4,* 59
Rane, A and Sjöqvist, F (1972) *Pediatric Clinics of North America, 19,* 37
Rane, A and Wilson, JT (1976) *Clinical Pharmacokinetics, 1,* 2
Reinicke, C, Rogner, G, Frenzel, J, Maak, B and Klinger, W (1970) *Pharmacologia Clinica, 2,* 167
Schanker, LS (1971) In *Fundamentals of Drug Metabolism and Drug Disposition.* (Ed) LaDu, Mandel and Way. Williams and Wilkins, Baltimore. Page 22
Sereni, F and Principi, N (1965) *Pediatric Clinics of North America, 12,* 515
Sereni, F and Principi, N (1968) *Annual Review of Pharmacology, 8,* 453
Sereni, F, Perletti, L, Manfredi, N and Marini, A (1965) *Journal of Pediatrics, 67,* 299
Sereni, F, Perletti, L, Marubini, E and Mars, G (1968) *Pediatric Research, 2,* 29
Sereni, F, Mandelli, M, Principi, N, Tognoni, G, Pardi, G and Morselli, PL (1973) *Enzyme, 15,* 318
Short, CR, Sexton, RL and McFarland, I (1975) *Biology of the Neonate, 26,* 58
Silverio, J and Poole, JW (1973) *Pediatrics, 51,* 578
Sjöqvist, F, Bergfors, PG, Borga, A, Lind, M and Ygge, H (1972) *Journal of Pediatrics, 80,* 496
Smith, CA (1951) In *The Physiology of the Newborn Infant, 2nd Edition.* Charles C Thomas, Springfield, Illinois. Page 180
Starinsky, R and Shafrir, E (1970) *Clinica Chimica, Acta, 29,* 311
Thiessen, H, Jacobsen, J and Brodersen, R (1972) *Acta Paediatrica Scandinavica, 61,* 285
Weber, WW and Cohen, SN (1975) In *Concepts in Biochemical Pharmacology, V 28(3), Handbook of Experimental Pharmacology.* (Ed) Gillette and Mitchell. Springer-Verlag, Berlin. Page 213
Wettrell, G (1976) *Acta Pediatrica Scandinavica, Supplement 257*
Widdowson, EM (1974) In *Scientific Foundations of Pediatrics.* (Ed) Davis and Dobbing. Heinemann, London. Page 153
Wilson, JT (1970) *Nature, 225,* 861
Yaffe, SJ, Rane, A, Sjöqvist, F, Boréus, L-O and Orrenius, S (1970) *Life Sciences, 9 (Part II),* 1189
Zamboni, L (1965) *Journal of Ultrastructure Research, 12,* 509

Acknowledgment

The authors are grateful to Dr Valeria Gianni for her contribution collecting bibliographic references.

The Value of Breast Feeding

MAVIS GUNTHER
Esher, Surrey, England

The value of breast feeding is taken to mean an assessment of those specific effects of the milk and the act of giving the breast which can be mimicked only to a limited extent or not at all by the provision of substitute milk. Few can still question whether there are indeed such specific qualities, for we now recognise several components of milk as well as of colostrum which protect the baby from infection and these cannot at present be safely provided from the milk of other mammals. Foremost, by present assessment, are the immuno-globulins, IgA, a little IgG and, at the outset, IgM. These recapitulate the mother's antigenic experience and are brought up to date by her further infection. The IgA augments the baby's own secretions in the nasopharynx and the gastro-intestinal tract and is known to protect against viruses to which the mother has antibodies. This is presumably the most specific quality of human milk in that it deals with the viruses of *human* infections. The immuno-globulins also have their effects in controlling bacterial infection and some of the mechanisms involved are coming to be understood. Here again the anti-bodies tend to be specifically suited to human babies, partly because the nature of the symbiosis with the intestinal flora differs from one type of mammal to another and the respective milks conform. The anti-bacterial antibody action of human milk is increased many times by its collaboration with lactoferrin, a protein with very high affinity for iron. Lactoferrin hinders the multiplication of bacteria by denying them iron (Bullen et al, 1972). Other protein components also influence bacterial multiplication. Lysozyme with complement can lyse E.coli (Glynn, 1969). Two carrier proteins for B_{12} and folate are absorbed intact through the gut wall and provide the vitamins for the baby but deny them to the gut flora (Ford et al, 1972).

Those who enjoy what seems like nature's ingenuity will appreciate the fact that these proteins serve not only in their special capacities but also as nutrients to the baby; and the milk provides an antitrypsin which ensures that some survive digestion and are effective throughout the length of the alimentary canal.

Two practical points arise: first, some workers are now studying ways of increasing the mother's anti-E.coli antibody by oral vaccination in pregnancy (Hanson, 1976). Secondly, these anti-infective substances in human milk are proteins. It may be possible to keep them in active form in breast milk banks by careful pasteurisation (Ford et al, 1976). This is far less likely to be safe or practicable in dealing with cow's milk, and without extensive trial, the proteins being foreign, must be expected to be antigenic to the baby. This point leads to another aspect of breast feeding. It appears that in the first six months of life when the baby's own supply of IgA is low, foreign proteins are much more likely than they are later in life to lead to allergies (Taylor et al, 1973). Human milk proteins are virtually non-antigenic to humans and possibly the IgA of the milk helps the baby's immune system to deal with other antigens without leading to allergy.

The influence of these protective substances on the health of the baby is hard to assess numerically. Surveys show that the breast fed baby is less likely to develop pneumonia, gastroenteritis or measles. Their value to the baby depends on the risks inherent in the place where they live — the hotter the country the greater the benefit. In England and Wales there are estimated to be about 3000 'cot deaths' a year. Although the cause or causes are unknown some statistics about the subject are certain. Babies of low birth weight are in most danger; viral infections are found in the lungs at autopsy in about half and the disaster is far commoner among bottle fed babies (Tonkin 1975). It seems that whatever the cause the immunological package in human milk has a preventive action. Protective qualities are important to the baby but so too is the need to grow well. The supply of milk should be ample, balanced in the proportions of its constituents and comprehensive to meet all nutritional requirements and this brings us to the positive and negative values of human milk compared to other forms.

The amount of milk a woman secretes is not necessarily enough for her child. The inception of lactation can be delayed as happens often, for instance, when the baby is delivered by caesarean section. A dogmatic ruling that 'nature's way' must be adhered to can then have serious results if there is a risk that the baby may develop hypoglycaemia. Some lactations set out abundantly and then falter for no known reason; the inadequacy in these circumstances is usually so clear that the baby is soon fed with other types of milk. But the situation is more dangerous where the secretion is enough for the mother to persuade herself that it is adequate when it is not. Although it is difficult to get sutiable data about the effects of prolonged underfeeding on the child's subsequent performance, it is likely from the findings in animals that the brain is then smaller and the intellectual capacity less than in those who had been well fed. The choice of method of feeding should then be for ample feeding. Only if the home circumstances make aseptic techniques too difficult should reluctance to feed the baby partly or wholly by bottle be countenanced. The disadvantages of inadequate breast feeding are not only that the baby is going short but that many mothers who have struggled through early difficulties by great determination or who have been misled by the idea that breast secretion responds to demand join with those with a mystical reverence for breast feeding. It is hard to persuade them that they must do better for the baby. It was partly their unhappy experiences with mothers who had been overpersuaded to breast feed their babies twenty or thirty years ago which led Western paediatricians often to prefer that a baby should be bottle fed from the beginning. In Britain severely underfed babies with falsely confident mothers are back again with us. Mothers should be taught that a baby's weight must be watched and that only rarely can an inadequate secretion be made abundant once the lactation is past the first two or three weeks; more frequent feeding has little effect.

Other risks brought by the mother's ideas have to be recognised too in our assessments. This applies to the balance in the proportion of the constituents of milk. Breast milk has the enormous advantage here in that its composition cannot be altered profoundly by anyone's ideas. The balance of solutes to water in it ensures that provided the baby is taking a fair amount of his normal daily volume he will not be dehydrated by fever or hot weather. Only when his appetite fails is he likely to be in danger (Shaw et al, 1973). On the other hand in bottle fed babies there is a real risk of raised plasma concentration of sodium and urea if the mother, wishing as much as possible for her baby, puts too much dried milk powder into the volume of water of the feed. There was until recently a widespread failure to recognise that the right proportion of water is as important as that of any other constituent. This disadvantage of bottle feeding is not a necessary one.

The amounts of protein and lactose in breast milk are not normally altered by the mother's diet; the fatty acid composition of the fat is. One cannot lay down a definition of the right composition for it is affected by the mother's recent intake and by her ever-changing body fat composition. There are consequently big differences in the milk from women in different parts of the world without apparently any effect on the babies' health and who shall say which is correct? The advantage in breast milk here comes from the range of kinds of fats the mother eats and it is highly likely that the supply of essential fatty acids will be adequate. The addition of vegetable oils containing only a limited range of even unsaturated fatty acids seem less sure of providing the baby's needs than the random range in breast milk.

There are circumstances where the breast milk is unsuited to the baby; it cannot be modified to the baby's necessary restrictions in the rare metabolic disorders such as galactosaemia or some aminoacidaemias. Drugs taken by the mother are secreted in her milk, sometimes making breast feeding unwise. In some parts of the world beriberi is still a potential danger. If the mother is short of thiamine not only is the baby short of it too but the faulty metabolites resulting from the mother's deficiency are passed in the milk to the baby. In such deprived circumstances the urgent need is of course to give the vitamin to both mother and baby rather than resort to substitute milk, for in areas of grave food shortages where beriberi is likely to be found the loss of the protective qualities of breast milk can spell death. Infection in infancy in any part of the world should be viewed nutritionally as an adverse factor leading to reduced intake and failure of absorption, exaggerating any existing shortage.

Breast milk does not contain enough of some substances for a baby born prematurely to derive from it the amounts he would have done transplacentally if he had continued in utero. The premature baby needs and can use more vitamin D and calcium than there is in the maximum volume of breast milk he can take. Without supplementation he will be deficient in iron, magnesium, zinc and tin (Shaw, 1976). Technical means of giving extra quantities of these elements are needed whether he is fed with human or cow's milk.

Such immune globulins as a baby possesses at birth are received transplacentally or are developed in the last three months of pregnancy. A baby born prematurely lacks even the normal small quantities and the contribution offered by breast milk is proportionately more important to him, provided that the proteins in the milk have not been denatured by heat treatment. The milk antibodies act locally in the alimentary canal but they are not absorbed in large enough quantities to make up the baby's deficiency in his body proper.

The financial value of breast milk is uncertain when not estimated on its sale price but on its cheapness in the mother's total expenditure. The mother who feeds her baby uses some of her nutritional reserves built up in pregnancy but she also eats more. Nutritionists know it is possible to think up very economical ways of covering her needs but in practice the cost depends on the family's usual way of living. The mother eats more of her usual diet. She is likely to spend more on clothes and their washing than she otherwise would while the bottle feeding mother spends on the milk, the bottles, teats, sterilising equipment and fuel for heating and re-heating. Economy of time gives the advantage clearly to breast feeding; the preparation of bottle feeds does take time. Also, once the first, sometimes struggling, days are over breast feeding is usually quicker. A baby often takes the first part of his feed from the breast at the rate of 2oz (50ml) a minute. A baby finds it uncomfortable to drink at that rate from a bottle.

One of the arguments put forward by those advocating breast feeding is that it induces a closer emotional bond between mother and baby. I have heard the belief proclaimed with as cruel an effect as one may see between one woman and another — the other having chosen to feed by bottle. If it is true, it makes only a small contribution to the mother's delight in her baby and can be readily overtaken by other factors. The evidence drawn from mothers is unreliable as the mother who chooses to feed her baby herself is likely to be different in personality and in attitude to motherhood from one choosing the other way. Arguments derived from experimental effects of hormones on, say, nest building in animals remind one that the exceptional emotional state of the newly delivered mother in the first days coincides with a time of cataclysmic reversal of her pregnancy balance of hormones. One may suspect that the inception of lactation, being part of hormonal physiology, may play a part in maternal emotions. The first days appear to be specifically important in building in the mother's responsiveness to her baby. It seems fair to guess that this is a time of hormonally induced sensitivity, possibly marginally influenced by lactation. Early frequent handling of the baby appears to be the most potent help in building mother-child relationship. Those who eventually assess the contribution which the act of breast feeding makes here will have taken into account that the baby whose difficulties due to prematurity or illness prevent the mother from taking care of him from the beginning is the one who is for the same reasons most likely to be bottle fed.

The emotional effect of breast feeding can be the reverse of that desired. Mothers with an intense antipathy to breast feeding have commented to me that they only started to enjoy their babies when they had been allowed to stop breast feeding.

It must be clearly stated that those who live in temperate climates, with the advantages of health education, a high level of public hygiene and with access to antibiotics and milks processed by modern technology, have a high probability of being able to bring up their babies very well by feeding them by bottle. And in an assessment it must be remembered that some women cannot lactate successfully; for them comparative evaluation does not apply.

A woman who is *fully* breast feeding a child is less likely than she would otherwise be to conceive again during the first 8—10 months of lactation. This contraceptive effect is enormously important in many parts of the world where infection, food shortages, lack of hygiene and poverty threaten for if pregnancy comes the lactation soon becomes inadequate for the first child; and the survival of both infants is put at risk where the mother has two very young ones to look after. Modern contraceptive methods are more reliable than lactation in preventing conception and in the first months pills containing progestogens only do not seem to reduce the secretion of milk. But for very many women the cost of the pill is too great. The lactational delay in conception must be ranked as one of the most beneficial effects of breast feeding.

In conclusion, how does the balance stand? The measure is in probabilities and this is one of the difficulties for few of us have an innate sense about them. Should the recognition of the risk of cot death drive a woman to breast feed? If public concensus ruled that she should, the sorrowing mother's searching of herself for what she did wrong could be gratuitously made more agonising because here the smaller the baby the greater the value and, unfortunately, the greater the difficulty in succeeding. The protective qualities of the milk are paramount where infection is a continual hazard; the unresponsiveness of the mammary gland to increasing demand makes an inflexible attitude to breast feeding a risk in its own right. There is a very real risk of a woman bearing a second child within 11 months where lactation is suppressed and other contraceptive methods are not available. The professional adviser needs to be able to offer a wise and kindly representation of the risks ahead for the newly delivered woman and her child. There seems to be no justification for imposing suppression of lactation or for compelling a woman to feed her baby herself without her considered decision.

References

Bullen J J, Rogers H J, and Leigh L (1972). *British Medical Journal 1*, 69

Ford J E, Knaggs G S, Scott K J, and Salter D N (1972) *British Journal of Nutrition, 27*, 571

Ford J E, Law B A, Marshall V M E, and Reiter B. *Journal of Pediatrics* (In Press)

Glynn A A (1969). *Immunology, 16*, 463

Hanson L A. *Personal communication 1976*

Shaw, J C L, Jones A and Gunther M (1973). *British Medical Journal 2*, 12

Shaw J C L (1976) *Pediatrics, 57*, 16

Taylor B, Norman, AP, Orgel H A, Stokes C R, Turner M W, and Soothill J F (1973). *Lancet, ii*, 111

Tonkin S (1975). *Epidemiology of SIDS in Auckland, New Zealand. SIDS 1974. Proceedings of the Francis E Camps International Symposium on Sudden and Unexpected Deaths in Infancy*. The Canadian Foundation for the Study of Infant Deaths, Toronto 1975.

Artificial Milks and Their Effects on the Composition of the Infant

ELSIE M WIDDOWSON
University of Cambridge, Cambridge, England

In the developed countries of the world there must be dozens of different dried milk preparations being produced and sold, all intended to serve as the sole source of nutrients for babies during the first months after birth. Some of these are whole or partially defatted cow's milk. Some have lactose or other carbohydrate added. Some use whey, a by-product of the cheese industry, as the protein base, and in some all the fat originally in the milk may have been removed and replaced with a mixture of other fats. Vitamins A, D, and C are added to some, and they may or may not be fortified with an iron salt. A few contain added copper.

A few years ago we analysed 32 of these preparations, on sale in seven European countries (Widdowson et al, 1974a) and found large differences between them. Protein for example varied from 10 to 29 g per 100 g of powder, fat from 8.5 to 31 g/100 g and total carbohydrate from 37 to 67 g/100 g. The energy value of the milks depended largely upon the percentage of fat. The lowest was 389 kCal per 100 g and the highest 527 kCal per 100 g. Many of these milks, made up according to the manufacturer's instructions, contained far more per 100 ml of some constituents than human milk — protein, sodium and calcium are examples, and if we take human milk as our standard it is generally excesses we have to consider rather than deficiencies. Whether an excess of a constituent of the food is likely to affect the chemical composition of the baby's body, or of any particular part of it, depends upon (1) whether the net absorption from the intestine exceeds the baby's requirements and if it does, (2) whether the baby is able to excrete the excess in the urine, or by some other route, or to metabolise it. If the answer to the first is yes, and to the second no, then the composition of the baby's body must become different from that of one that is breast fed. Of

71

course an excess, for example of protein, may possibly make the baby gain weight faster, so we have to take this into account.

Fat A fundamental change that is sometimes made to cow's milk in preparing infant formulas from it is to remove the milk fat and replace it with other fats or oils. In some preparations the fat mixture is chosen so that the fatty acid composition resembles that of human milk fat. In others no attempt is made to do this, but the fat or fats are those that are known to be readily absorbed by young infants. Table I shows the major fatty acids in the fat in some of these milk foods, with human and cow's milk for comparison. The greatest difference found by us

TABLE I. Major Fatty Acids in Milk Containing Animals and Vegetable Fats (g/100 g total fatty acid)

Milk	Country of Purchase	C14:0	C16:0	C18:0	C18:1	C18:2
SMA	UK	6	13	7	39	13
Nativa	France	9	22	7	35	13
Almiron B	Holland	Trace	11	2	27	58
Frisolac	Holland	3	32	4	38	16
Similac	Holland	7	9	3	19	40
Milumil	Germany	7	35	8	32	10
Nan	Germany	11	31	9	24	16
Pelargon	Italy	8	25	11	30	17
Plasmolac	Italy	8	25	8	47	6
Auxolac	Italy	8	26	10	37	11
Eledon	Denmark	8	27	9	25	22
Pelargon	Denmark	9	24	11	31	15
Pelargon	Switzerland	2	24	11	30	17
Guifolac	Switzerland	6	33	6	38	14
Humana 1 & 2	Switzerland	7	23	7	43	14
Human milk		6	24	7	37	9
Cow's milk		12	30	14	31	2

was between the full cream cow's milk fed to infants in Britain, and the Dutch preparation Almiron, in which the cow's milk fat is entirely replaced with corn oil. Linoleic acid in these two infant foods made up 2% and 58% of the total fatty acids respectively. The percentage for human milk fat is 9. This led us to wonder what effect this was having on the body fat of infants in the two countries, so we investigated it (Widdowson et al, 1975). The British babies receiving only cow's milk fat always had 1—2% of linoleic acid in their body fat, while breast fed babies had 3—4%. In contrast, by 6 weeks Dutch babies had 25% of linoleic acid in their body fat, and by 12 weeks up to 46%. If linoleic acid is so high a percentage of the total fatty acids, others must be correspondingly lower.

For example the percentages of myristic acid and stearic acids in the fat of Dutch babies were considerably lower than those in the fat of British babies. Does all this matter? Are Dutch babies any better or worse off at that time or later for having a highly unsaturated body fat in infancy? Does the degree of saturation of body fat affect cell multiplication and the likelihood of obesity? Some French authors believe that it does, but we have been unable to confirm this. Are lipids other than those in the depot fat, for example those in the arteries and cell membranes, influenced by the nature of the fat in the diet? Animal experiments suggest that they are, and if so does this alter the fragility of the red blood cells, or the permeability and function of the membranes, or their behaviour in the presence of disease? Is the nature of the lipid deposited in the brain during the first months after birth affected by a large intake of linoleic acid? This seems rather unlikely, but until it has been investigated we cannot be sure.

Nitrogen I am now going to tread a well worn path and consider once again the apparent effect of different intakes of nitrogen on the composition of the baby's body. Babies on cow's milk formulas containing over 3% protein have invariably been found to absorb and retain more nitrogen than babies having human milk with 1.2% protein. Babies fed on cow's milk may gain weight a little faster than breast fed babies, but this may be due to the fact that they are given more milk and more calories, as well as more protein, than the babies having human milk. The problem, which as far as I am aware has never been satisfactorily solved, is set out in Table II. This is taken from publications of Fomon and his co-workers and summarised by Fomon (1974). It shows intakes and retentions of nitrogen from breast milk and cow's milk by babies studied between birth and 4 months of age, calculated as total retentions of nitrogen over the whole of the first 4

TABLE II. Retention of Nitrogen by Babies Between Birth and 4 Months

	Human Milk	Cow's Milk
N intake in 4 months g	187	499
N retention in 4 months g	73	246
Total N in baby's body (3.5 kg) at birth g	67	67
Total N in baby's body (7 kg) at 4 months g	140	313
N in body at birth g/kg	19	19
N in body at 4 months g/kg	20	45
N in body at adult g/kg	29	

months after birth. The babies receiving human milk retained a total of 73 g of nitrogen from a total intake of 187 g. The full term baby at birth contains about 67 g of nitrogen, so with the 73 g of nitrogen retained it will have 140 g of nitrogen in its body at 4 months, or 20 g/kg, a concentration similar to the value at birth. Fomon (1967) has suggested that the percentage of nitrogen, or of protein, in the body does not change greatly between birth and 4 months, any fall in the percentage of water being compensated by an increase in the percentage of fat. The balances of babies fed breast milk confirm this suggestion.

But now we come to the difficulty. The babies being fed on cow's milk preparations took in their food more than twice as much protein and nitrogen as the babies having breast milk. They absorbed most of it, but their urinary excretion of nitrogen, although higher, was not high enough to match the intake, and the babies appeared to retain three times as much nitrogen as the babies fed on breast milk. Only about 0.5 g of this was accounted for by a higher concentration of urea in the serum and the rest of the body water (Table III), but the

TABLE III. Serum Urea of Infants Fed Human or Cow's Milk (mg/100 ml)

Age days	Serum urea	
	Human Milk	Cow's Milk
15 – 42	17	57
43 – 70	14	56
71 – 98	14	47
99 – 126	15	40

destination of the remainder is unknown. If these results are true, the cow's milk fed babies would have 45 g of nitrogen per kg of body weight – and an adult has only 29 g/kg. There is clearly something here that needs an explanation, and yet the mysterious thing is that everybody who makes metabolic studies on babies having breast and cow's milk and measures the nitrogen intake and excretion finds the same sort of thing. We did ourselves for babies one week old (Slater, 1961). The most obvious explanation is that it is due to technical errors. If the baby regurgitates some of its feed, or a little is split you think the baby has had more than it did. If you lose a little urine or faeces you think the baby has excreted more than it did, and both of these lead to falsely high positive balance. Errors are generally due to losses and all the losses in a metabolic balance tend to be cumulative, and together give high retentions that are not correct. The balance periods on which I have based these calculations were not necessarily continuous and another possible explanation is that the baby retains more nitrogen during balance periods than between them. However, the results for human milk seem to come out about right.

Calcium   There is a similar difficulty over calcium. Although we know that calcium exerts vital functions in cell membranes all over the body, only very small amounts of it are required there, and 98–99% of the total amount of calcium in the body is found in the skeleton and other calcified structures. Fomon's results, calculated as the cumulative intakes and retentions of calcium by normal full term babies during the first 4 months after birth are shown in Table IV.

TABLE IV.   Retentions of Calcium by Babies Between Birth and 4 Months

	Human Milk	Cow's Milk
Ca intake in 4 months g	39.5	194
Ca retention in 4 months g	18.5	66.6
Ca in baby's body (3.5 kg) at birth g	28.4	28.4
Ca in baby's body (7 kg) at 4 months g	46.9	95.0
Ca in body at birth g/kg	8.1	8.1
Ca in body at 4 months g/kg	6.7	13.6
Ca in body of adult g/kg	18.6	

Some were having human milk and others full cream cow's milk. The full term baby at birth has about 28 g of calcium in its body. The babies fed on breast milk received 39.5 g calcium in 4 months; of this they absorbed and retained 18.5 g. This, added to 28.4, comes to 47 g altogether, or 6.7 g/kg, considerably less than the 8.1 g/kg in the body at birth. This fits in very well with Stearns' (1939) calculations made nearly 40 years ago. She concluded that the full term breast fed baby does not absorb and retain enough calcium to maintain the concentration of calcium it had in its body at birth. The total amount of calcium in the body increases, but not as fast as the body weight, and the percentage of calcium in the body must fall. Even by 4 months of age the percentage has still not reached the level at birth. But again we are in difficulties over the babies having cow's milk. Their intake of calcium was nearly 5 times that of babies having human milk and their retention between 3 and 4 times as high. If we add the 66.6 g retained to the 28.4 g in the body at birth, the total of 95 g in the body at 4 months is equivalent to 13.6 g/kg or more than twice the 6.7 g/kg in the breast fed baby. This is not as high as the adult value, so it is possible, but such large differences in the calcification of the bones of thriving human infants according to the way they are feed seem very remarkable and are physiologically unlikely. They are the more unlikely in view of the results obtained by Dickerson (1962) for the composition of femurs obtained from infants that had died during the first 4 months after birth, as compared with those of immature fetuses and stillborn infants. The degree of calcification of the bone rose during fetal life, but was lower in infants of 2–4 months than in stillborn infants at term. There was no information about the feeding of the infants, but it seems improbable that they had all been entirely breast fed.

Sodium Sodium is the element in infant formulas that has perhaps caused the most concern in Britain in recent years. Cow's milk contains considerably more sodium than human milk, 25 compared with 6.5 mEq per litre. Unlike adults, infants do not rapidly excrete a sudden excessive intake of sodium ions because, for some time after birth, the infant kidney reabsorbs sodium ions from the glomerular filtrate more completely than the adult kidney. For the first 10 days or so after birth, the kidney of the infant also rids the body of an excess of water much more slowly than that of the adult, but the age we are interested in at the moment is not the immediate neonatal period. We are concerned with the age when the kidney is still immature with regard to the excretion of sodium, but not of water. If therefore a breast fed infant is changed to a cow's milk preparation, particularly if this is made up too strong, much of the sodium may be retained and relatively little water to match it, and the serum sodium rises. However, there is at the same time an increase in the amount of water being absorbed and the consequence is hypertonic expansion of the body fluids. The extracellular fluid volume is expanded and the concentration of sodium in it is raised. This is the change in composition that takes place in the body of a healthy baby, and the higher the intake of salt and the younger and more immature the baby, the bigger is the effect (McCance & Widdowson, 1957). If the baby has an infection there will inevitably be an increased loss of water through the skin and lungs, and the baby becomes more dehydrated and the tonicity of its body fluids may rise to lethal levels if it is not given plenty of water.

Some of the infant formulas on sale nowadays are made from whey which is electrodialysed to remove the sodium, and then some skimmed milk powder is added so that the sodium content resembles fairly closely that of human milk. This is an expensive process and the formulas made in this way are correspondingly costly. Other manufacturers mix the dried cow's milk with carbohydrate and the concentration of sodium in the prepared feed is thereby reduced to about halfway between that in human and cow's milk.

Potassium Babies absorb potassium readily, and they are able to excrete potassium ions more easily than sodium ions. The higher concentration of potassium in whole cow's milk preparations as compared with human milk (36 mEq/l compared with 14) does not present a problem. The amount of potassium in the baby's body should not be affected by the type of milk fed, although balance studies on one-week old babies showed that those receiving a cow's milk preparation appeared to retain more potassium than those who were breast fed (Slater, 1961).

Iron It has been known for many years that milk contains far too little iron for the growing baby if the concentration of haemoglobin in its blood is to be maintained even at the level reached after the immediate post-natal fall. At one time it was thought that the liver at birth was equipped with a store of iron, but we now know that it does not contain enough to make much contribution to the needs of the rest of the body (Widdowson et al, 1974b). Fomon (1974) calculated that the increment of iron in the body over the first year should be about 200 mg, of which 100 mg should be retained over the first 6 months. If this is so, then the average daily increment should be 0.55 mg. The iron intake of a baby living on human or unfortified cow's milk would be about 0.33 mg a day, varying with the age of the baby and the volume of milk taken. The baby will not absorb the whole of its intake, and balance studies with ^{59}Fe when infants were given milk from a cow infused with the isotope, suggested that absorption of 10% of the intake is a reasonable estimate after 3 months of age (Schulz & Smith, 1958). Thus a retention of 0.55 mg a day requires an intake of 5.5 mg of assimilable iron, considerably more than the 0.33 mg contained in milk. Manufacturers of some infant foods add an iron salt to their preparations and the daily intakes of iron from these would vary from about 4 mg to 8 to 10 mg.

There is another side to this however. Human and cow's milk are not peculiar in containing little iron. The milk of all well-known species contains too little iron for the young to maintain the concentration of haemoglobin in their blood at birth while they double their birth weights. The haemoglobin level always falls. One wonders how necessary it is to keep up the haemoglobin level of the human infant by artificial means.

Copper Values given for the concentration of copper in milk vary considerably from one analyst to another, but all agree that it is very low, and that cow's milk contains less (30 μg/100 ml) than human milk (40 μg/100 ml). The baby born at term would need considerably more than the amounts provided by either milk to maintain the concentration of copper in its body, even if all the copper in the milk was absorbed. This may not matter for the human liver at birth contains astonishingly large amounts of copper. The concentration is more than 10 times that in an adult's liver, and the total amount of copper in the liver of the full term baby is about one-and-a-half times the amount in the liver of an adult. In fact copper in the liver accounts for at least half the copper in the baby's body (Widdowson et al, 1974b). The copper is in the mitochondria as a specific copper-protein complex, which seems to be a storage compound. This breaks down and the copper released is used for the needs of the rest of the body during the first months after birth. Thus even if the baby does not absorb any copper from its milk while doubling its weight it has enough stored in its liver to maintain the copper concentration in the extrahepatic tissues at their newborn level.

Zinc The concentration of zinc in both human and cow's milk falls during lactation from over 20 mg/l in colostrum to 3–4 mg/l after several months (Berfenstam, 1952). Mature human milk, and mature cow's milk which is used for preparing the dried milk preparations, would provide enough zinc for the term baby to maintain the concentration of zinc in its body at birth (16 mg/kg) if about 15% of the daily intake of 3.3 mg was absorbed and retained. However, metabolic

77

studies have shown that the zinc balance of breast-fed babies is negative at the end of the first week after birth (Cavell & Widdowson, 1964), and negative or only slightly positive during the whole of the first 4 months, at any rate in infants fed formulas on sale in the United States (Fomon, 1974). If this is so then the concentration of zinc in the infant's tissues must fall. Hambidge et al (1972), also working in the United States, found that the concentration of zinc in hair was lower in older infants than it was in the newly born, and they attributed this to the low zinc concentration in some American infant milk formulas. British infants fed on cow's milk formulas had a higher concentration of zinc in their hair. Whether American infants are fed on milks containing much less zinc than British infants I am not sure. What I am sure about is that the trend towards greater processing of infant milk foods, for example by using whey from the cheese industry as the starting material, brings new problems. The minerals attached to casein in the original milk will be removed with the cheese. Dialysis of the whey will remove water soluble inorganic constituents, and he is a brave man who will guarantee to return to the product all the trace elements and other substances that were present in the original milk.

References

Berfenstam, R (1952) *Acta Paediatrica, Stockholm, 41, Suppt.* 87
Cavell, PA and Widdowson, EM (1964) *Archives of Disease in Childhood, 39,* 496
Dickerson, JWT (1962) *Biochemical Journal, 82,* 56
Fomon, SJ (1967) *Pediatrics, 40,* 863
Fomon, SJ (1974) *Infant Nutrition, 2nd Edition.* WB Saunders, Philadelphia
Hambidge, KM, Hambidge, C, Jacobs, M and Baum, JD (1972) *Pediatric Research, 6,* 868
McCance, RA and Widdowson, EM (1957) *Acta Paediatrica, Stockholm, 46,* 337
Schulz, J and Smith, NJ (1958) *American Journal of Diseases of Children, 95,* 109
Slater, J (1961) *British Journal of Nutrition, 15,* 83
Stearns, G (1939) *Physiological Reviews, 19,* 415
Widdowson, EM, Dauncey, J and Shaw, JCL (1974b) *The Proceedings of the Nutrition Society, 33,* 275
Widdowson, EM, Dauncey, MJ, Gairdner, SMT, Jonxis, JHP and Pelikan-Filipkova, M (1975) *British Medical Journal, 1,* 653
Widdowson, EM, Southgate, DAT and Schutz, Y (1974a) *Archives of Disease in Childhood, 49,* 867

Special Problems Arising in the Nutrition of Very Small Prematures and Their Subsequent Growth

J H P JONXIS
State University, Groningen, The Netherlands

In recent years the death rate of very small prematures has fallen and their chances of surviving the first critical days of extrauterine life have greatly increased. This has stimulated the paediatrician's interest in the nutritional problems of infants with a very low birth weight. The normal growth rate during the last months of gestation is about twice as high as that of the full term infant during its first months after birth: 13 g compared with 6 g/kg body weight/day. The composition of the fetal body, moreover, alters during the last months of gestation. The percentage of fat increases from 3 to 16%. In the low birthweight infant sufficient amounts of nutrients and calories must be provided to allow a rate of growth similar to what it would be if the baby was still in the uterus. During the last months of intrauterine life about 3 g of body fat per kg body weight (equivalent to 27 kCal) are formed daily, whereas in the full term infant during the first months after birth it amounts only to about 1 g (9 kCal).

An important question is whether the growth rate of the premature infant during its first months of extrauterine life needs to be as high as the normal intrauterine growth rate. There is up till now no proof that such a high growth rate has particular advantages. Many small prematures have become normal individuals with normal intellects on a formula with a nutritional value which has allowed a growth rate of only about 6 g/kg bodyweight/day. In the past the high percentage of prematurely born infants who later became mentally and neurologically defective is more likely to have been due to anoxia and hypoglycaemia in their first days after birth than to a low caloric intake and a slow growth rate. Nevertheless, the very rapid growth and development of the central nervous system during the last months of intrauterine life form a strong argument for trying to achieve a high rate of growth in these infants, if possible similar to the normal intrauterine growth rate. To reach such a growth rate it is necessary to give a formula which provides an ample supply of energy and nutrients.

If the environmental temperature is lower than the neutral temperature of the child, metabolic rate increases (Table I). Even the very small premature baby

TABLE I. O_2 Uptake ml/kg/min. Infants birthweight $<$ 1250 g

Age in days	In metabolic chamber at neutral temperature $\pm$ 35.3°C	In metabolic chamber at 5°C below neutral temperature
4	4.8	7.1
8	5.7	9.7
12	6.8	9.6

is able to increase its metabolic rate by 80% when the environmental temperature falls as little as 6–7°C below the neutral temperature. We should therefore nurse the infant near to its neutral environmental temperature in order to keep its rate of metabolism as low as possible. Less of the caloric value of the food will then be used to maintain the body temperature within normal limits and more will be available for growth. The neutral environmental temperature of the small premature is 35–36°C. To prevent energy losses by infra-red radiation the temperature of the inside of the wall of the incubator should also be kept at 35–36°C.

In infants with a birth weight of over 1500 g the insensible water loss by evaporation at a relative humidity of 50% is not very large. In the very small premature baby who weighs only 1000 g, the loss is much larger owing to the very thin epidermis (Table II). In these infants the evaporation increases more than

TABLE II. Weight Loss by Evaporation

	$g/m^2/day$		$g/kg/day$
	Age 0–7 days	Age 8–16 days	Age 5–10 days
$<$ 1.1 kg	558	440	50
1.25 – 1.75 kg	408	430	29
1.75 – 2.25 kg	283	327	22
2.25 – 3.00 kg	261	282	15

Table II would lead one to expect. In the conventional incubator with a relatively high rate of air flow, water loss is high, even when the relative humidity is higher than 50 per cent and this has an important bearing on the fluid intake of very low birth weight infants.

Silverman et al (1958) were among the first to describe the advantages of nursing children at temperatures not far below their neutral temperature (±35°C). They found that by doing so they could reduce the death rate considerably. In our premature nursery at Groningen we use incubators with heated walls and without forced ventilation. Sterile air or gas mixtures with a known oxygen concentration flow into the incubator at a rate of only 2 to 3 litres per minute, at a humidity of about 50%. To prevent as far as possible a rise in the metabolic rate when the incubator has to be opened for nursing and handling purposes, the room temperature of the air conditioned nursery is kept at 32°C, humidity 50%. The oxygen uptake of very low birth weight infants in our type of incubator is not much higher than that in a metabolic chamber at neutral temperature. Moreover, the rise may be due to the higher energy intake and expenditure of the

TABLE III. O_2 Uptake ml/kg/min

Days of life	Full term infants at neutral temp. in metabolic chamber	Infants birth weight < 1250 g at neutral temp. in metabolic chamber	Infants birth weight < 1250 g, 35°C in heated wall incubator
2	5.4	4.4	6
4	5.4	4.8	7
6	5.6	5.5	7.2
8	6.1	5.7	7.2
10	6.3	6.4	7.5
12	6.2	6.8	8.1
14	6.5	6.9	8.3
	Caloric intake at 14 days 100 kcal/kg	Caloric intake at 14 days 100 kCal/kg	Caloric intake at 14 days 140kCal/kg

infant (140 kCal per kg body weight), as compared with 100 kCal for infants of the same size (Table III).

Even when the energy expenditure of the premature baby is reduced as far as possible a diet must be given which contains sufficient nutrients to cover not only the metabolic needs of the child, but also a growth rate of 13 g/kg/day. The caloric intake of the premature infant should therefore be higher than that of the full term infant as stated just now. The protein content of the formula should allow the formation of new tissues at a rate about twice as high as that of the full term infant. In the full term infant there should be a positive protein balance of about 0.7 g/kg/day, whereas in our tiny prematures this amounts to about 1.5 g. The estimated protein requirement of the full term infant is 1.6 g/kg/day, the advisable intake 1.9 g. Therefore the protein requirement of the very low birth weight infant is probably of the order of 2.4 g and the advisable intake 2.7 g/kg/day.

81

In the low birth weight infant the mucosa of the gastrointestinal tract and its secretory and absorbing functions are better developed than the supporting musculature. Distention often occurs, especially when air is swallowed with the food. Gastrointestinal motility should induce a rather rapid passage through each portion of the tract, but a certain amount of the food tends to lag behind. Digestive enzymes for the nutrients in milk are always present at birth and are secreted in sufficient amounts by the smallest prematures. This applies even for lactase, although this enzyme appears rather late among the disaccharidases.

Even in full term infants the digestion of fat, and especially that of cow's milk is not complete. This is more marked in premature infants, and even the absorption of human milk fat is less complete than it is in full term infants. Cow's milk fat is very poorly absorbed. The absorption of vegetable oils rich in linoleic acid may equal that of human milk fat. The absorption of medium chain triglycerides (MCT) appears to be almost complete. Tantibhedhyangskul and Hashim (1975) ha have recently demonstrated that when a mixture of vegetable oils with a high percentage of linoleic acid and MCT was given to premature infants the absorption of the total mixture amounted to ± 90%.

After birth the supply of nutrients is usually temporarily interrupted. Perhaps the colonisation of the intestinal tract with micro-organisms should precede the intake of food. In the premature infant the period of starvation should not be longer than 12 hours, and often intravenous fluid administration should be started even earlier, especially when there is a certain degree of dysmaturity. During the first 24 hours we administer 75–100 ml/kg body weight/day; at the age of 5 days we give 150 ml and after about 10 days a maximum of 200 ml/kg is reached. The high losses of water by evaporation in infants with a very low birth weight should be countered by a sufficient intake. When intravenous fluid is necessary we generally give a 5% glucose solution, or if the blood sugar concentration is low, 10% and in exceptional cases a 15% solution. In the premature infant the glycogen stores are small and are probably exhausted a few hours after birth; glycogenesis is then the only protection against hypoglycaemia. In the premature baby glycogenosis is not yet fully developed, and it is therefore preferable not to delay the administration of sufficient amounts of carbohydrate even when the blood sugar value is not particularly low.

The fall of the respiratory quotient after birth indicates that the body fat quickly becomes the main source of energy. In the premature infant the amount of body fat is rather limited. Even when the child is causing us anxiety for other reasons, we start gavage feeding (25 ml/kg/24 hours). When administration of larger amounts of milk has to be postponed we continue the administration of small amounts by gavage feeding, adding to it a mixture of vitamins and minerals (see Tables IV, V and VI), while intravenous fluid administration is continued.

In the premature infant protein digestion and absorption are not limiting factors. Although the amount of pepsin produced seems to be less than in the full term infant, the production of trypsin and enterokinase is adequate and

TABLE IV. Composition of Mineral Mixture. 1 ml contains:

Na	11.5	mg
K	25.5	mg
Mg	3.7	mg
Ca	35	mg
Zn	0.12	mg
Fe	0.3	mg
Mn	15	μg
I	0.8	μg
Al	0.06	μg
Co	0.15	μg
Cu	38	μg
Mo	0.4	μg

TABLE V. Vitamin Solution. 0.1ml/kg body weight

calciferol	100 IU
vitamin A	600 IU
tocopherolacetate	4 mg

TABLE VI. Vitamin Mixture. Administration 45 mg/kg body weight

Thiamin	0.1	mg
Riboflavin	0.05	mg
Pyridoxine	0.025	mg
Niacin	0.5	mg
Folic acid	0.1	mg
Choline	4	mg
Ascorbic acid	10	mg
Para-amino-benzoic acid	1	mg
Menadiol	0.1	mg
Inositol	2	mg
Vitamin B$_{12}$	0.2	μg
Biotin	5	μg

administration of hydrolysed proteins does not seem to have any advantage.

I have already said that the minimal protein requirement for a growth rate of 13 g per kg body weight is about 2.2 g and the advisable intake 2.7 g. The margin between the two may be rather narrow. The plasma amino acid levels of the premature infant tend to be higher than those of the full term baby with the same protein intake per kg. The tyrosine level especially tends to rise when the protein intake is increased. In the literature there are conflicting opinions as to whether high tyrosine levels and moderately high phenylalanine levels may damage the brains of these infants. Until this point has been settled, the protein intake should not be much higher than the protein requirement.

We have given alternative formulas that provided 100 or 180 kCal and 2.7 g or

4.7 g of protein per kg body weight to 10 infants weighing 1300–1800 g during their 3rd to 7th week of life. The children who got 180 kCal and 4.7 g of protein gained 16.9 g daily; those who received 100 kCal and 2.7 g of protein gained 7.6 g daily. These values suggest that a formula with a protein content of 2.7 g per kg body weight is sufficient to obtain a safe rate of growth if the energy intake is 180 kCal.

The plasma amino acid levels of babies fed on these formulas were compared with the amino acid levels in cord blood and with the amino acid levels of full term infants at the age of two weeks, fed on a formula providing 100 kCal and 2.7 g of protein per kg body weight per day. The free amino acids were determined on heparinised plasma. Details are given in Table VII. Compared with the values

TABLE VII. Plasma Aminoacid Levels

| Aminoacid μmol/ml | Prematures, birthweight 1300–1800 g | | | Full term babies |
	100 kCal 2.7 g of protein	180 kCal 4.7 g of protein	180 kCal 2.7 g of protein	
Ornithine	8	9	7	6
Lysine	16	23	14	15
Histidine	8	11	10	7
Tryptophane	2	3	3	4
Arginine	8	7	6	5
Threonine	27	33	21	12
Serine	17	22	22	14
Glutamic asparagine	50	55	60	44
Proline	33	42	31	17
Glutamic acid	17	16	17	18
Citrulline	3	3	3	2
Glycine	30	32	30	24
Alanine	30	43	41	25
Valine	22	30	19	18
Methionine	4	7	6	3
Isoleucine	8	9	7	5
Leucine	13	14	7	8
Tyrosine	27	36	25	6
Phenylalanine	8	9	8	4

found in the full term infants the plasma values for threonine, proline, tyrosine and phenylalanine were higher in the premature infants. An increased protein intake of 4.7 g and a high caloric diet produced a rise in the plasma concentrations of many amino acids, especially of tyrosine. When we compared the values during the periods in which the children had an intake providing 180 or 100 kCal/kg/day (both with 2.7 g of protein) we found that in the period of the high caloric intake, in which the growth rate equalled the rate of growth in utero, the concentrations of the essential amino acids, leucine, valine and threonine, tended to be somewhat lower than in infants on the lower caloric intake.

Recently we tried to find out whether it was possible to lower the protein content of the formula without changing the growth rate. Instead of 2.7 g of cow's milk protein alone we gave 2.2 g of cow's milk protein with a whey protein/casein ratio of 1. Preliminary results gave a slight decrease in weight gain and somewhat lower plasma amino acid levels. In our experiments we have not included human milk protein. The concentration of protein in human milk is only 1.1−1.2 g per 100 ml. To cover the minimal requirement of 2.2 g an intake of 200 ml of human milk would be sufficient but the caloric intake might be marginal.

Human milk is rich in carbohydrate as lactose. Should a formula for premature infants primarily contain lactose or dextri-maltose? There are several formulas on the market whose carbohydrate is lactose only. We, however, prefer a formula with less lactose to which dextri-maltose has been added. This is a precautionary measure. Virus infections of the intestinal tract sometimes occur in premature nurseries. The lactase activity is then more severely affected than that of maltase and isomaltase. In the very small infant, moreover, we cannot be sure that lactase activity will yet be fully developed. As already stated absorption of fat, even human milk fat, is far from optimal in the young premature infant. Since vegetable oils rich in polyunsaturated fatty acids are better absorbed than cow's milk fat, most humanised milk formulas contain vegetable oils. In the formula that we normally use milk fat has been replaced by maize oil. The absorption of fat by infants weighing 1200−1500 g is 75−80%. When maize oil is partly replaced by MCT the total fat absorption is increased considerably. Our special formula for small prematures contains 4.4% of fat, of which 60% is maize oil and 40% MCT and with this formula fat absorption in infants weighing 1200−1500 g is 90%. We have determined the fatty acids in the faecal fat. Most of the fatty acids were probably derived from the maize oil. Of the medium chain fatty acids the C8 was completely absorbed, but small amounts of C10 were found in the faeces.

The percentage of fat in the fetus rises during the last months of intrauterine life, but the extent of the rise varies. The average increase is from 7% at a weight of 1500 g to 16% in the full term infant of 3700 g. About 550 g of fat are thus stored in the last 50 days of intrauterine life. The presence of some linoleic acid (an essential fatty acid) in the fat of the fetus and newborn indicates that some transport of fat or fatty acids must take place across the placenta.

We have recently determined the composition of the body fat of infants, mainly those of low birth weight. All babies received the same formula, Almiron, in which the fat is maize oil which contains 57% of linoleic acid. Owing specially to the rapid accumulation of fat, it is likely that the composition of the body fat resembles to a certain extent the fatty acid composition of the fat in the food (Table VIII). Some of the older infants were already on a mixed diet. The concentrations of plasma cholesterol (106 mg/100 ml, range 70−158) were low compared with those found in children on other formulas (170 mg/100 ml). The

TABLE VIII. Fatty Acid Composition of the Body Fat of Babies

	At birth	0–4 weeks	4–16 weeks	6–12 months
C 14:0	3.3	3.15	2.54	4.8
C 16:0	45.8	39	37.1	29.7
C 18:0	3.8	3.4	2.2	2.9
C 16:1	15.2	13.8	10.9	13.8
C 18:1	29.0	27.7	27.9	40.8
C 18:2	2.9	11.4	28.8	8.0

significance of this is uncertain, but at present we think it is more likely to be an advantage than a disadvantage. We know little, however, about the influence of fatty acids in the food on the composition or behaviour of the cell membranes. Preliminary investigations of the fatty acid composition of the erythrocyte membranes suggest that the fatty acids in the membranes may influence their behaviour but that the effect is small.

The minerals of human milk are suitable enough for the moderate growth rate of the full term infant but it must be admitted that the concentrations of Ca, P, Na and Fe are rather low. For a premature baby with a growth rate twice as high, the amounts of these minerals in human milk are not enough to maintain the mineral composition of the body at its correct level. A regime fully adequate for the needs of a small premature should cover the requirements of the child (see Table IX).

TABLE IX. Amounts of Minerals in 13 g of the Body Tissues of a Premature Infant Compared with the Amounts Provided by its Daily Food

	Na	K	Ca	P	Mg	Fe	Zn
13 g premature infant tissue	30	26	90	50	3	0.9	0.2
200 ml human milk	30	100	60	30	8	0.2	0.8
200 ml Almiron	30	100	100	50	10	0.8	0.8
200 ml Nenatal	40	110	200	100	20	1.6	1.6

Cow's milk contains more minerals than human milk and the concentrations of some of them, Ca, P and K, for instance, are so high that the milk has to be partly demineralised before it can be used for a tiny premature baby. The high phosphate content of cow's milk may cause hyperphosphataemia and tetany. In a full term infant the calcium content of the bones decreases if the child is breast-fed, even when it is given additional vitamin D, yet its development seems to be otherwise normal. Nevertheless it seems advisable to feed the premature infant with a formula that contains enough minerals to allow normal growth without

86

deficiencies.

Recent studies have revealed that the small premature infant is able to synthesise considerable amounts of haemoglobin, partly of the fetal, partly of the adult form. When the iron, copper and vitamin requirements are covered the haemoglobin level remains stable at 9—10 g/100 ml, even when the rate of growth is high. The iron stores of the premature are small and are soon exhausted, and at least 0.8 mg iron/100 ml should therefore be added to the formula.

The quantities of vitamins in human milk are sufficient for the requirements of the premature infant; manufactured formulas contain about twice as much to allow for losses during storage. To the premature infant an extra supply of certain vitamins may be an advantage (Table X), especially vitamins D, E, C, folic acid

TABLE X. Vitamins in 200 ml Human Milk and Formulas

		Human milk	Almiron	Nenatal
Vitamin A	mg	0.15	0.14	0.16
Vitamin D	units	2	160	240
α-tocopherol	mg	0.4	4	8
Thiamine	mg	0.04	0.08	0.16
Riboflavin	mg	0.06	0.12	0.24
Niacin	mg	0.35	0.8	1.6
Pantothenic acid	mg	0.5	0.5	1
Pyridoxine	mg	0.04	0.06	0.12
Vitamin B_{12}	μg	0.08	0.16	1
Folic acid	μg	10	13	26
Biotin	μg	0.4	1	2
Ascorbic acid	mg	9	10	24

and vitamin B_{12}. In Northern latitudes the vitamin D requirement of the full term infant is about 60 IU/kg but an intake of 120 IU/kg/day is advisable. In the Netherlands the normal infant formula is fortified with 800 IU of vitamin D per litre, and we do not see either rickets or hypercalcaemia. In the rapidly growing small premature infant the requirements are probably higher and twice as much should be given to them during the first months of life.

The influence of vitamin C on the metabolism of phenylalanine and tyrosine is well known, and the premature infant requires more ascorbic acid than the baby born at full term. A formula for prematures should contain about twice as much vitamin C as human milk and to give more will not further reduce the excretion of tyrosine.

The requirement for vitamin E is related to the amounts of polyunsaturated fatty acids (mainly linoleic acid) in the formula. The ratio vitamin E (mg) to polyunsaturated fatty acids (g) should not be lower than 0.5. In the premature infant the plasma vitamin E levels (1 mg/100 ml is normal) tend to be low and the erythrocytes survive a shorter time than in full term babies and there is a secondary reticulocytosis. The vitamin E content of a special formula for premature infants should therefore contain sufficient vitamin E, 2—4 mg alpha-tocopherol per 100 ml, to keep the plasma concentrations within their normal range.

The requirement for folic acid is uncertain, but is higher in full term infants than in adults, and higher still in premature babies. Some authors consider that if 0.1 mg of folic acid is given daily to premature infants their red cells contain more folic acid and their concentrations of haemoglobin are higher than those of the control group. My own experience is that with a formula containing 13 μg of folic acid/100 ml we see less anaemia in our premature babies even in periods of rapid growth. Table X gives the vitamin concentrations in the formulas we use.

The caloric intake per kg body weight of a child of 1—1.5 kg after it has reached its maximum fluid intake of 200 ml/kg should be higher than that of the full term infant whose intake is 100—120 kCal/kg. However, when the caloric value of the food is increased the osmotic pressure is also raised, except when fat or protein are added. A formula with a high osmotic pressure may cause diarrhoea and the caloric value of the formula cannot be raised above 80—90 kCal/100 ml. For routine feeding we use a formula with a caloric value of 80 kCal and a protein content of 1.8 g/100 ml. When 200 ml/kg body weight/day of this formula is taken, the growth rate of most infants with a birth weight between 1000 and 1500 g is 13 g/kg body weight/day, but when a formula with a caloric value of 90 kCal per 100 ml is given it is 16 g/kg/day.

Most premature babies with a birth weight lower than 1500 g are unable to suck. We feed them continuously through a thin indwelling polyvinyl nasogastric tube and an important advantage of this method is that the hands of the nurse need not go into the incubator so often and this reduces the risk of infections. The volume of the sterile formula is measured with a calibrated burette and the whole system is replaced every 12 hours to reduce the risk of infection. Bottle feeding is tried when a weight of 2000 g has been reached, the nurses being more fond of early bottle feeding than I am myself.

How do the very small prematures we have treated grow? Are the results we are obtaining today better or worse than those we were getting ten years ago? At that time we gave less food and the temperature in the incubator was somewhat lower. It is difficult to come to a conclusion because these are not the only procedures that have changed; obstetrical treatment for instance has also changed and our obstetricians are more prepared now to try to save an unborn child in distress by performing a caesarean section.

We can now keep alive many newborn infants with respiratory distress whose chances of survival were low five years ago. In my department the mortality rate of newborn infants with a birth weight of less than 1100 g has dropped from 85%

ten years ago to 50% more recently. On the other hand the mortality rate of infants with a birth weight between 1100 g and 1500 g, which amounted to about 15% ten years ago, has risen to 20%. The number of admissions over the last ten years has doubled, whereas the birth rate in the Netherlands has fallen. Many infants of low birth weight, born in the local hospitals of the Northern Netherlands, are now referrred to our neonatal unit already critically ill. These trends influence not only the mortality rate of our admissions but also the prognosis of the survivors.

The family background of our children has changed too. Ten years ago the majority of them were born of multiparae from normal working class families. Now they are often the first child, in some cases of very young unmarried women, and others the offspring of marriages with a very low fertility. When we try to compare the results of our treatment in the past with those of today therefore, we have to consider differences in the backgrounds of the children admitted.

There is still one more thing that makes it very difficult to decide whether recent changes in our treatment have been, as we hope, improvements. Not until the child has reached the age of 5–6 years and goes to the primary school is it possible to decide, with the help of neurologists and psychologists, whether the development of the child has been normal. We cannot however wait for 5 years before making a change in our treatment. Most of us make alterations which we hope will be improvements before we have had time to evaluate our earlier results, and hence these earlier results are of only limited help in planning the next step.

With these limitations in mind I would like to tell you something about the growth and development of the very small prematures we have treated. Ten years ago their growth rate was lower than now. At that time we gave 100 kCal/ kg/body weight/day, but the formula had the same composition as the one we have used recently. The environmental temperature in our incubators was 1–2°C lower than it is now. The rate of growth was below that which is normal in utero. Very few infants showed any 'catch-up' growth during the months they stayed in hospital, and owing to their slow growth rate their stay was much longer, which may have delayed their mental development. At that time we did not measure the length of the children at regular intervals and I, therefore, have only a few figures on the rate of their growth in length, but these figures indicate that their length lagged behind less than their weight. Recently I have been able to see a group of young people 15–20 years old who had once been treated under my care in our premature nursery (birth weight under 1800 g). The group was small (about 20) and not all whom I asked to come did so. Some of those who did not come may not have done so well as the others. The average height of the group I saw (we only asked males to visit us) was only a few centimetres less than that of the average young Dutchman of the same age. One was fairly severely mentally retarded, four had minor signs of neurological damage, ranging from slight spasticity to moderate defects in learning. One, who had weighed 1100 g at birth had become particularly bright and had entered university; his father was a high school teacher. The rest (13) were well adapted to normal life.

In the last few years we have collected data on weight, length and head circumference; in 80% weight, length and head circumference increased quite normally during the first 6 weeks after birth as they should have done if the child had not been born prematurely; 20% lagged behind but this group included many children with congenital malformations and some who had had respiratory distress. The weight loss that is normally seen in the full term infant was less in most, probably because of the intravenous administration of fluid. Practically all the children were gaining weight by the 7th to 10th day. In none of them was there any sign of rickets or of hypercalcaemia during the whole period of observation (first year). There was hypocalcaemia, often combined with hypoproteinaemia, in the first weeks after birth but the serum phosphate was within the normal range or slightly higher. The haemoglobin concentration decreased during the first weeks after birth to 9–10 g/100 ml, and remained in that range in spite of gains of weight of the order of 13 g/kg/day. After some months, when the rate of growth had slowed down, the concentration of haemoglobin showed a tendency to rise. If at an early stage blood had to be withdrawn, for example for repeated blood gas analysis, a progressive anaemia developed and blood transfusions became necessary.

There was no catch-up growth in length, weight and head circumference in 20%. In most of these infants birth weight was very low because of the combination of prematurity and dysmaturity caused by intrauterine malnutrition.

The best results were obtained in the group of dysmature full term infants with birth weights between 1800 and 2200 g. The catch-up growth in head circumference began about 3 weeks after birth and was complete by the age of 25 weeks and in length and weight started about 6 weeks after birth and finished about 30 weeks after birth. By the age of one year the length, weight and head circumference of most of these children were between the 10th and 50th percentiles.

Our very small prematures who were not dysmature began to catch up in weight about 2 weeks later than the full dysmature infants; their rate of gain in weight was about 13 g/kg body weight/day. Their length velocity followed the normal percentile line. Their head circumference showed a tendency to grow more rapidly and had already begun to show catch-up growth by the 2nd week. At the age of one year length was usually between the 10th and 50th percentile lines, and head circumference on the 90th percentile line.

In the group of children who were born prematurely and whose birth weight was low for their gestational age, catch-up growth did not begin much before 12 weeks but continued until the 58th week. Most of these children, however, only reached the 10th percentile for weight, usually higher for length. Catch-up growth of head circumference was usually under way 2–3 weeks after birth, and by the age of one year the average circumference was often over the 90th percentile, about 4 cm larger than it should have been for children of their length.

The oldest children have now reached the age of 2½ years, but it is still uncertain what their neurological and mental development will be when they are 5–6 years old. At the age of one year many of the very small dysmature infants were retarded in their neurological development and had some spasticity which, however, was diminishing, and by 2 years 50% had little or no signs of neurological retardation. In the group of infants with a birth weight of less than 1000 g the number of permanent mentally defective children is likely to be rather high, although some of them show a satisfactory neurological and mental development. We have no case of retrolental fibroplasia in our recent group; this has necessitated many blood gas analyses and, subsequently, blood transfusions.

We shall have to wait for at least five years to learn whether our treatment today is better than it used to be. I am sure, however, that within a year we shall be making further changes in our treatment which we hope will be improvements. Scientifically this is not a very satisfactory procedure; clinically, however, it is normal and inevitably we must console ourselves the adage that "what the weaver weaves he seldom knows".

References

Silverman, WA, Fertig, JW and Berger, AP (1958) *Pediatrics, 22,* 876
Tantibhedhyangkul, P and Hashim, SA (1975) *Pediatrics, 55,* 359

See also the following literature –

Fomon, SJ (1974) *Infant Nutrition, 2nd Edition.* WB Saunders, Philadelphia
Review (1976) *Medium chain triglyceride absorption by preterm infants.*
    Nutrition Reviews, 34, 71
Smith, CA (1976) In *The Physiology of the Newborn Infant, 4th Edition.*
    (Ed) CA Smith and NM Nelson. Charles C Thomas, Springfield, Illinois

Surgical Rescues and Their Subsequent Growth

A W WILKINSON
Institute of Child Health, University of London, England

The human neonate is very tough and will stand a great deal of surgical operative treatment. After many of the operations which are necessary for the relief of congenital abnormalities of the alimentary tract anatomical and functional deficiencies may make it necessary to feed babies intravenously, by gastrostomy or by jejunostomy, sometimes for weeks or months. An abnormally short small intestine, disaccharide intolerance, enterocolitis, E coli enteritis, peritonitis and secondary obstruction due to adhesions are all liable to interfere with the normal feeding of human or modified cow's milk by mouth. Once the child is through such complications as these in the early months there may be an intermediate stage when growth is slow because the intake of food is poor because of physical and sometimes psychological reasons. The remarkable capacity of the human alimentary tract to undergo modifications after extensive resections of parts of it are well known but defects of the absorption of Vitamin B_{12}, bile salts and fat may all cause serious disturbance and although these are rare they must be remembered and anticipated after certain types of surgical treatment.

Some of our patients are born prematurely and are abnormally low in weight, and the odds against their survival are increased. It seems unlikely that any remarkable improvement in surgical technique is likely to make much difference in the results at present achieved in the treatment of major congenital abnormalities in the newly born. There is no doubt at all, however, that better understanding of the normal physiology of the human neonate and its application to the clinical management of such patients is likely to produce considerable improvements. Control of the environment, the modification of milks, the provision of even better preparations for the maintenance of intravenous feeding, and more knowledge of the requirements for trace elements are all likely to be beneficial.

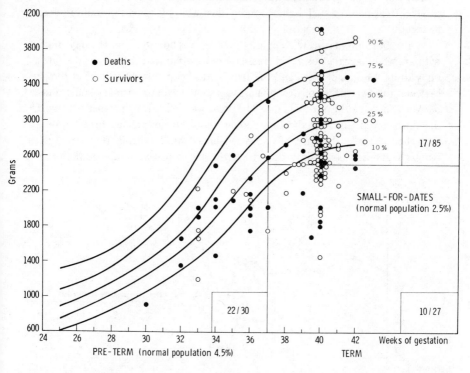

Figure 1. Birth weights and gestational ages of 142 neonates with oesophageal atresia plotted on Lubchenko's length and weight curves (from Cozzi & Wilkinson, 1974, with permission)

The birth weight and length of gestation were known in 142 out of 153 patients with oesophageal atresia treated in the Professorial Unit of The Hospital for Sick Children, Great Ormond Street, London between January 1959 and December 1973 [Figure 1] (Cozzi & Wilkinson, 1974). Thirty patients (21 per cent) were preterm, being born before 37 weeks of completed gestation with a mean weight of 2.08 kg, 27 others (19 per cent) were small for dates when born after 37 weeks with a mean weight of 2.23 kg so that in this series of babies with oesophageal atresia there were nearly five times as many babies who were preterm and eight times as many babies who were small for dates as would be found in a population of normal neonates (Butler & Bonham, 1963). Similar incidences of preterm and small babies are found in association with anorectal anomalies and with abnormalities of the small bowel. For example, out of 300 neonates with intestinal obstruction admitted under my care during the same period, 54 (18 per cent) were preterm and another 51 (17 per cent) were small for dates. In addition, there is a high associated incidence of potentially fatal anomalies in the cardiovascular and genito-urinary systems.

93

The nutritional problems which may be encountered during and after the surgical treatment of such babies can be illustrated by some representative case histories.

A girl, born prematurely, weighing 1.28 kg was admitted on the day of birth with an oesophageal atresia and tracheo-oesophageal fistula.She was operated on within 24 hours of birth and the fistula was ligated and divided but the gap between the two pieces of oesophagus was so wide that a primary anastomosis between them could not be made. The child was fed through a gastrostomy from the third day of life, for the first sixteen days with expressed breast milk and then, because of a shortage of expressed breast milk, with S26 fortified with Benger's. It was fifteen days before weight began to rise on an intake of over

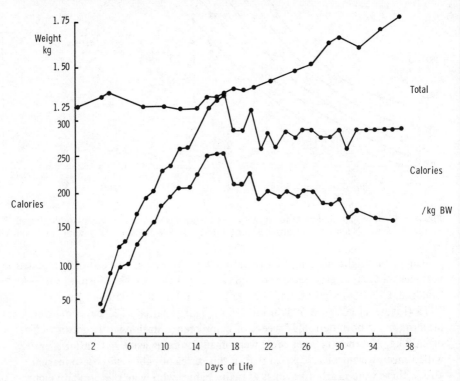

Figure 2. Weight changes and calorie intake of girl who was born weighing 1.28 kg with oesophageal atresia and tracheo-oesophageal fistula

300 kcal or 240–250 kcal per kg body weight (Figure 2). The feeds could not be increased any more because of reflux into the feeding tube. Bouts of cyanosis aroused the suspicion that there was some major cardiac anomaly and this is believed to be a ventricular septal defect. Even after full digitalisation the cyanosis intermittently recurred and it was not possible to increase the feeds

94

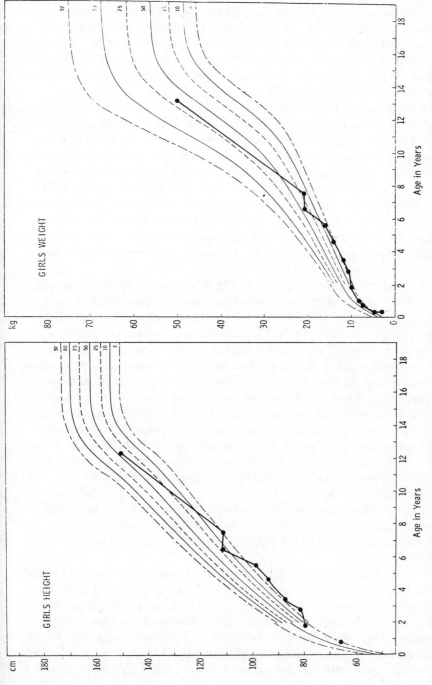

Figure 3. Heights and weights of girl who was born weighing 1.42 kg with oesophageal atresia and tracheo-oesophageal fistula treated by primary anastomosis

as fast as we would have liked. At the age of 3 months her weight was 3.1 kg and the chest was re-opened but the gap between the two pieces of oesophagus was still too wide to make an anastomosis and the upper pouch was brought out in the left side of the neck. Even the most enthusiastic attempts at abundant feeding may be defeated by the effect of associated anomalies and by the inability of the baby to tolerate the quantities of milk which are necessary for normal gains in weight.

A girl (Figure 3) was born weighing 1.42 kg at the 32nd week of gestation, that is to say about two months prematurely and when her weight was on the 25th Lubchenko percentile. She suffered from oesophageal atresia which was treated by division of the fistula and a primary anastomosis of the pieces of oesophagus and she has since been followed for almost 13 years. At the age of 13 weeks, a month after she should really have been born, she weighed 4.2 kg. She was a poor eater and her height and weight both moved steadily up the 3rd percentile until the age of 7 years. However, now at the age of 12½ years her height is on the 50th and her weight just above the 50th percentile. She has a small mother and seems at present to be following the genetic pattern of her father rather than her mother.

A boy (Figure 4) who weighed 2.475 kg at birth was admitted the same day with an oesophageal atresia and tracheo-oesophageal fistula. The fistula was divided and because of the wide gap between the two pieces of oesophagus it was impossible to make a primary anastomosis and he was fed at birth by a gastrostomy. Nearly 7 weeks later a delayed primary anastomosis was made but the anastomosis leaked causing a pneumothorax and it was necessary to re-open the chest, close the lower piece of oesophagus and bring the upper piece out in the neck. A year later the two ends of the oesophagus were joined together with a piece of transverse and descending colon. Following the first stage of this anastomosis he had some convulsions and a cerebral thrombosis but two months later it was possible to complete the upper anastomosis. He had some post-operative stridor after this but after another two months was taking all his food by mouth. At the age of almost 4 years his height is just below the 50th percentile and his weight is on it.

These patients show that even extensive major operations and the complications associated with them do not prevent normal growth according to the inherent genetic pattern of the child, if an adequate intake of food can be achieved.

At birth a girl, the second of twins, probably uniovular, weighed 2.44 kg and was 53 cm in length and her older twin was 2.32 kg and 52 cm in length. She had intestinal obstruction due to a high jejunal atresia and 34 cm of jejunum were resected; the length of the remaining small intestine was not accurately measured. There was difficulty with feeding for 12 days. A further laparotomy was necessary for a secondary intestinal obstruction and following this she was fed intravenously with a mixture of amino acids, fructose and fat emulsion until

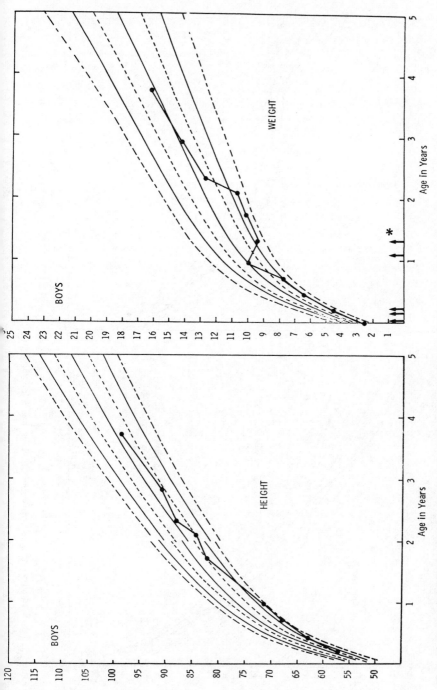

Figure 4. Heights and weights of boy treated by colon replacement for oesophageal atresia with wide gap

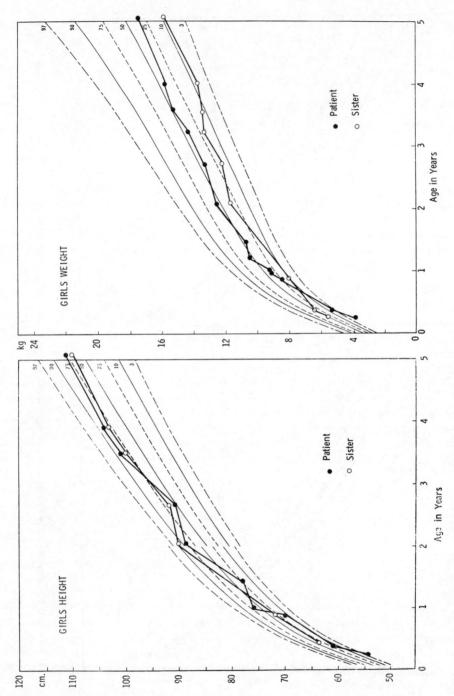

Figure 5. Heights and weights of twins, one of whom had a jejunal atresia

she was able to take milk by mouth. When discharged three months after birth she weighed 3.5 kg. Her subsequent progress was very similar to that of her twin (Figure 5). The amount of bowel resected was not great, perhaps 20 per cent of the total, and this would not be expected to have a great deal of effect on this child's growth and development.

A boy was born 11 days post-mature weighing 2.97 kg. He bagan to vomit the day after birth and the next day the vomits became bile-stained and he passed meconium mixed with dark blood. On admission he weighed 2.27 kg. He had a volvulus of the midgut and almost the whole of the intestine was gangrenous. The gangrenous bowel was resected, leaving 32.5 cm of jejunum and 12.5 cm of terminal ileum. He had to be maintained by intravenous infusion for four days and then hourly feeds of expressed breast milk were started but had to be stopped because of further vomiting. Subsequently, however, he made good progress on expressed breast milk and was discharged 22 days after admission but he was still passing loose stools. He was readmitted a week later because he passed a loose stool immediately after every feed; the mouth to anus transit time for carmine was 30 minutes and he was found to have a lactose and galactose intolerance so he was fed on various feeds such as skimmed milk, Prosperol, Casilan and fortified milk with arrowroot and Benger's and his stools gradually became rather less frequent and much less watery. The progress of this child during the next 6 months until he was discharged home is shown in Figure 6. During the latter part of this time he was fed on lean meat, rusks, skimmed milk, cereals, baby rice and medium chain tryglycerides and 40 ml olive oil per day. He was not given vegetables, fruit juice or animal fats, all of which caused diarrhoea.

When he was just over three a Vitamin B_{12} absorption test, with intrinsic factor showed a 37 per cent absorption, the normal range being 35–40 per cent. His serum folic acid was just over 18 mμg per ml the normal range being 0.9 to 21. His red cell folate was over 450 mμg per ml and the serum Vitamin B_{12} assay was 657 mμg per ml. A fat balance showed that he was absorbing about 75 per cent of the fat he consumed, even though MCT gave him diarrhoea and he was intolerant to sugar. Even at the age of 5 years he had acute disturbances if he ate sugar and cream.

A girl was born weighing 3.01 kg with an ileal atresia; after resection of the atresia 115 cm of small intestine remained of which only 10 cm was terminal ileum. She was fed intravenously for two days and then by mouth with milk. Subsequently her length went up fairly consistently along the 3rd percentile. At about the age of 2 years and 5 months her weight did not increase for almost 8 months and she was found to have a haemoglobin of 7.5 per cent with a low Vitamin B_{12} absorption, the serum iron was only 17 μg per 100 ml (normal of 60–200 μg per 100 ml) but the serum folate was within the normal range. She was given iron by mouth and injections of Neocytamin and made a remarkable improvement in both height and weight. This child has been followed for over

99

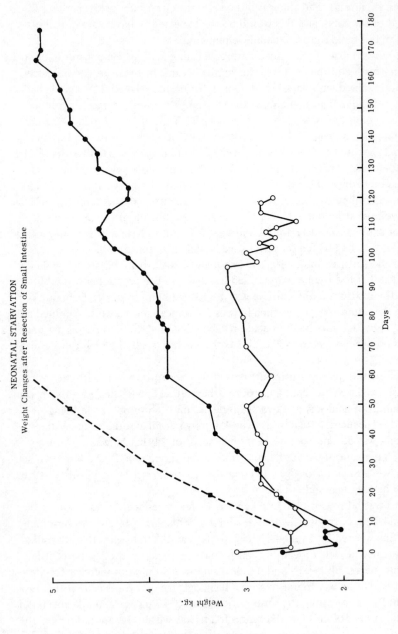

Figure 6. Weight changes. ●— — —● 50th centile curve of normal neonate. ●———● neonate with 32.5 cm jejunum and 12.5 cm terminal ileum who survived. ○———○ similar neonate with a short small bowel whose treatment was not successful and who died at 123 days weighing less than at birth but whose length had increased throughout

NEONATAL STARVATION
Weight Changes after Resection of Small Intestine

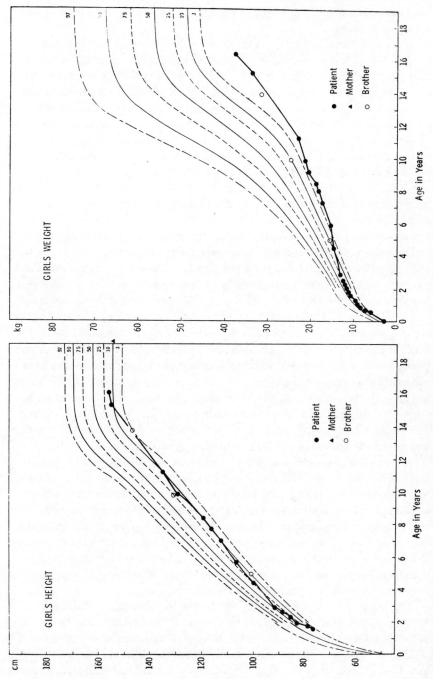

Figure 7. Height and weight changes in a girl who had only 60 cm proximal jejunum and 10 cm terminal ileum

101

three years, and now passes normal stools and eats anything she is offered. All her family are small but this child at the age of two was nearly as tall as her sister who was four.

A girl who was admitted on the first day of life had been born prematurely, 21 days before term, weighing 2.95 kg, above the 50th percentile. She had an ileal atresia and an antenatal peritonitis as the result of gangrene of the ileum and after operation only 10 cm of terminal ileum and 60 cm of proximal jejunum remained. She has now been followed for 15½ years (Figure 7). After operation her feeds were modified. Animal fat was removed as completely as possible, the milk was pre-digested, sweetened with glucose and olive oil was added. A month after birth she was getting 430 kcal per 24 hours and her weight was about 3 kg. Her bowel moved after every feed and she passed explosive, gassy stools but after about 7 weeks the number of these and their nature improved and she was eventually discharged home 3½ months after admission.

Subsequently she was difficult to feed and needed supplements of vitamins and amino acids as well as Benger's, arrowroot and olive oil; gradually soya flour and egg yolk were introduced and so on through a variety of modifications and she made satisfactory progress along the 25th percentile for the first three years. Then gradually her weight fell off below the 3rd percentile although her length remained along the 10th to 25th percentile until she was 12 or 13 years. At the age of 16½ years, after years of dietary restriction, she is now eating any food which is on the table, meat, eggs, milk, butter, cream, chocolate and green vegetables, some of which earlier would have caused prostrating diarrhoea and yet she passes only one very large, pale formed stool every day. Her height is almost the same as her mother's, although her weight is about 15 lb less, but there has been little difference in her progress with only 70 cm of small intestine and her younger brother with an intact bowel, and they are both probably following the height and weight behaviour of their genetically similar mother.

Another girl (Figure 8) who is now 13½ years was admitted with multiple small intestinal atresias of the jejunum and ileum and after two operations was left with only 27 cm of jejunum joined to her ascending colon that is without any ileum or ileo-caecal valve. She also had a complicated course involving many modifications of her feeds but she now attends a normal school, enjoys all the normal activities of her age, eats freely of any food she can get without any of the former restrictions, and passes one huge and very foul-smelling pale stool each day. She also has been proved to be unable to absorb any Vitamin B_{12} and is on injections of Neocytamin every second month.

The small intestine has remarkable potential for adaptation after resection and this is most evident in the ileum and seems to be related to age. In the baby adaptation seems to be acquired about the age of 4 months after a neonatal resection and becomes more firmly established and less likely to be disturbed by variations in the diet as time passes. It has been claimed that such compensation

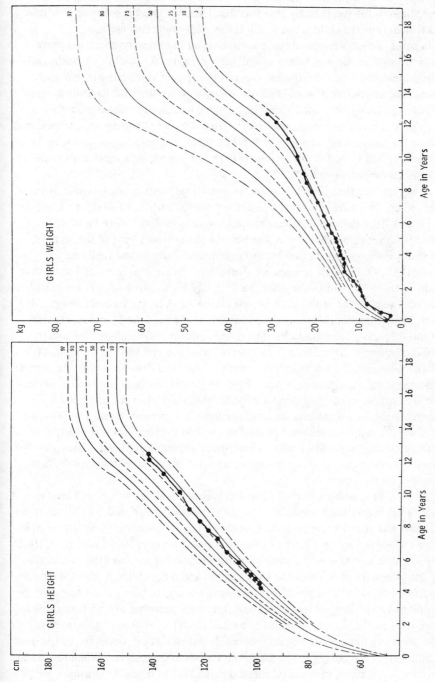

Figure 8. Heights and weights of a girl who had only 27 cm jejunum

depends partly on the maintenance of nutrition by intravenous feeding in the early stages but it seems likely that it is the efficiency and the plane of nutrition rather than how the child is fed which is the most important factor.

In some neonates repeated complications after the primary operation prevent the institution of the oral intake of milk in some form for weeks or months and such babies must be fed by the intravenous infusion of synthetic l-amino acids, glucose and emulsions of soya bean oil. A boy who weighed 2.2 kg at birth was admitted 24 hours later with a very high jejunal atresia and midgut malrotation. The partly gangrenous atresia was resected and 156 cm of small intestine remained. During the next 7 weeks he required five further operations for recurrent obstruction and he had to be fed intravenously (Figure 9) and later a jejunostomy was established for enteral feeding.

It was noticed that this child repeatedly suffered from hypoglycaemic disturbances when the intravenous infusion did not contain sufficient dextrose. Candida was grown from the blood culture and intravenous feeding had to be stopped after 79 days. Stilton cheese was given by the jejunostomy tube in the hope of recolonising the gut with more normal commensal bacteria and replacing the candida. The child began to improve thereafter, especially as more and more milk could be taken by jejunostomy. By the 75th day his weight had at last regained the birth weight, and at this time he was taking 200 kcal per kg body weight. It seems likely that this child was copper deficient at about the 50th day. He was fed more or less continuously by intravenous infusion of Vamin or, for a short period, Aminosol, 20 per cent soya bean oil emulsion and various strengths of glucose solution for 79 days, but for much of this time it was not possible to give him enough calories to achieve a good gain in weight. We have the clinical impression that copper deficiency developed in another baby after she had been fed intravenously for 3½ months, because persistently recurrent anaemia improved when copper supplements were given. Poor weight gain by the same child, in spite of an apparently adequate intake of carbohydrate, may have been related to selenium deficiency and there seemed to be some improvement when selenium supplements were provided.

Another interesting aspect of nutrition is appetite about which we know very little. When newly born babies are offered expressed human milk ad libitum from 12 hours after birth some begin to take it at once but in others there is a variable delay and some may take little or none for up to four days (Wilkinson et al, 1962). It is as unfair as it is wrong always to blame the mother and her milk production for the poor consumption of the baby. Babies and older children who are recovering from a period of malnutrition, whether it was due to tropical marasmus or the complications of surgical treatment have voracious appetites and will consume far more food and calories than their theoretical capacity; intakes of 150 or more calories per kg per day are not only desirable but should be striven for to the limit in such babies if recovery in the minimum time is to be achieved. When restoration of tissue is complete, in neonatal surgical patients as in tropical marasmus, the

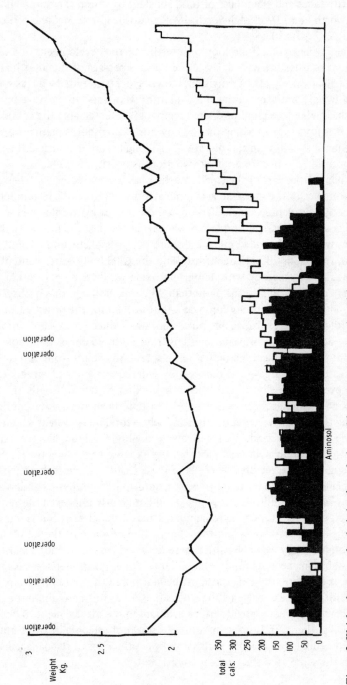

Figure 9. Weight changes and calorie intakes of a boy with a gangrenous atresia of jejunum and malrotation of midgut.
■ = calories administered by intravenous infusion. □ = calories taken by mouth or by jejunostomy

105

appetite fades and the intake of food subsides to within the normal range (Ashworth et al, 1968; Ashworth, 1969; Rutishauser & McCance, 1968; Figure 2, Figure 9).

The presence of a blind loop of intestine or the development of a dilated segment of intestine with delay in the onward passage of the intestinal contents may also adversely affect nutrition; patients and pigs with such stasis are ravenously hungry but after taking a few mouthfuls of food stop eating and appetite vanishes. When the blind or dilated segment is resected appetite returns to normal. It is no less astonishing that a baby born two months prematurely weighing less than 2 kg will take and digest milk so long before the normal time instead of continuing to live for another two months off the placenta.

When a large part of the small intestine has been resected, or when treatment of anomalies of the intestine is complicated by enterocolitis or temporary disaccharide intolerance, malnutrition and the loss of gastrointestinal secretions will cause rapid wasting and loss of weight. In the past the mortality in such babies was 75 per cent or more and there was gross distortion of body composition. In a group of patients of this kind the total body water content measured by the dilution method with deuterium oxide was over 85 per cent in 17, over 90 per cent in 9, in 3 it was more than 95 per cent and in one it was 97.5 per cent. The exchangeable sodium was about normal for the observed weight of the child but the exchangeable potassium was reduced by a third or more. In a 2.5 kg baby a change in water content from 80 to 95 per cent without a change in body weight indicates a reduction in total body solids from 500 to 125 g, but with satisfactory treatment such a baby will recover and will subsequently grow and develop normally. It is also remarkable that growth in length, the only form of growth which can conveniently be measured in such patients, continues even during the most severe deprivation and while total body weight declines. We must assume that other kinds of growth also probably continue, like the maintenance of daily metabolism, at least partly at the expense of existing tissues. When adequate nutrition is restored the cells of these tissues can be replenished. The maintenance of nutrition by the intravenous infusion of synthetic l-amino acids, glucose and an emulsion of soya bean oil has greatly improved the survival rate of such patients. It must be remembered that in its present forms intravenous feeding is still very crude and the composition of many of the solutions which are commercially available which were designed for use in adults makes them unsuitable for neonates and young infants. When intravenous feeding is the sole form of nutrition the longer it must be continued the more important the trace elements become as the existing stocks present at birth are diminished and this is becoming an increasingly serious problem in the management of neonatal surgical patients. In Europe marasmus is now not uncommon after initially successful neonatal emergency surgery and the principles of its management are much the same as in the tropical countries.

Acknowledgments

I am indebted to the Editor and Publishers of the Archives of Disease in Childhood for permission to include Figure 1.

References

Ashworth, A, Bell, R, James, WPT and Waterlow, JC (1968) *Lancet, ii,* 600
Butler, NR and Bonham, DG (1963) *Perinatal Mortality.* Livingstone, Edinburgh
Cozzi, F and Wilkinson, AW (1974) *Archives of Disease in Childhood, 50,* 791
Rutihauser, IHE and McCance, RA (1968) *Archives of Disease in Childhood, 43,* 252
Wilkinson, AW, Steven, LH and Hughes, EA (1962) *Lancet, i,* 982

Progress after Experimental Intestinal Resections

R A McCANCE
University of Cambridge, Cambridge, England

A newborn pig is about the size of a premature infant. An infant, if it does well might weigh 12kg by the time it is one year old. A large white pig anything from 160–180kg. In both all the requirements in the shape of food for maintenance and growth have to be ingested, absorbed and metabolised. The pig, therefore, should be a very satisfactory model on which to carry out gastrointestinal operations which are similar to those often required to save an infant's life, for one can study the subsequent progress of the animal so much more easily and rapidly than that of the child. The growth requirements of the pig moreover, make much greater demands upon its intestinal tract than those of the infant. Yet pigs have been little used. They cost more to feed than rats for one thing, and, if they do well, they get rather large and heavy as laboratory pets.

There is another very good reason for venturing into pigs for intestinal work. The effects of intestinal resections and by-pass operations on the subsequent growth and behaviour of the gut has been a matter of dispute for nearly 100 years. Does the remainder, if functional, hypertrophy in weight and length, and, if non-functional, atrophy. Could there be species differences in this matter which have not been explored?

THE OPERATIONS

The operations were carried out on pigs when they were about 10 days old. Those to be operated upon were removed from the sow early in the morning and kept warm in a covered box till they were to be used, which was usually between 09 30 and 14 00. The piglets were anaesthetised with ether using a simple mask held over the nose and mouth. After the operation was over the piglets were placed in a second box with straw in it and kept warm. In an hour or two they

108

were moving about and trying to get out of the box. After the animals to be used that day had all their operations, they were kept together in a warm place till the following morning, and then returned to the sow. They at once began to feed with the piglets that had not been selected for operation.

The following operations have been carried out from time to time:
1. removal or bypass of the ileum and its bypass; 2. removal of the colon with end to end anastomosis of the terminal ileum to the descending colon; 3. total removal or bypass of the jejunum, or of the jejunum and half the ileum.

Results

The incision was always a midline one and although this had an advantage, for it made the operations almost bloodless and thus avoided any need for blood transfusion, it also led to a somewhat weak scar and a hernia sometimes began to develop a week or so later and might become large and sacculated. Some were successfully repaired, and in a few the protruding intestines became strangulated, but in most the hernial sac began to regress after a time and caused no further trouble and two sows with hernias subsequently had several litters.

The operations were always followed by diarrhoea but by the end of a week the animals were often slowly gaining weight. Progress however might be very slow, particularly if only half the ileum had been left functional. During this prolonged period of slow growth we lost a number of animals from lung infections, sometimes initiated by round worm infestations. These are very difficult to eradicate in undernourished animals and one mature worm can produce a great many eggs. Crhonic swine erysipilas, usually presenting as swollen joints, has been another trouble.

Many of the animals, grew well even if they had made a slow start and became fully functional, if rather small adults. We have reared three generations of female animals. The mother and grandmother both made good breeding sows. If the operated animals were kept unmated when they were mature they tended to get very fat if fed to capacity.

THE ABSORPTION OF FOOD

While the animals were alive rough absorption experiments were carried out on them by feeding healthy animals on the same quantities of food and collecting several samples of faeces from each of them. These samples of faeces were then analysed for their content of water, protein, fat, and the minerals sodium potassium, calcium, magnesium and phosphorus, and the results compared. Three ages were chosen for study, piglets aged 5 weeks while still suckling, aged 8 weeks when being slowly weaned and adults. At five weeks the piglets usually had diarrhoea and in some experiments the healthy littermates were also passing loose motions. By eight weeks the experimental animals were usually passing more normal stools but both at 5 and 8 weeks the percentage of fat in the faeces of the experimental animals was considerably higher than in those passed by the normal littermates. These differences were statistically significant but the corresponding reductions in the percentage of water and protein were not, although they were in the expected direction. The adults were fed on (a) the stock diet, (b) the same diet made up to contain 12.5% of fat and (c) to contain 20% of fat. As the percentage of fat in the diets was raised the percentage of fat in the faeces of the experimental animals rose, and the increases were statistically significant. The percentages of water and protein in the faeces fell and those of water significantly so.

When the animals were slaughtered the whole intestinal tract was carefully dissected and completely cleared of its adhesions, which were always numerous, particularly round the anastomosis. The gut was then laid out on a bench and the lengths of the functional gut, the blind arm and the large intestine measured. Healthy animals, often littermates and always of similar age and size, were killed on the same day and the gut handled similarly. There was no significant difference between the *total* lengths of the small intestine of the two groups and no significant difference between the weights of the duodenum, or similar stretches of ileum after they had been carefully emptied and washed. Any interference with normal movement and function by reason of adhesions, however, was always followed by some, and often great, hypertrophy. The blind arm was invariably much thinner and lighter than the functional jejunum of the control animals. We concluded that *in pigs* (a) removal of large portions of the gastrointestinal tract does not lead to measurable hypertrophy of other portions except when there was partial obstruction caused by adhesions; (b) growth in length of the intestine, whether functional or not, depends upon genetic inheritance whereas growth in girth and weight depends largely upon functional use.

The activities of three enzymes, lactase, amylase, and acid phosphatase were measured in the non-functional blind arms and compared with those in those found in the functional jejunum of the controls. The upper middle and lower stretches were measured separately. No significant difference was found in the activities of amylase and phosphatase per g of mucosal protein, either between the upper middle and lower stretches or between the blind arms and the functional jejunum. The activity of lactase fell as the distance from the duodenum increased in both the functional and non-functional jejunum. The activity of the lactase, however, was greater in the non-functional blind arms than in the normal jejuna and the differences were fully significant.

Our work has been limited to the pig. There is some evidence, direct and indirect, that the intestine of the rat may behave differently. Hypertrophy of the residual intestine has also been reported in dogs after massive resections but the findings require confirmation.

References

McCance, R A, Stoddart, R W, Artavanis, C and Wilkinson A W (1976)
Biochemical Society Transactions 4, 151
McCance, R A, Stoddart, R W, Artavanis, C and Wilkinson A W (1976)
(In press)
McCance, R A and Wilkinson, A W (1967). *British Journal of Nutrition 21*, 731
Wilkinson, A W and McCance, R A (1971). *Proceedings of the Nutrition Society 30*, 26A
Wilkinson, A W and McCance, R A (1973). *Archives of Diseases in Childhood, 48*, 121
Wilkinson, A W and McCance, R A (1976). (In press)

Genes, Clocks and Circumstances—the effects of over and under nutrition

B A WHARTON
Queen Elizabeth Medical Centre, Birmingham, England

The effects of under and over nutrition are protean. There are early adaptive changes in metabolism often within days of a change in the diet and usually weeks or months before the individual can be considered malnourished; later growth velocity both of the whole body and of individual tissues and cell changes and the biological clock of development gains or loses time; finally if rehabilitation occurs recovery may be complete or in some there may be permanent sequels. There are many recent reviews concerned with particular aspects of these processes, e.g. learning processes (Birch, 1972); cell growth (Winick & Brasel, 1973); metabolic changes (Wharton, 1973), or with the overall effects of one particular variety of malnutrition; vitamin A deficiency (Srikantia, 1975); protein-energy deficiency (Waterlow & Alleyne, 1971); obesity (Garrow, 1974).

This review will not therefore be concerned with any particular process within the individual nor with any particular variety of malnutrition; rather it aims to examine those factors which mould and modify within the individual the overall effects of a particular nutritional environment. Three factors are considered, the genetic endowment of the individual, the stage of development he has reached, and other factors within his environment apart from nutrition.

GENETIC ENDOWMENT

In a sense all our nutritional processes depend on our genetic endowment. We must by genetic selection have developed processes of ingestion, assimilation and so on which have enabled us to use, with success and without reaction, the animal and particularly the plant foods which are available. Some, for example those with coeliac disease, are not genetically endowed to do this completely. Four examples of the way in which the genetic endowment may 'modify' the effect of malnutrition are discussed, two from the developing world, and two of importance in Western Europe.

Jejunal Lactase Deficiency

Jejunal lactase arises in the fetus shortly before birth and reaches a peak shortly thereafter (Aurichio et al, 1965). In the majority of the people of the world it then falls to reach insignificant levels in later childhood, but this does not commonly occur in northern Europeans, Arabs, or Nilo-Hamitic Africans (Cooke, 1972). The aetiology of these differing patterns is genetic and probably the mutation to maintain jejunal lactase in adult life occurred as man moved out of the tropics and became a milk drinker. The nutritional implication is that because of their genetic endowment the ability to handle a lactose load normally is considerably impaired in some children well before the first birthday, at a time when breast feeding is almost essential for survival in that environment (Cooke, 1967). In a few children the inability to handle lactose will be so severe as to cause diarrhoea after each feed. The majority however will probably make reasonable progress until a further stress such as an intestinal infection occurs. The episode will then be more severe, more prolonged and rehabilitation slower. The intake and retention of food and nutrients diminish and the long road to nutritional marasmus begins.

At a later age kwashiorkor may occur associated with a reduction in the activity of all the disaccharidases, including lactase, so that some children have both a genetically and environmentally induced fall in lactase. Probably the majority of children escape intolerance of dietary lactose when only one of these influences operates, but when both are present a proportion develop severe food intolerance which is difficult to treat (Wharton et al, 1968).

Kwashiorkor and Growth Velocity

When 56 Jamaican children were followed up 2—8 years after an overt episode of kwashiorkor they had broader chests, thicker limbs, and were a little heavier and taller than their siblings. Garrow and Pike (1967) speculated whether these children had been genetically endowed to grow more rapidly and hence had been more susceptible to the adverse nutritional environment than had their more slowly growing brothers and sisters. I speculated further as to whether this was a sign that the malnourished child was inappropriately trying to grow. Perhaps this was why children with kwashiorkor had a high rate of collagen turnover as reflected in their excretion of hydroxyproline, but a higher death rate compared to those with kwashiorkor who had the expected reduced excretion of hydroxyproline (Wharton, 1973). In retrospect, I think this raised excretion reflected a pathological breakdown of collagen containing tissues and was, therefore, merely

113

a non-specific biochemical indicator of the severity of the malnutrition. It is interesting, however, that a fall in growth velocity may not occur until some time after a reduction in the plasma albumin (Whitehead et al, 1971).

Rickets

It may be wrong to regard nutritional rickets as an environmental disease alone. All children with nutritional rickets have a tubular aminoaciduria (Jonxis et al, 1952). Although in the majority this disappears with treatment (Jonxis & Huisman, 1953), it may persist in up to 60% in a recent series from Greece (Doxiadis et al, 1976). A number of these children and their parents show evidence of a persisting tubular leak of aminoacids and phosphate. The developing thesis therefore is that these children have a genetic susceptibility to rickets which becomes manifest only in an adverse solar and dietary environment.

Hyperlipaemia

The association between hyperlipaemia and coronary artery disease is well established both within the individual and within populations. Plasma lipid concentrations reflect the intake and quality of dietary fat and carbohydrate, but the effect of the diet varies according to the genetic make up of the individual. While many adults will eat a diet containing 100 g of saturated long chain fat each day without any undue elevation of their plasma cholesterol concentration, in the heterozygote for familial hypercholesterolaemia (Type II) it will be well over 300 μg per 100 ml, and in the homozygote much higher concentrations together with xanthelasma will occur. Similarly if adult men increase their carbohydrate intake to over 500 g per day their fasting plasma triglyceride may increase by up to 170 mg per 100 ml, but in those with Type III hyperlipaemia, which is probably recessively inherited, it increases by 2–3 times this amount, while the increase in those with Type II is essentially normal (Glueck et al, 1969). In lipid metabolism during infancy the dietary environment dominates genetic expression, so that it is not possible to diagnose heterozygous familial hypercholesterolaemia until around the first birthday. Before then a 'higher than average' plasma cholesterol concentration probably indicates that the child is receiving breast milk (as opposed to an infant feeding formula containing cow's milk or vegetable oils) rather than indicating an inborn error of metabolism (Darmady et al, 1972).

STAGE OF DEVELOPMENT

The individual receives genes at conception and then blends and interacts with diet during development in utero, postnatal maturation and eventually ageing. The stage of development modifies the effect of nutritional stress on firstly the 'distance' the individual has reached at a certain age (e.g. in height, number of

114

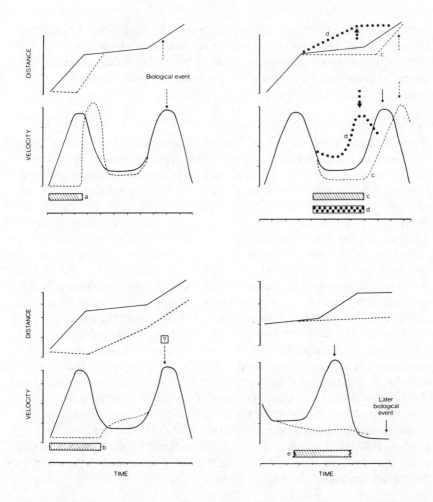

Figure 1. Nutrition and the stage of development: the effects of nutritional stress in an early period (a and b), in the mid term (c and d) and at a later stage (e) on distance travelled, velocity, and biological events in the development of an individual

cells in various organs – Figure 1), and secondly, the velocity or rate at which the 'distance' is covered, e.g. height velocity, peaks of growth rate in cells and tissue. Some aspects of development seem to occur in one stage or phase only such as lymphoid tissue in the later toddler and early school years; others may occur in two or more stages; height and weight velocity have two peaks during infancy and at puberty, and probably a peak occurs also earlier still in the mid trimester of pregnancy. Superimposed on these continuous variables, such as height and so on and partly programmed by them, are discrete biological events, such as eruption of teeth, the ability to walk upright, the arrival and departure of fertility and so on. The diagram shows a theoretical measurement (it might be height or cell number or whatever) which has two peaks of velocity with a relatively quiescent period in between, a gradual increase in distance covered, and a biological event (e.g. menarche) occurring during the second peak.

Early Stress

Insult 'a' occurs during part of the first growth spurt but when it is over there is still time for an acceleration in velocity which, although delayed, is sufficient for the individual to experience 'catch up growth' on the distance chart. By the time insult 'b' has ceased, however, the opportunity for a substantial acceleration of velocity has passed by and so although there is some acceleration and some catch up growth it is too little to make up for what has been lost. An example of 'a' is the light for dates baby in whom the onset of intrauterine growth retardation occurs in later pregnancy perhaps in association with maternal pre-eclampsia. When this nutritional constraint is relieved at birth then there is sufficient time for a catch up acceleration of stature or glial cells in the brain. There is therefore an opportunity post-natally to make up for the poor nutritional environment in middle and late pregnancy; it may be that we do not make the most of this opportunity. The prolonged undernutrition occurring throughout infancy and into the early toddler years which occurs in a number of developing countries, particularly in urban areas as an example of 'b' (Graham, 1968). These prolonged episodes of undernutrition lead to delays in some biological events due to occur during the period of restriction. Eruption of teeth may be delayed although this delay is usually not so marked as the restriction in the length of the jaw so that when eruption eventually occurs the teeth may be crowded and misplaced (Owens, 1968). The effect on biological events timed for some years later has, as far as I know, not been observed, e.g. the age of menarche in babies who were born small for dates or in children who had kwashiorkor.

Mid-term Stress

Insults 'c' and 'd' occur during a period of steady velocity such as in stature during the toddler and earlier school years. In addition to altering the velocity rate the stress also advances or retards the biological clock so that the second peak velocity and its associated biological events are moved to a different point in time.

The biological events of puberty are susceptible to the nutritional environment. Obesity in childhood leads to an earlier puberty (Wolff, 1955) while undernutrition delays it. The trend for menarche, the most easily timed event of puberty, to occur at an earlier age is almost certainly the effect of an increasing plane of nutrition. The exact mechanism by which nutrition affects the 'triggering' of the hormonal events behind menarche is unknown but Frisch (1972) has suggested that menarche most commonly occurs at a body weight of approximately 45 kg.

What is the effect on the final distance travelled if the biological clock is altered? As menarche has occurred earlier in Western society there has been a contemporary increase in adult height (Tanner, 1962), and this trend has on occasion been halted following prolonged periods of nutritional stress in a community, such as in war time Greece (Valaoras, 1970). It might seem generally then that an advancing biological clock led to an increase in the final distance achieved. However, in a series of obese children in whom puberty had been advanced, the final adult height was a little below the reference standard used (Lloyd et al, 1961), i.e. an advanced biological clock was associated with a reduction in total distance covered. We might speculate from these observations: suppose there is a time set genetically for a biological event, commonly the plane of nutrition delays the clock and reduces the final distance covered; as nutrition improves the biological event occurs earlier and distance covered increases. Eventually, however, nutritional influences lead to the event occurring *before* the genetically set time; when this occurs the final distance achieved is less.

Later Stress

Insult 'e' occurs throughout the second peak velocity of the whole organism, individual organ or tissue. The velocity and distance charts are both affected and immediate biological events are delayed — the zinc deficiency in Persia which leads to short stature, hypogonadism and delayed puberty is an example (Sandstead et al, 1967). The subsequent reproductive histories of the zinc-deficient young men of Persia or of the adolescent children caught in the Dutch 'hunger winter' have not been recorded. Similarly our observations of biological events occurring some time after growth is over are limited. The age of menopause has attracted the attention of the developmental biologist much less than has the age of menarche. Possibly the menopause occurs earlier in women of developing countries (WHO, 1969) but if so is this genetic or environmental?

The Critical Period Hypothesis

The long term effect of nutritional stress depends then at least partly on its timing; the importance of timing particularly in relation to weaning was demonstrated in a variety of animals in Cambridge twenty years ago, and was reviewed by McCance (1962). These, and similar observations, have been used to support the critical period hypothesis of development. This was probably first stated by Moulton (1923), but more recently has been elegantly stated by Dobbing (1968) as follows: "if a developmental process be restricted by any agency at any time of its fastest rate, not only will this delay the process, but will restrict its ultimate extent, even when the restricting influence is removed and the fullest possible rehabilitation obtained". The hypothesis in relation to cell growth and multiplication was developed particularly by Winick and Noble (1966) and has recently been re-viewed (Winick & Brasel, 1973).

The hypothesis is, of course, well known to embryologists where undoubtedly a 'restricting agency' applied at a critical period will have a permanent effect, for example the effect of fetal rubella in the first trimester on development of the heart, but it is clear that the hypothesis cannot be applied so absolutely to situations where the restricting agency is more gradually perceived by the individual, and the developmental process has fewer discrete and marked changes than in embryological life. Nutritional stresses occurring during post-natal life and after the first trimester of pregnancy in the human might therefore not follow the hypothesis as closely as embryological events.

This caveat may be self evident but three examples will illustrate its force. Firstly, although we predicted from critical period theory that recovery from insult 'a' will be complete, we know that the majority of small for dates term babies do not catch up completely in stature and yet after birth there is at least one year of peak velocity in stature left; is this because many of the small for dates babies had suffered restriction probably of a non-nutritional nature from very early in pregnancy? Does this observation disprove the theory or do we fail to rehabilitate adequately *throughout the first year of life* our small for dates babies? Secondly, adipose tissue increases greatly during the first year of life and before puberty and there is some evidence that at these times the adipose cells are particularly susceptible to hyperplasia (Brook et al, 1972; Salans et al, 1973), that is to say according to the hypothesis these are critical periods; there-fore, if hyperplasia had not occurred by the time the second period was over it would never do so (Grinker, 1973), and extrapolating a little, such people would not develop obesity in adult life. There is however adequate evidence from many sources that people who have remained slim until their 20s may still subsequently become obese *and* have an increase in the number of adipocytes, i.e. hyperplasia (as well as hypertrophy) has occurred after the supposed critical periods (see development of this argument by Garrow, 1974). If these difficulties apply when considering a relatively homogeneous tissue, such as the adipose organ, how much more must they apply to organs as heterogeneous as the brain. The third example therefore concerns the brain; it is well known that malnutrition during the growth spurt in rodents reduces brain weight and cell number, but malnutrition *before* the growth spurt also lowers the ultimate size of the brain even though nutrition was adequate *during* the growth spurt (Bush & Leathwood, 1975).

The effect of 'time' on 'food' and 'growth' is unquestionably important and the 'critical period' is a useful concept but we should not apply it uncritically.

OTHER ENVIRONMENTAL CIRCUMSTANCES

The genes of the individual have interacted with his nutritional environment and the effects have been modified by the time at which nutritional stresses have occurred. What other factors in the individual's environment operating at the time of, or after, a nutritional stress will mould and modify the response to it?

Microbiological Environment

The interactions between nutrition and infection are clinically obvious and the immunopathology of this interaction is becoming clearer. The public health aspects of this interaction are discussed elsewhere, but a particular example of interaction between intestinal flora and nutrition, is considered in more detail here.

Malnourished children in Guatemala have very high counts of both anaerobic and facultative bacteria in the fluid in the duodenum and jejunum but this is not due to malnutrition per se since the same degree of bacterial contamination also occurs in well nourished children from the same environment (Mata et al, 1972). This bacterial contamination of the upper small bowel which is found in many children of developing countries has at least two nutritional implications.

Firstly, the bacteria split the bile salts to give free bile acids and so the ability to form micelles for the solubilisation of lipids within the duodenum is restricted

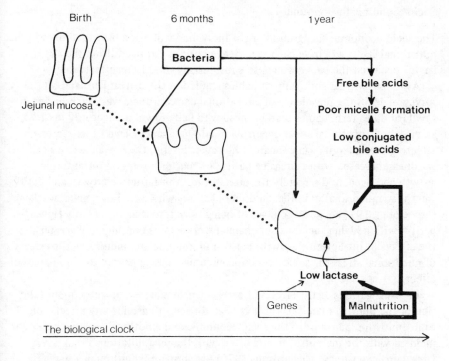

Figure 2. The interplay of genes, nutrition, and the microbiological environment on jejunal morphology, bile acid metabolism and jejunal lactase

119

in all of these children, malnourished or not. In addition the malnourished child has a much lower concentration in the duodenum of conjugated bile salts, probably because of reduced hepatic synthesis (Schneider & Viteri, 1974). The bacterial environment and the nutritional stress therefore synergistically reduce micelle formation in these children so that hydrolysis of fat by lipase is considerably reduced.

Secondly, children in developing countries are born with finger shaped villi in the jejunum, but within a few months varying degrees of villous atrophy are found and these changes progress with age (Chacko et al, 1969; Cooke et al,1969) (Figure 2). The cause of these changes is not absolutely clear but is probably increasing bacterial contamination of the small intestine which affects both bile acid metabolism and jejunal morphology. If the child becomes malnourished further villous atrophy may result, the disaccharidases including lactase will fall (Wharton, 1975) and so will the production of bile salts. Furthermore, many children at this time will be experiencing a genetically induced fall in their lactase activity. In this combination of genetic, microbiological and nutritional influences abnormal function of the gut occurs in very many children

Socio-economic Background

The socio-economic background of the individual will often have dictated whether nutritional stress will have been experienced or not but in addition the stress having occurred the background can substantially modify its effect.

At the seven year follow up of babies studied in the British Perinatal Mortality survey of 1958 the prevalence of educational backwardness was much higher in small for dates term babies than in those who had grown satisfactorily *in utero,* an effect of nutritional stress occurring in late pregnancy. Two other factors affecting the outcome were apparent however. Firstly, the prevalence of backwardness increased with increasing parity, no matter how good intrauterine growth had been, and secondly the effect of both intrauterine growth and parity were very much smaller in the children of fathers who were not manual workers (Davie et al, 1972). The advantages of being born into a smaller family (lower parity) with a higher income (non-manual worker) was considerably greater than the effects of intrauterine growth. Far from moulding and modifying the effects of nutritional stress the socio-economic circumstances appeared to dominate their effect.

In investigations of the effects of early nutritional stress on subsequent function of the brain in man it has always been difficult to ascribe any effects found to malnutrition per se or to the socio-economic and emotional circumstances coincident with the malnutrition and often with the rehabilitation. From a very large Jamaican survey Richardson (1976) has shown that although a previous episode of overt malnutrition and continuing undernutrition thereafter (as shown by height) affected IQ at 6–10 years of age and a favourable social background did much to counteract these effects and was the dominant factor. Some years ago I expressed uncertainty about the validity of the far reaching conclusions being drawn at that time from brain function studies (Wharton, 1970).

Even in the 'purer' circumstances of the animal experiment it is not clear whether permanent changes in behaviour induced by malnutrition before weaning are the effects of malnutrition alone or the effects of a disturbed mother-pup relationship induced by the experiment. It seems that disturbing mouse litters before weaning induces just as much disruption of subsequent learning ability as does malnutrition during that period; when applied together the effects were additive (Leathwood et al, 1975).

We are told "Give me neither poverty nor riches; feed me food convenient for me: (Proverbs, 30:8). Appropriate food is indeed important but perhaps the socio-economic circumstances are important too.

Personal Environment

The child has little control over his personal environment. An important factor in the personal environment of people in the Western world is their chosen diet; does it contain too *much* energy, too *little* fluoride, or an inappropriate *quality* of fat? Other factors in the personal environment, however, modify nutritional effects. The mother who smokes produces a small for dates baby and even after allowing for the smaller size at birth and the likely lower social class of the mother, the child at seven years is a little shorter and educationally a little slower (Davie et al, 1972). In adult life the chosen diet may by itself, or together with a genetic susceptibility, result in hypercholesterolaemia and an increased risk of coronary artery disease; but this nutritional effect is compounded and heightened if the man smokes too (Joint Working Party, 1976). Another important modifying influence of the personal environment is alcohol — at levels of intake well below those when alcoholism might be considered. Digestive enzyme production is increased then falls; the intestinal transport of nutrients, such as thiamin and iron, are altered; intermediary metabolism of galactose is inhibited; the excretion of common metabolites, such as uric acid, is reduced (Sinclair, 1972).

The circumstances of an individual cannot turn a nutritional catastrophe into a success, but they go a long way in modifying its sequels.

THE CONCERT

Nutritional stress therefore has a number of effects; some are almost immediate and temporary; some appear later, some may be prolonged and on occasion permanent. These effects are however moulded and modified in their expression partly by the genetic endowment of the individual, partly by their timing in relation to the biological clocks of the individual, and partly by the other circumstances, particularly socio-economic in which the individual either finds or places himself during the stress and the period of rehabilitation. The nutritional stresses are moulded and modified in concert by his genes, his clocks, and his circumstances.

Acknowledgments

I am grateful to the Medical Illustration Department, Birmingham Children's Hospital, Signor T Barktziris and to Mrs Peggy Cox for their help in preparing this chapter.

References

Auricchio, S, Rubino, A and Murset, G (1965) *Pediatrics, 35,* 944
Birch, HG (1972) *American Journal of Public Health, 62,* 773
Brook, CGD, Lloyd, JD and Wolff, OH (1972) *British Medical Journal, 2,* 25
Bush, MS and Leathwood, PD (1975) *British Journal of Nutrition, 33,* 373
Chacko, CJG, Paulson, KA, Mathan, VI and Baker, SJ (1969) *Journal of Pathology,98,* 146
Cooke, GC (1967) *British Medical Journal, 1,* 527
Cooke, GC (1972) *Symposium of the Swedish Nutrition Foundation No.XI,* 52
Cooke, GC, Kajubi, SK and Lee, FD (1969) *Journal of Pathology, 98,* 157
Darmady, JM, Fosbrooke, AS and Lloyd, JK (1972) *British Medical Journal, 2,* 685
Davie, R, Butler, NR and Goldstein, H (1972) *From Birth to Seven.* Humanities Press, New York
Dobbing, J (1968) In *Applied Neurochemistry.* (Ed) AN Davison and J Dobbing. Blackwell, Oxford. Page 289
Doxiadis, S, Angelis, C, Karatzas, P, Vrettos, C and Lapatsanis, P (1976) *Archives of Disease in Childhood, 51,* 83
Frisch, RE (1972) *Pediatrics, 50,* 445
Garrow, JS and Pike, M (1967) *Lancet, i,* 1
Garrow, JS (1974) *Energy Balance and Obesity in Man.* North Holland Publishing Company, Amsterdam. Page 248
Glueck, CJ, Levy, RI and Fredrickson, S (1969) *Diabetes, 18,* 739
Graham, GC (1968) In *Calorie Deficiencies and Protein Deficiencies.* (Ed) RA McCance and EM Widdowson. Churchill, London. Page 301
Grinker, J (1973) *Journal American Dietetic Association, 62,* 30
Joint Working Party (1976) *Journal of the Royal College of Physicians of London, 10,* 213
Jonxis, JFP, Smith, PA and Huisman, THJ (1952) *Lancet, ii,* 1015
Jonxis, JHP and Huisman, THJ (1953) *Lancet, ii,* 248
Leathwood, PD, Bush, MS and Mauron, J (1975) *Psychopharmacologia, 41,* 105
Lloyd, JK, Wolff, OH and Whelan, WS (1961) *British Medical Journal, 2,* 145
Mata, LJ, Jimenez, F, Cordon, M, Rosales, R, Priera, E, Schneider, RE and Viteri, F (1972) *American Journal of Clinical Nutrition, 25,* 1118
McCance, RA (1962) *Lancet, ii,* 671
Moulton, CR (1923) *Journal Biological Chemistry, 57,* 79
Owens, PDA (1968) *Calorie Deficiencies and Protein Deficiencies.* (Ed) RA McCance and EM Widdowson. Churchill, London. Page 341

Richardson, SA (1976) *Pediatric Research, 10,* 57

Salans, LB, Cusham, SW and Weismann, RE (1973) *Journal of Clinical Investigation, 52,* 929

Sandstead, HH, Prasad, AS, Schulert, AR, Farid, Z, Miale, A, Basilly, S and Darby, WJ (1967) *American Journal of Clinical Nutrition, 20,* 422

Schneider, RE and Viteri, FE (1974) *American Journal of Clinical Nutrition, 27,* 777

Sinclair, HM (1972) *Proceedings Nutrition Society, 31,* 117

Srikantia, SG (1975) *World Review of Nutrition and Dietetics, 20,* 185

Tanner, JM (1962) *Growth at Adolescence, 2nd Edition.* Blackwell, Oxford

Valaoras, VG (1970) *Human Biology, 42,* 184

Waterlow, JC and Alleyne, GAO (1971) *Advances in Protein Chemistry, 25,* 117

Wharton, BA (1970) In *Modern Trends in Paediatrics.* (Ed) J Apley. Butterworth, London. Page 191

Wharton, BA (1973) *Journal Royal College of Physicians, 7,* 259

Wharton, BA (1975) In *Paediatric Gastroenterology.* (Ed) CM Anderson and V Burke. Blackwell, Oxford. Page 569

Wharton, BA, Howells, G and Phillips, I (1968) *British Medical Journal, 4,* 608

Whitehead, RG, Frood, JDL and Poskitt, EME (1971) *Lancet, i,* 287

WHO (1969) *Biological Components of Human Reproduction. Technical Report Series No.435.* WHO, Geneva

Winick, M and Noble, A (1966) *Journal of Nutrition, 89,* 300

Winick, M and Brasel, JA (1973) In *Modern Nutrition in Health and Disease.* (Ed) RS Goodhart and ME Shils. Lea and Febiger, Philadelphia. Page 506

Wolff, OH (1955) *Quarterly Journal Medicine, 24,* 109

Growth Before Puberty—Catch-up Growth

W A MARSHALL
Institute of Child Health, University of London, England

Observations of children's growth are widely used as indices of nutrition and general well-being. It is certainly true that undernourished children suffer impairment of growth, although there are many other causes which may produce the same effect.

Inadequate nutrition which is not sufficiently severe to cause manifest deficiency diseases is often associated with impaired growth in stature. However, it is usually difficult to distinguish the effects of undernutrition per se from those of poor hygiene and other adverse environmental conditions which nearly always accompany it. Optimal nutrition in an otherwise satisfactory environment will permit optimal growth as ordained by the child's genotype. Overnutrition will not lead to greater stature than that determined genetically. It will lead only to obesity. This is often demonstrated in the more prosperous parts of the world where the parents of genetically small children sometimes over-feed their offspring in the belief that this will make them grow, but only succeed in making them obese.

In many developing countries babies have mean birth weights similar to those of children in more economically prosperous communities but, after the first six months, their weight gains diminish (Eveleth & Tanner, 1976). This failure to sustain a high rate of weight gain is probably due mainly to undernutrition although other factors, such as infection, may also play a part.

In some communities, the fall in rate of weight gain becomes apparent at the age of weaning, when breast milk is replaced by foods high in starch and low in protein. A study in the West Indies (St Vincent) showed that infants were, on average, near the 50th centile of the Harvard weight standards during the first six months of life, but had dropped to the 15th centile by the age of 18 months.

Those children who were considered to have grown satisfactorily were weaned at an average age of 12.7 months while those with poor growth were weaned at about six months (Antrobus, 1971).

The impairment of growth resulting from malnutrition appears to be more or less uniform throughout the body and does not alter the relationship of the length of the limbs to that of the trunk.

In most highly developed countries, the stature of children at any given age has increased considerably over the last hundred years or so but, in general, the children of well-off parents are taller than those who are less privileged. Also children with several siblings are usually shorter than those from smaller families. Variations in nutrition are believed to play a part in creating these differences.

Thus, information about growth is helpful in assessing the nutritional status of both communities and individuals but the possible influence on growth of factors other than nutrition must be considered in each case. In addition to endocrine and chromosomal disorders specifically related to growth, almost any prolonged or recurrent illness may inhibit growth in stature. Similarly, endemic

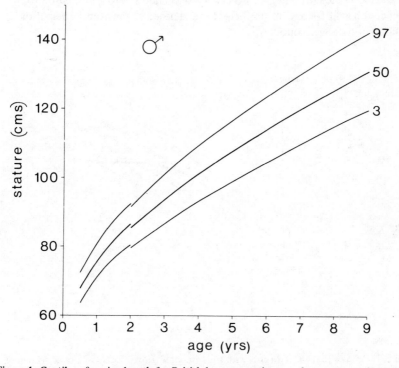

Figure 1. Centiles of supine length for British boys up to the age of two years and stature for British boys up to the age of nine years. The corresponding centiles for girls are almost identical. (Based on data from Tanner, Whitehouse and Takaishi, 1966)

disease may contribute to short stature in a population. Further, reliable deductions about growth can be made only from measurements which distinguish between skeletal growth and change in body composition. The extent of variation in the growth patterns of normal healthy children must also be fully appreciated.

Stature, provided it is correctly measured, is generally more satisfactory than weight as an index of growth. In very young children supine length may be used. The variation in stature of normal children at each age in a given population is usually expressed in centiles. The centiles for British children are shown in Figure 1 and are based on data from Tanner, Whitehouse and Takaishi (1966). By definition, 50 per cent of normal healthy children at each age have statures below the 50th centile and only 3 per cent have statures below the third centile.

Figure 1 shows that the normal variation in stature amongst children of any given age is much greater than is often realised. For example, the third centile stature for 9-year old boys is almost identical with the 97th centile stature for 5½-year old boys. In other words, a small, but normal, 9-year old boy is the same height as a rather tall, but entirely normal 5½-year old boy. Similar comparisons can be made between other ages. It is therefore relatively meaningless to talk about the normality, or otherwise, of a child's height in relation to his 'expected height for age' or his 'height age' defined as the average height of children in that age group.

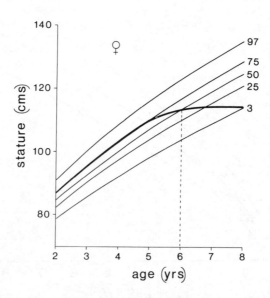

Figure 2. Centiles for stature in girls with superimposed growth curve of a child who grew up the 75th centile to age five years and then suffered from growth inhibition leading to a total cessation of growth by age six. At this age her stature was still at the 50th centile and did not fall to the 3rd centile until she was eight years old

126

A single measurement of a child's stature is never a sufficient basis for deciding whether or not his growth is normal. Stature at any given time represents the end result of all the growth which has occurred since conception and does not give an adequate measure of what has happened in the immediate past, or is likely to happen in the immediate future. A child whose stature is exactly average, or even above average, for his age may be suffering from serious growth failure. For example, a rather tall girl (Figure 2) grew steadily, with a stature in the region of the 75th centile, until she was 5 years old. At this point, her growth began to slow down. By her sixth birthday it had stopped completely and yet a single measurement at that time would have shown her stature to be at the 50th centile, i.e. 'normal'. If there was no further increase in her stature it would be

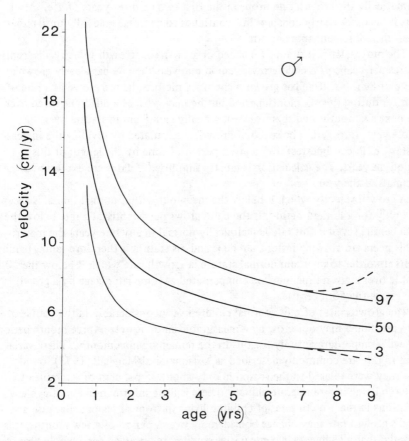

Figure 3. Centiles for stature velocity in boys up to the age of nine years. The corresponding centiles for girls are identical up to age seven when the 3rd centile and the 97th centile become further apart as shown by the interrupted lines. (Based on data from Tanner, Whitehouse and Takaishi, 1966)

127

two or more years (if she survived for that length of time) before her stature would fall below the third centile and before this gross abnormality could be detected in a single measurement.

In order to recognise abnormally slow growth in a child whose stature has not yet fallen below the third centile, it is essential to have repeated measurements from which we can decide whether or not he is growing at a normal speed. If the child's growth rate is grossly abnormal, this will become apparent as the repeated measurements are plotted on a centile chart for stature. Each plot will be at a lower centile than the previous one. This drop in status is more difficult to detect if the stature is already well below the third centile, or if the growth rate is only slightly subnormal. It is then helpful to use a chart which gives the centiles of growth rate in normal children of different ages (Figure 3). Note how dramatically the growth rate drops in the first two or three years of life. After this, it becomes nearly constant but continues to decrease gradually until puberty, when the adolescent spurt occurs.

The most satisfactory unit for speed of growth (or 'growth velocity') is 'centimetres per year'. If a child grows 8 cm in one year then he has clearly grown at a rate of 8 cm/yr. If he has grown 4 cm in six months, he has grown at a rate of 8 cm/yr during this six month period but he may grow at a different speed over the next six months and therefore not actually gain 8 cm in stature over the whole year. In general, the speed of growth is calculated by dividing the increase in stature (in centimetres) over a given period of time by the length of this period, in years. The calculation is greatly simplified if dates are expressed as decimals of the year.

A growth velocity which is below the mean but within normal limits, is acceptable only for a limited period. If the child grows persistently at a rate below the 50th centile (even if this rate is technically normal in any one year) the majority of his peers are growing faster than he is and his stature is therefore falling behind theirs. In order to maintain normal stature, a growth rate which is below the 50th centile over a given time must be compensated at some later stage by a growth rate above the 50th centile.

The growth rates of most normal children vary considerably in the course of the year. Some may not grow by a measurable amount over a three month period, but will compensate entirely for this in the remaining nine months. These variations in rate are commonly described as 'seasonal' but Marshall (1975) found that they were related to the season in only about 35 per cent of a sample of children living in a temperate climate. There is little information about cyclic variations in the growth rates of children living in tropical regions. Because a child's growth rate may change considerably over a period of a few months, it is essential that all subjects in comparative studies are observed for a whole year. No valid conclusions can be drawn over a shorter period. In order to assess the effect on a child's growth of a modified diet, or other treatment, the increase in stature over a whole year of treatment must be compared with that during the whole of the preceding or following year.

The discussion so far has been based on the measurement of stature but much of it applies equally to weight. However, stature and weight are not comparable measurements and the latter is a less satisfactory index of growth. A child may gain weight by becoming either obese or oedematous with very little or no increase in stature. Alternatively, quite normal growth in stature may be accompanied by very little gain in weight, or even loss in weight, if fat is being lost rapidly at the same time.

However, if it is not possible to measure a child's stature accurately, his weight may have to be used as the only index of his growth. Centiles for weight in boys

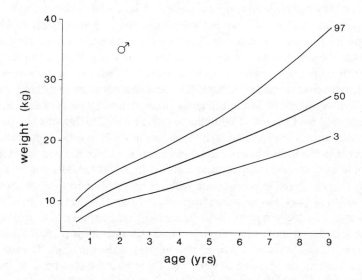

Figure 4. Centiles for weight in boys up to age nine years. (Based on data from Tanner, Whitehouse and Takaishi, 1966)

are therefore shown in Figure 4. It should be noted that the third centile is not a constant percentage of the 50th. Thus, a 2-year old boy is underweight (below the third centile) when his weight is 17 per cent below the 50th centile, but an 8-year old is not in a comparable situation until his weight is 24 per cent below the 50th centile. Thus it is fallacious to regard any fixed percentage of 'ideal' weight as the basis for suspecting undernutrition. Also, as with stature, the normal variation in weight at any given age is enormous. A heavy (97th centile) 4-year old is the same weight as a third centile boy at the age of 8½, yet both these boys may be entirely normal, healthy and obtaining optimum nutrition. On the other hand, the heavy one might be obese, with relatively short stature. The lighter one might be very thin, if his stature were normal but he might even

129

be obese if his stature were for some reason below the third centile. We cannot choose between these alternatives on the basis of weight alone.

Despite the above reservations about the interpretation of a single measurement of a child's weight, it is generally true that failure to gain weight over several months is indicative of undernutrition or disease. As in the case of stature, the rate of gain is much more significant than the absolute value.

The most satisfactory way of assessing a child's growth in both weight and height is to observe his progress on the stature and weight centile charts independently. A child suffering from undernutrition may be extremely small in stature for his age. In such a case, the defect in weight for height might be much less extreme than that in either height or weight alone. Even amongst healthy children, of any given age and stature, there may be a wide difference in body weight between stocky, muscular individuals and those of more linear build.

Weight in children is no more valid as a measure of obesity than it is an index of growth. The simplest way to decide whether a child is too fat or too thin, and whether he is gaining or losing fat, is to measure the thickness of folds of skin and subcutaneous fat at selected sites. Special instruments are available for this purpose and centiles of skinfold thickness from birth to 19 years of age have been published by Tanner and Whitehouse (1975) who also describe the technique of this measurement. This technique does not give results of an accuracy comparable to the measurement of stature, but it is a much more satisfactory index of obesity or deficiency in total body fat than is the child's weight, even when this is considered in conjunction with his height. The 50th centile of subcapular skinfold thickness increases from about 7 mm at birth to 9 mm at six months and then declines until about the eighth year. However, the 'normal' range of variation at any age is very wide. In 8-year old girls it is approximately 4 to 20 mm as compared to 3.5 to 12 mm in boys of the same age. The use of the word 'normal' here is open to question. Those near the upper end of the range might be described as obese.

The norms of height, weight and skinfold thickness which we have mentioned so far are based on samples of healthy British children. It may be assumed that few, if any, were suffering from any degree of undernutrition although a measure of overnutrition is much more likely. The same standards could be applied with reasonable confidence to most populations in North West Europe but it would be necessary to check their validity before applying them to other groups.

However, although children of different races and cultures may vary in their absolute size, the general pattern of rapid but decelerating growth in the first year or two with a more gradual decrease in speed thereafter seems to be universal in pre-adolescent children.

Catch-up Growth

If a child's growth is inhibited by malnutrition or illness the effect is not

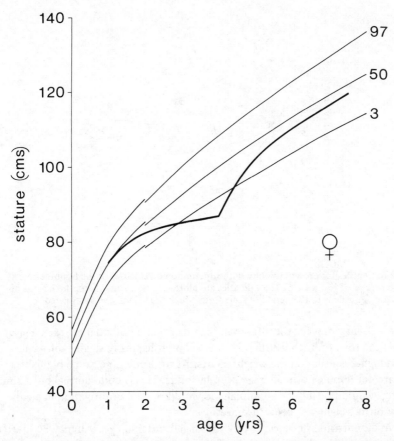

Figure 5. Centiles for stature with superimposed growth curve of a hypothetical girl who suffered severe growth inhibition up to the age of four when catch-up growth began

necessarily permanent. When an adequate diet is provided or health is restored, the child will grow at a speed greater than the average for his age. His stature therefore approaches the level it would have reached if the setback had not occurred. As the growth curve approaches its original trajectory, there is a gradual deceleration so that future growth follows a close approximation to its original channel on the centile chart (Figure 5). The high speed of growth which restores the curve to its original path has been termed 'catch-up growth' by Prader, Tanner and von Harnack (1963). During 'catch-up' the child's growth rate may reach two or three times the average for his chronological age (see Figure 6).

Babies born at term (40 weeks) with birth weights below average (but not abnormally so) usually gain weight more quickly in the first six months of life than those who were heavier at birth. This is probably an example of catch-up growth and reflects the fact that intrauterine growth is limited by maternal fac-

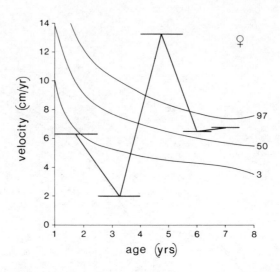

Figure 6. Centiles for growth velocity with superimposed velocities of the hypothetical child represented in Figure 5. The velocities are plotted as horizontal lines, the lengths of which are equivalent to the period of time from which the velocity was estimated

tors which may prevent the infant realising its genetic potential to reach a given size by the time of birth. During the first six months, many small babies will rise to higher centiles on the weight charts. At the same time, some big babies who are developing normally may drop in status. This is quite normal but a similar drop would possibly be abnormal and would require investigation in a child whose birth weight was below average.

If undernutrition or illness is very prolonged, catch-up growth may be insufficient to enable the child to reach his full potential for growth and his final stature will be diminished.

The mechanism responsible for catch-up growth is not known. Tanner (1963) has suggested that the central nervous system may receive information about the difference between a child's actual stature and the stature he would have reached if his growth had not been impaired. The growth rate is then adjusted so as to reduce this difference. This hypothesis, however, has not been tested and the possibility of a peripheral mechanism cannot be excluded at present.

References

Antrobus, ACK (1971) *Journal of Tropical Paediatrics and African Child Health,* 17, 187
Eveleth, PB and Tanner, JM (1976) *World Wide Variation in Human Growth. International Biological Programme Series.* Cambridge University Press
Marshall, WA (1975) *Annals of Human Biology, 2,* 243
Prader, A, Tanner, JM and von Harnack, GA (1963) *Journal of Paediatrics, 62,* 646

Tanner, JM, Whitehouse, RH and Takaishi, M (1966) *Archives of Disease in Childhood, 41,* 454, 613

Tanner, JM and Whitehouse, RH (1975) *Archives of Disease in Childhood, 50,* 142

Some Nutritional Problems in Infants

D HULL
University Hospital Medical School, Nottingham, England

Rearing infants is a mixture of an art, a craft and a science, with strong cultural overtones. The clinical problem called 'failure to thrive' is relatively common, although often 'failure to rear' would be more appropriate for the difficulty may be as much with the parent as the child.

Of the 1350 children admitted to the medical wards of the Nottingham Children's Hospital in 1975, drawing from a population of about 500,000, 5 per cent were admitted with 'failure to thrive'. A further 2 per cent had feeding difficulties. None of these infants had responded to simple out-patient measures, or were sufficiently ill when they first presented to demand immediate in-patient care. It is pertinent to note that an analysis of the length and weight of all infants (0–5 years) admitted to hospital for whatever reason showed them on average to be undersized compared to the children in the community and there was a preponderance from social classes IV and V (J Wynne, personal communication).

Sometimes in infants with 'failure to thrive' there was a fault in bodily function, but often factors in the infant, the parents and the home were involved and to try to place the child into a single medical diagnostic category was neither appropriate nor helpful. After investigation and assessment of their response to medical care, the infants fell into a number of broad and overlapping groups (Table I).

The care of these infants can be reviewed only briefly here and I shall discuss mainly those questions I would ask myself about each infant. Inevitably, this reflects a personal approach and the discussion of individual disorders is superficial, but I have tried to include the commoner conditions and to recall those rare conditions which in my experience have responded dramatically to dietary adjustments.

134

TABLE I. The Number of Infants Admitted to the Nottingham Children's Hospital with 'Feeding Problems' and 'Failure to Thrive' in 1975

'FEEDING PROBLEMS'

Infants – minor difficulties	10	
Mother – inexperienced unhappy	12	
Poor Social conditions	4 =	26

'FAILURE TO THRIVE'

Social

Poor conditions and inadequate parents	10	
Severe deprivation	6	
Severe deprivation with non-accidental injuries	4 =	20

Disease

Swallowing difficulty, e.g. cleft palate etc	3	
Cystic Fibrosis	2	
Coeliac Disease	6	
Acrodermatitis Enteropathica	1	
Delayed recovery from Gastroenteritis including 2° lactose intolerance	7	
Severe systemic disease	3 =	22

No Cause Found

Improvement in hospital	10	
No improvement in hospital	10 =	20

	TOTAL	88

Is the Infant Being Offered Sufficient Food?

It is exceedingly rare in the UK for a mother not to have sufficient of an appropriate food to offer her child and failure to give sufficient is usually due to neglect either because of ignorance, ineptitude or illness in the parents, or by deliberate intent. The latter is now a well-recognised form of child abuse (Barbero & Shaheen, 1967). The complexity of the relationships between the parents, particularly the mother and their neglected offspring, has been the subject of a number of studies (Glaser et al, 1968; Pollitt & Eichler, 1976; Fischoff et al, 1971). The parents occasionally have unrealistic views on what the relatively helpless infant can or cannot be expected to do. Simple statement on 'how to feed your baby' will not solve their problem. Often, however, parents with limited abilities in poor social circumstances have a fair idea of what to do, but for one limitation or another are unable to give their infant what is needed; with help they may manage. On the other hand some parents who could cope deliberately neglect their infants for a variety of real or imagined reasons. The infants I have called deprived (Table I) were taken out of their parents hands 'into care'. On admission to hospital they often show other signs of neglect, especially of the skin, particularly over the scalp and buttocks. There may be even more overt evidence of injury, but more often the possibility of abuse is suspected from the features of the history and the social report. Some but by no means the majority of infants subject to non-accidental injury are undersized. Whether unfortunate circumstances or unfortunate parents lead to the child failing to thrive, once the infants are in the ward they respond over the first few days to gentle handling by accepting more food, but the body weight may not increase for 2—3 weeks. When it does it may be dramatic. Infants who have been or who are difficult to rear, such as pre-term infants, are more likely to be neglected or injured.

Is the Infant Able to Take in All the Food Offered?

Sucking and swallowing problems are common in pre-term, brain damaged, hypotonic and abnormal infants (e.g. Down's syndrome and infants with cleft palate). Together these form a small but important group demanding considerable nursing skill and maternal determination if they are to be reared satisfactorily. But these infants apart, there are occasionally those who have specific problems with swallowing in whom oesophageal incoordination may be demonstrated by cine radiography, who need to be recognised and offered the same intensity of attention. They may present with respiratory difficulties due to repeated aspiration of milk and clinically this condition might be confused with cystic fibrosis.

Is the Infant Able to Digest the Food he is Given?

Many of the inherited disorders of digestion, for example monosaccharide intolerance, primary disaccharide intolerance, primary lipase deficiency, and enterokinase deficiency, present with intractable diarrhoea from the first few days of life. Diagnosis depends on the awareness of these and other possibilities. Unfortunately, the clinical need to give clear fluids to improve the infant's condition often obscures the diagnosis initially. Sometimes no diagnosis can be made and the child may be sufficiently ill to justify a period of total parenteral nutrition (Green et al, 1975). In most instances dietary adjustments alone allow the infants to thrive, though rearing infants on unusual diets, for example on fructose as a sole source of carbohydrate, has its hazards. Figure 1 shows the response of two infants with monosaccharide intolerance when they were given a glucose-free diet. As these infants grow older they tolerate more and more glucose in their diet. One rare condition in this category, acrodermatitis enteropathica, has recently been shown to respond dramatically to supplements of zinc (Moynahan, 1974).

136

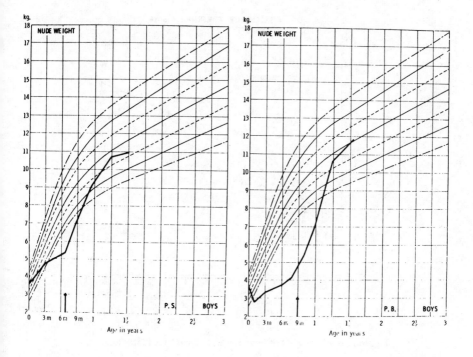

Figure 1. The growth curve of the two patients with glucose-galactose malabsorption. The arrow indicates when the infants were placed on a glucose-galactose-free diet

The two medical conditions that most clinicians wish to exclude when they admit an infant who is not thriving are cystic fibrosis and gluten enteropathy. The former is easily identified by a sweat test but the latter is a more difficult problem. It is the author's current practice in all but the weakest infants to observe the child's initial response to a normal gluten containing weaning diet. If the child continues to grizzle and does not thrive then a duodenal biopsy is performed and the infant is given a gluten-free diet. The weaker infants of low body weight are started immediately on a gluten-free diet and the response of the child to the gradual introduction of gluten is observed once he is of reasonable size and weight. Transient gluten sensitivity may occur. The diagnosis might be confirmed later by a xylose test (Rolles et al, 1975; Lamabadusuriya et al, 1975).

Infants often fail to thrive after an episode of gastroenteritis and this may be due to secondary disaccharide intolerance. It is of interest that infants with low body weights before they develop gastroenteritis are more liable to develop secondary disaccharide intolerance (Figure 2 – Bartrop & Hull, 1973). Factors other than disaccharide intolerance may contribute to failure to thrive with or

137

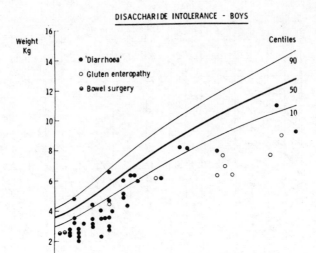

Figure 2. Body weights of boys found to have lactose intolerance

without initial gastroenteritis and many will respond to removing milk protein
from their diet (Kuituren et al, 1975; Walker-Smith, 1975).

Is the Infant Able to Metabolise the Food he is Given?

There is a wide range of enzyme defects, particularly in protein metabolism,
which lead to a variety of signs and symptoms from vomiting to fits, from derma-
titis to thrombocytopenia, and they are often associated with failure to thrive.
The signs and symptoms are often at their worst in the first few days or weeks
of life. In many instances little can be done except to reduce the protein intake
to critically low levels. A good response occasionally occurs when the appropriate
co-enzyme is given, as for example Vitamin B_{12} in methylmalonic aciduria, thiamine in maple syrup urine disease, biotin in propionic acidaemia (for a full discussion see Scriver, 1973).

Relatively simple dietary adjustments have perhaps their best effects in phenyl-
ketonuria and galactosaemia, but these disorders, which were among the first of
the inherited metabolic disorders to be described and in which the response to
treatment led to such high hopes of dietary management of inherited disease,
are not common.

If an Infant Digests and Metabolises Adequate Nutrients and Still Fails to Thrive, What Then?

By the time the medical enquiry has reached this stage, serious disorders of the heart, lung, kidneys and brain, and intractable infections will have been excluded. There will still be some problem infants left in whom no cause is found (Table I). Half respond to care in hospital, suggesting some transient illness in the child or problem in the home. But some undersized infants do not thrive with the best of care. Initially, they may have been of low birth weight for gestational age, or they may have had an early disturbance in, or have a fundamental disorder of growth in their bones, muscle or adipose tissue. Many of these infants 'thrive' in infancy as much as they ever thrived subsequently. Medical enquiry does little to help, although it may allay parental or medical anxiety.

In summary, an infant who 'fails to thrive', or a parent who 'fails to rear' presents a fascinating challenge to the paediatrician. In some infants too much investigation may do more harm than good, whereas in others early recognition of an underlying defect may suggest simple dietary adjustments which lead to dramatic improvement. A careful enquiry about the child, his family and his home with the various alternatives in mind should avoid unnecessary investigations and lead to the early introduction of appropriate management.

References

Barbero, GJ and Shaheen, E (1967) *Journal of Paediatrics, 71,* 639
Bartrop, RW and Hull, D (1973) *Archives of Disease in Childhood, 48,* 963
Glaser, HH, Heagarty, MC, Bullard, DM and Pivchik, EC (1968) *Journal of Paediatrics, 73,* 690
Greene, HL, McCabe, DR and Merenstein, GB (1975) *Journal of Paediatrics, 87,* 695
Jischoff, J, Whitten, CF and Pettit, MG (1971) *Journal of Paediatrics, 79,* 209
Kuitunen, P, Visakorpi, JK, Savilahti, E and Pelkonen, P (1975) *Archives of Disease in Childhood, 50,* 34
Moynahan, EJ (1974) *Lancet, ii,* 399
Pollitt, E and Eichler, A (1976) *American Journal of Diseases of Childhood, 130,* 24
Rolles, CJ, Anderson, CM and McNeish, AS (1975) *Archives of Disease in Childhood, 50,* 259
Scriver, CR (1973) In *Treatment of Inborn Errors of Metabolism.* (Ed) JWT Seakins, RA Saunders and C Toothill. Churchill Livingstone, Edinburgh and London
Walker-Smith, J (1975) *Archives of Disease in Childhood, 50,* 347

Nutrition and Infection—the community implications

B A WHARTON
Queen Elizabeth Medical Centre, Birmingham, England

During childhood two great ages of man occur, the suckling and the weanling. During the first age the child has only one food and it is all liquid but with the arrival of the second, the progress to a mixed adult diet commences. This review considers the interplay of nutrition and infection on child health during these two ages of man.

THE SUCKLING

The major nutritional variation for the suckling is whether he or she is breast or bottle fed. Although there has been a recent renaissance of breast feeding, the majority of children in Britain and many other Western Countries are never breast fed, whereas in the developing world almost all children are, and the infective implications of these differing practices are important.

Mechanisms

Breast feeding as a method has certain anti-infective advantages. Only the mother will feed the child and this may reduce the amount of handling of the child by other people and so reduce the opportunity for cross infection. Apart from its emotional and logistic considerations this anti-infective view is a potent argument for keeping newborn babies by their mothers if they are in a maternity hospital. The clearest anti-infective advantage of this method is that the hygienic preparation of bottles, teats and infant feeding formulas is not necessary, nor is the associated expense. Generally, chemical methods of sterilisation (usually with hypochlorite solutions) have proved bacteriologically safer than boiling.

It is doubtful how effective such sterilisation processes can be in the average domestic conditions of the developing world. In these circumstances there is conflicting evidence on whether boiling is superior to chemical methods and whether, if the child cannot be breast fed a cup and spoon should be used rather than a bottle since they are easier to clean.

Breast milk itself has certain anti-infective properties. Breast milk contains more lactose than can be handled by the small intestine of most babies and hence some passes into the large bowel where lactic acid is formed by bacterial action. This is not well buffered and the acid environment together with the lactose favours the growth of the commensal anaerobes, lactobacilli. Cow's milk contains less lactose and so very little is available for lactic acid production and that which is, is rapidly buffered by the higher phosphate and to some extent by the higher casein content of cow's milk (Bullen & Willis, 1971). In these circumstances E coli thrives – an organism which may be pathogenic within the gut and is always so elsewhere in the body.

Apart from these chemical differences there are others in composition which have anti-infective implications. Human milk contains lactoferrin which binds the small amount of iron in breast milk so that it is unavailable for bacterial multiplication (Bullen et al, 1972). Human milk also contains maternal antibody in the secretory IgA form which is not digested and is still immunologically active even in the faeces. The child that is breast fed has not only received a transplacental immunological endowment (as IgG) from his mother in late pregnancy but continues to receive further immunological protection (as secretory IgA) post-natally (Kenny et al, 1967). These two substances, lactoferrin and secretory IgA, act synergistically against bacteria and probably play an important role in vivo. Other substances such as lysozyme and complement are present too, but their exact role within the gut is not completely certain. Nor is the role of the white cells present in breast milk understood. The macrophages and lymphocytes are living and may well have an anti-infective role within the intestine, but this has not been demonstrated. The anti-infective properties of breast milk have been reviewed by Hansen and Winberg (1972) and Goldman and Smith (1973).

Developing Countries

These differences in the anti-infective qualities of the two methods of feeding are reflected in the vital statistics of child health. The relevant vital statistics are the neonatal mortality rate (the number of deaths in the first 28 days of life per 1,000 live births), the post-neonatal mortality rate (the number of deaths between 28 days and the first birthday per 1,000 live births) and these two together make up the infant mortality rate. It is clear from Table II that in England and Wales, despite the low incidence of breast feeding death rates are much lower than in many countries where breast feeding is common during the first year of life and often longer. Similarly death rates from enteritis which breast feeding might particularly have prevented, were much higher in the developing countries. Since the environments are so different, apart from breast feeding, this inter-country comparison may be too crude to show the differences we are seeking. It is necessary to compare the effects of bottle and breast feeding within the same microbiological and socio-economic environment. There seems to be no doubt that within the average conditions of a developing country, bottle feeding is associated with a much higher mortality rate than is breast feeding. Crude comparisons must be looked at in detail, however, since the reason the child was bottle fed may indicate some other adverse factor in life expectancy, such as death or severe illness of the mother. With this in mind, however, there are many comparisons; in 7 Punjabi villages Gordon et al (1963) showed that of 20 bottle fed children only one was alive at one year (15 had died during the neonatal period) whereas of 739 breast-fed 650 survived infancy. Morley (1973) has summarised other similar evidence and the anti-infective advantages of breast feeding in developing countries is well proven. In Punjabi breast-fed children however the infant mortality rate was 120 per 1,000 (46 during the neonatal period) so that breast feeding is by no means a panacea for child health in the developing world.

The Western World

In Western European countries finer differences are expected. Table I summarises three investigations of the association between the method of feeding and

TABLE I. Breast Feeding and Infection in Western Countries

| Birmingham Children's Hospital[1] | Incidence of breast feeding (%) at ages in months | | | |
	1 – 4	5 – 8	9 – 12	13 – 14
Admission diagnosis:				
Diarrhoea and vomiting	11	0	0	4
Chest infection	36	17	10	8
Non-infective illness	46	12	6	8
Liverpool Infant Welfare Clinic[2]	Number of babies	Morbidity per 1000	Mortality per 1000	Case fatality
Breast fed > 6 months	971	219	8	4%
Breast fed < 1 month	854	570	53	9%
Norboten Community Study[3]	Length of breast feeding in weeks			
	< 3	3 – 10	11 – 26	> 26
Number of infective illnesses during infancy	2.4	2.1	2.4	2.05

1. Asher, 1952. 2. Robinson, 1951. 3. Mellander et al, 1959

142

infection. At the Birmingham Children's Hospital many fewer than expected of the children admitted with diarrhoea and vomiting (probably due to intestinal infection were breast fed. At a Liverpool Child Welfare Clinic in breast-fed babies the incidence of illness was half and the mortality one-sixth what it was in bottle-fed babies. Finally, the large Norboten study on a whole community showed that children breast fed for longer than six months had significantly fewer infections during infancy than those breast fed for less than three weeks. However, although the difference between 2.4 and 2.05 infections per year in the Norboten study may be statistically significant, such a small difference is of doubtful clinical significance. The Liverpool study in 1951 showed that such factors as social class did not account for the extremely low mortality of the breast-fed group.

While accepting these criticisms however, it may be that for this problem the study of a whole community may be less efficient than a study of selected groups. The Liverpool mortality statistics may be significant because this study had in effect excluded many early neonatal deaths which had nothing to do with feeding, e.g. congenital malformations, intrapartum asphyxia, etc. Similarly, the Birmingham study in effect selected socio-economic groups at special risk in that they needed admission to hospital for management of common infection.

On balance I feel the anti-infective properties of breast feeding in the Western world can be stated to the mother with some support, but the epidemiological background is by no means sufficiently strong to make this, by itself, an overriding factor in the decision she makes.

THE WEANLING

Breast feeding ceases at different times throughout the world. In Uganda conception of another child was the time to wean the previous one, usually around the age of one year. In Johannesburg weaning has become earlier and earlier as mothers want to go back to work (Wayburne, 1968) and the trend to earlier weaning has become a feature of urban society in the developing world (McLaren, 1966).

What are the death rates during this time of life and what contribution does the relationship between nutrition and infection make to them?

Post-neonatal and Toddler Mortality

Table II shows the number of deaths a cohort of children might experience during the first month of life, from then till their first birthday, and from their first to their fifth birthday. In England and Wales the total number of deaths becomes progressively smaller but in the developing countries the peak number of deaths occurs either in the post-neonatal period or in the toddler years. Probably many African countries have the Honduras pattern, for example Uganda and Malawi (Wharton, 1971, 1972) and many Middle Eastern countries have the Chilean one, but their statistics are not currently accepted for publication in the WHO Demo-

143

TABLE II. Mortality Rates Due to Malnutrition and Certain Infections

Causes of death	Mortality rates per 100,000		
	Neonatal (1)	Post-neonatal (2)	Toddler (3) (1-4 yr rate x 4)
England and Wales (1972)			
a) All causes	1154	568	299
b) Malnutrition (A65)	0.1	1	0.1
c) Diarrhoea (A5)	8	33	15
d) Measles (A25)	–	1	1.6
e) Tuberculosis (A6–10)[4]	–	–	0.4
Honduras (1971)			
a) All causes	959	2990	3324
b) Malnutrition	2	17	64
c) Diarrhoea	85	550	489
d) Measles	2	65	232
e) Tuberculosis	–	1	4
Trinidad and Tobago (1971)			
a) All causes	1615	1233	856
b) Malnutrition	7	95	60
c) Diarrhoea	150	550	184
d) Measles	–	–	–
e) Tuberculosis	–	4	2
Chile (1972)			
a) All causes	2901	4207	1024
b) Malnutrition	24	285	32
c) Diarrhoea	146	1030	108
d) Measles	8	88	80
e) Tuberculosis	–	9	6

1. Deaths below 28 days of life per 100,000 live births.
2. Deaths between 28 days and first birthday per 100,000 live births.
3. Deaths per year of 1–4 year olds per 100,000 in age group – rate multiplied by 4 to give additive figure throughout the toddler years.
4. Rates for neonatal and post-neonatal period are for all forms of tuberculosis (A6–10); for toddler years rate is mean of rates for respiratory (A6) and meningitic (A7) forms.

graphic Statistics Annual and, therefore, are not quoted in this exercise.

There is a considerable amount of epidemiological evidence to show that the high toddler mortality in developing countries reflects a high prevalence of malnutrition during these years (Behar et al, 1958; Wills & Waterlow, 1958) and this probably applies to some extent to the post-neonatal deaths too. The mortality rates due to malnutrition in each age group are generally highest at the same time as the overall death rate.

144

The differing ages for the peak mortality both overall and specifically for malnutrition probably reflect different times of weaning, although epidemiological evidence on the age of weaning in different countries is scanty. At weaning, which may often be traumatically sudden, the child if he receives maize may have great difficulty in eating sufficient to meet his energy requirements and if he receives plantain or cassava, even if he met his energy requirement, he would not meet his protein requirement. In addition, weaning imposes a much greater bacterial load with many effects on the jejunal mucosa and intraluminal digestion. These nutritional and microbiological stresses result in diarrhoea going on to malnutrition, and from this course of events Gordon et al (1963) developed the concept of 'weanling diarrhoea', "Transition to adult food is of minor importance in human populations with good nutrition and sound understanding of infant feeding". Indeed although there are worries in the Western world concerning weaning such as osmolar load, obesity, and early onset coeliac disease (DHSS, 1974) infection is not one of them.

Apart from diarrhoea another infective disease which interacts substantially with malnutrition is measles. Case fatality rates may be as high as 5% in malnourished communities and the prolonged anorexia which ensues from severe measles may precipitate an overt episode of kwashiorkor in some children who were previously growing reasonably (Morley, 1973). This severe or 'black' measles was well known in Europe of the nineteenth century and was described in Dudley as follows:

> "The measles have a dark coloured eruption in the bad
> localities I have named, instead of the usual red and more
> healthy colour; in such places measles are frequently fatal"
> Johnson (1852)

Diarrhoea, Measles and Malnutrition

If the interrelationships of diarrhoea and measles with malnutrition are strong then they may be reflected in the vital statistics of the countries concerned. Figure 1 shows the ratio of the infant mortality rate: the 1–4 year old (toddler) mortality rate for malnutrition, diarrhoea, and measles for all countries in the WHO Statistics Annual where the death rate due to malnutrition was greater than 10 per 100,000 during both infancy and the toddler years. Generally it seems there is a relationship between the age at which malnutrition strikes and the age at which deaths from diarrhoea and measles are most common. Countries with high infant:toddler ratios for malnutrition generally had higher infant:toddler ratios for diarrhoea and malnutrition too.

The infant mortality rate is expressed per year and covers one year of life, whereas the 1–4 year old mortality rate is expressed per year and covers 4 years of life. Therefore, where the ratio is less than 4 then the total number of deaths during the 4 toddler years exceeds the number of deaths during infancy. There-

145

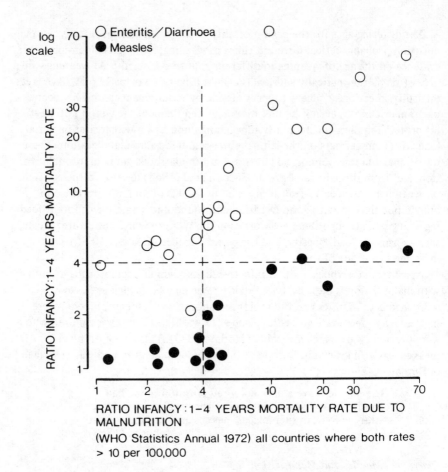

Figure 1. Ratio of mortality rates :: infancy : 1–4 year olds for malnutrition, diarrhoea and
measles in countries where malnutrition rate exceeded 10 per 100,000 at both ages.
Where the ratio exceeds 4, the total number of deaths during the toddler years exceeded
the total in infancy. Source: WHO Demographic Statistics Annual 1972

fore, although the timing of both diarrhoeal and measles deaths are related to the
timing of malnutrition, nevertheless, diarrhoeal deaths in most countries occurred
predominantly in infancy (i.e. the ratio is usually above 4) while measles deaths
occurred predominantly in the toddler years (i.e. the ratio is usually below 4). It
seems that diarrhoeal and measles deaths have their own age specificity which is
partly modified by the age of malnutrition.

This conclusion may be applied to the data in Table II. Line (c) for each
country shows the number of deaths due to diarrhoea. Generally the post-neonatal
period is the predominant time for diarrhoeal deaths, but in Honduras, where the
majority of malnutrition deaths were in the toddler years, there was also a sub-

stantial number of diarrhoeal deaths (nearly half of the total) in the toddler years as well. In contrast line (d) for each country shows the number of deaths due to measles. The predominant time for measles deaths was the toddler years but in Chile where the majority of malnutrition deaths were in the post-neonatal period there was also a substantial number of measles deaths (about a half of the total) at that time. Trinidad and Tobago recorded an insignificant number of deaths due to measles.

The relationship between malnutrition and diarrhoea and measles is, therefore, sufficiently strong to affect the pattern of childhood mortality in these countries, but the association with malnutrition does not completely obliterate the age specificity of the two infections.

Tuberculosis

It is difficult to use a country's vital statistics to examine the relationship between malnutrition and tuberculosis since recorded death rates from tuberculosis during childhood are very low (see Table II) although generally death rates from tuberculosis are higher at the age when death rates from malnutrition are also high. Hospital series, however, show a strong association between the two. In Uganda for example, of 401 children admitted to hospital for treatment of kwashiorkor or marasmus 13% had tuberculosis. This had been unsuspected at the time of admission and was often difficult to diagnose because of the anergic state induced by the malnutrition (Lloyd, 1968). In the same series a third of all children treated in hospital for tuberculosis had been admitted primarily for treatment of their malnutrition.

The decline in deaths due to tuberculosis in Britain occurred well before specific prevention (BCG) or chemotherapy was available and was also apparent well before the sanitary revolution of the nineteenth century. Demographic historians have ascribed this fall and that for many other diseases to an improvement in nutrition (McKeown, 1965), but this conclusion has been reached largely by a process of exclusion rather than by positive evidence. Certainly in some communities during the 19th Century a divergence in death rates due to measles and to tuberculosis can be shown which is difficult to explain if both were nutritionally conditioned (Wharton, 1975).

Clinically we have little doubt about the relationship of malnutrition and tuberculosis but it is difficult to detect any reflection of this in the vital statistics of a community.

TRIBULATION, FAMINE, AND PESTILENCE

Hesiod (c700BC) knew of the association between malnutrition and infection many years ago. He described it

"God cast down on them great tribulation, famine, and
pestilence; the people perished"

The association applies not only at times of famine but is also a feature of the
endemic malnutrition still found throughout the world. There is no doubt, however, that when *famine* and *pestilence* do occur together there is indeed *tribulation* and this is reflected in the vital statistics of the countries concerned.

Acknowledgments

I am grateful to the Medical Illustration Department, Birmingham Children's
Hospital, Senor T Barktziris and to Mrs Peggy Cox for their help in preparing
this chapter.

References

Asher, P (1952) *Archives of Disease in Childhood, 27,* 270
Behar, M, Ascoli, W and Scrimshaw, NS (1958) *Bulletin World Health
  Organisation, 19,* 1093
Bullen, CL and Willis, AT (1971) *British Medical Journal, 3,* 338
Bullen, JJ, Rogers, HJ and Leigh, L (1972) *British Medical Journal, 3,* 69
DHSS (1974) *Present Day Practice in Infant Feeding. Report on Health and
  Social Subjects No.9.* HMSO, London. Page 7
Goldman, AS and Smith, CW (1973) *Journal of Pediatrics, 86,* 1082
Gordon, JE, Chitkara, LD and Wyon, TD (1963) *American Journal of Medical
  Science, 245,* 345
Hanson, LA and Winberg, J (1972) *Archives of Disease in Childhood, 47,* 845
Johnson, WE (1852) In *Report to the General Board of Health on a preliminary
  enquiry into the sewerage, drainage and supply of water, and the sanitary
  condition of the inhabitants of Dudley in the County of Worcester.*
  W Lee, London. Page 18
Kenny, JF, Boesman, MI and Michaels, RH (1967) *Pediatrics, 39,* 202
Lloyd, AV (1968) *British Medical Journal, 3,* 529
McKeown, T (1965) *Medicine in Modern Society.* George Allen and Unwin,
  London. Page 48
McLaren, DS (1966) *Lancet, ii,* 485
Mellander, D, Vahlquist, B and Melbin, T (1959) *Acta Paediatrica (Suppl.116),
  48,* 1
Morley, DC (1973) *Paediatric Priorities in the Developing World.* Butterworth,
  London. Pages 100, 207, 213, 217
Robinson, M (1951) *Lancet, i,* 788
Wayburne, S (1968) In *Calorie Deficiencies and Protein Deficiencies.*
  (Ed) RA McCance and EM Widdowson. Churchill, London. Page 7
Wharton, BA (1971) *Journal of Tropical Paediatrics, 17,* (Monograph 13), 17
Wharton, BA (1972) In *Report to Freedom from Hunger Campaign on Child
  Health and Malnutrition in Malawi* – unpublished
Wharton, BA (1975) *Diploma in History thesis.* University of London. Page 53
WHO (1975) *World Health Statistics Annual 1972, passim.* WHO, Geneva
Wills, VG and Waterlow, JC (1958) *Journal of Tropical Paediatrics, 3,* 167

Critical Periods of Growth Early in Life. Later in Life

R A McCANCE
Sidney Sussex College, University of Cambridge, England

EARLY IN LIFE

You must all be familiar with the percentile lines of human growth. These lines have now been extended backward into fetal growth by weighing material obtained from well dated abortions and in living fetuses by ultra sound techniques. These lines are really nothing more than cross sectional growth curves and there are several reasons why any single child should not grow smoothly along the line on which he can be placed when first seen.

One is genetics. The size and stature of a mother is an important element in fixing the weight and size of her child but for the most remarkable demonstration of this one should turn to the work of Walton and Hammond (1938). These authors crossed large Shire stallions with tiny Shetland pony mares, and Shetland stallions with Shire horse dams. The size of the foals at birth were appropriate for the size of their dams, but, on rearing the foals, the influence of the sire made itself felt and the crosses grew into horses not very different in size. Similar effects have been described in cattle and one can expect them also if a tall and heavy man marries a tiny woman and vice versa.

The second is nutrition, and this is the one that will concern us most, but we must have a short digression first about illness. Each of the percentile lines should be taken to represent the growth of a healthy child. If the child falls ill it will for a time not be able to maintain its weight on the growth curve it has been following and will fall to a lower one. The same thing happens if a child does not get enough food to grow at the rate conferred upon it genetically. If now the child recovers from its illness it will begin to eat roughly what one would expect for its size (not its age), gain weight faster than its fellows of that age and rejoin its

149

original line of growth. It will not go above it as a rule unless it has already been doing so for genetic reasons. If faulty nutrition has been the cause of the trouble the child will eat to capacity as soon as the fault has been corrected and show what has been termed 'catch up' growth. If the child's desire to eat does not fall off after it has rejoined its original weight curve it may go above it, at least for a time, but overeating is most unlikely to make it exceed its height curve.

Catch up growth, or compensatory growth, is a common enough event of animal husbandry, for food supplies tend to vary from one time of year to another. The husband man is always torn between the dictates of physiology and of economics, and the gains in weight of growing animals are often much less in seasons of hunger than in those of plenty which is when the animals are likely to show their compensatory growth.

If rats are undernourished after weaning they invariably show 'catch up' growth if they are fed to capacity afterwards, but whether it is complete or not depends upon its timing and duration. Pigs and guinea pigs behave similarly if experiments of the same nature are made upon them and the phenomenon of 'catch up' growth is so familiar to everyone interested in nutrition or growth that it requires no further discussion at the moment.

If, however, two litters of rats born on the same day are mixed up together and suckled by one of the dams in a small group of three, and in a large group of 18 or so by the other one, the ratlets suckled in the small group will be two to three times the size of the others at weaning. If now all the rats are offered an unlimited and fully satisfactory diet, the small ones do not catch up or show any signs of doing so. Before explaining this a short digression must be made into developmental timing. There are certain milestones of development that are well known, events which are quite strictly clocked from the date of conception, and can be used to indicate the stage of development an animal has reached. Not so the date of birth, which, though equally well 'clocked', bears little or no relationship to the stage of anatomical and physiological development the young have reached when birth takes place. Compare for example the development at birth, already reached by the relatively mature foal, with that of the highly immature rat, kitten or kangaroo.

So far as the development of the nervous system is concerned, birth may be regarded almost as an incident, and Flexner (1955) writing about the critical time for the initiation of cortical function in mammals, calculated that stages of development that took place in the pig and guinea pig at about the beginning of the last trimester of gestation only took place at about 10 days after birth in the rat. The integration and commencement of hypothalamic function would be expected to precede these times, and experiments on rats indicate that this is so. Harris and Levine (1962) found that very small doses of testosterone given to a female rat on the 5th day after birth altered the animal's sexual behaviour for the rest of its life (Barraclough, 1961), but not the development of the genital tract, which had already been induced by the hormones proper to the animal's genetic sex (see also Harris, 1964). We know that these hormones operate through the hypothalamus, posterior pituitary and the adrenals, and the hypothalamus must therefore be functional at that time. We know also that there are neuronal 'centres' in the hypothalamus which co-ordinate many other aspects of behaviour – the drive to eat and drink for example and the control of respiration. The latter must be functionally complete at the time of birth in all mammals. The hypothalamus, however, is also concerned with the control of body temperature. One would expect all the hypothalamic functions of mammals to become functional in the same order, and, interestingly enough in the rat the regulation of body temperature is by no means complete at birth, though it is in the foal. In this species the function must lie dormant till birth. Alternatively, some of the incompleteness in the rat may be due to peripheral rather than central causes but we know nothing of this.

One would expect from the above that alterations in behaviour brought about by the way rats are treated after birth would only be brought about in pigs and guinea pigs by the appropriate treatment before birth, and this has now been shown to be the case.

The rate of growth of the fetus depends upon its genetic endowment and its supply of nutrients. These can only reach it through its blood supply. In some species, of which the guinea pig is one, the supply depends upon the nutrition of the mother, and large or small offspring can be produced by varying the amount of food provided for the pregnant dams. In other species nature sometimes makes a similar experiment for us for, if the blastocyst, derived from one of a large number of the ova discharged, imbeds in a part of the uterus where the supply of blood is poor, the fetus will get fewer nutrients through the placenta, and not grow so fast as one whose blastocyst has imbedded in a more favourable position. This happens sometimes in mice (McLaren & Michie, 1960) and is a well known phenomenon in pigs. We have used guinea pigs and pigs for our experiments and in both species we have obtained the expected results; i.e. no catch up growth if one of the newborn in a litter is very much smaller than the others (Widdowson, 1971; McCance & Widdowson, 1974). We are forced to conclude that there is a critical period of growth in all animals when the centres in the hypothalamus that control the drive to eat are being organised neuronically to conform with the size (or perhaps the surface area) of the growing organism at that time. Thereafter, the responsibility of appetite, whether conscious or unconscious, is to ensure that the intake of nutrients is sufficient for the animals' size, growth rate and activity. At what time before birth appetite could begin to function in pigs, guinea pigs or man we do not know, but it is certainly ready to come into action immediately after birth in all of them. We know too that it is not functional at the time of birth in rats but becomes so before weaning and we suggest that it is likely to do so about the fifth day after birth. Pigs and guinea pigs, therefore, born smaller than their littermates, and rats, made small by limiting their intake of nutrients during suckling, eat according to their size and activity and have no abnormal feelings of hunger. The small ones therefore, grow up, but they do not catch up (Widdowson & McCance, 1975).

One interesting point remains. Were these small rats, pigs and guinea pigs undernourished? They may have been but they showed none of the physiological criteria of it. They were not over-hungry; they showed no sign of catch up growth; they behaved as though they were genetically small, slow growing, but perfectly proportioned animals (McCance, 1975). The matter requires thought, but I suggest to you that we have brought to light something quite new to physiology.

LATER IN LIFE

It is well known that over the last 100 years the heights and weights of school children in Europe and North America have been increasing at each year of the school age. It has been demonstrated in London, Hamburg, Holland, Sweden, Australia and other places (Lenz, 1957a,b; Boyne & Clark, 1959; Sinclair, 1969). A similar increase has also been shown to have taken place in the growth of much younger children. Adults in these countries are also known to be taller than they used to be and to reach their mature height and weight at a younger age. An excellent description of the effects of this was given by Oppers (1963) for young Dutchmen who since the beginning of the last century have been called up for military service at the age of 18 and again for Home Guard duties when they were 25. Ziegler (1966) and Lenz (1959) have discussed the reasons and the last paper is a particularly valuable one, describing changes over the years long ago that have been documented only by archeological evidence (see also Coon, 1939).

Another change that has been taking place over the last 100 years is a fall in the age at which boys and girls attain sexual maturity. The aspect of this which is most easily dated is the age of menarche in girls, although it is not always so easy to get the desired information as it is to observe the burst of growth which is obvious at this time to the naked eye (Sinclair, 1969; Tanner, 1962). The age of menarche was about 17 a hundred years ago. The average is now below thirteen.

It is natural for those interested in nutrition to feel that these changes over the years in stature and rate of growth have been due to improvements in the food children have had to eat. This must certainly be taken into account, but since the opening of the present century there have been great advances in public health in all the western communities. Diphtheria and its complications and chronic tuberculosis are no longer with us, the intestinal infections that used to carry off more than half the children in the first five years of their lives have gone as well. Worms are no longer the scourge they were, and marasmus has been described in an extreme form in a child suffering only from scabies, and such infestations were the rule in children long after the first war. Till well on in the present century moreover few houses or schools were adequately warmed. On marginal intakes of food this must have called for the expenditure of much of a child's intake of energy and protein on keeping warm, and, on intakes of food that would have been insufficient even at the best of times the child's capacity for growth would certainly have been limited.

It was shown some time ago (Widdowson & McCance, 1960) that in rats some of the signs of development depend upon chronological age. The appearance of the teeth and the opening of the eyes are good examples. Others depend upon size rather than age, and into this category comes sexual maturation. The chemical development of the skeleton and muscles depend upon both size and chronological age and fall into an intermediate group. It was also discovered by these authors that after pigs had been severely undernourished from about 10 days after birth till they were a year old, and then rehabilitated, the animals became sexually mature when they were smaller, but nearly a year older than their normal littermates. Hence the generalisation made above about size and sexual maturity is subject to some experimental manipulation.

Girls begin to menstruate at the average weight of 47.8 kg and at 158.5 cm in height (Frisch & Revelle, 1971a,b). If, therefore, they have been growing more rapidly in weight over the years, as the secular trends show, this explains the earlier and earlier age of menarche. Further analysis has shown that weight is actually not the critical thing that determines the onset of menstruation, but the percentage of fat in the body. The composition of the body changes during the puberty growth spurt in a characteristic way, and from the time it starts, which is about a year before menstruation begins, the body weight and the lean body mass of both early and late maturers increases by about 42%, but their fat increases by 125% (Frisch, 1973; Frisch et al, 1973). Anorexia nervosa in adolescent girls is usually associated with amenorrhoea, and menstruation does not begin again till the weight of the patient has risen to about the mean weight of a healthy but otherwise matched group of the population (Crisp & Stonehill, 1971). This suggests that the composition of the patient's body and the percentage of fat in it will by then be roughly back to normal.

Malcolm (1970a,b) has published a very instructive study of an upland tribe in New Guinea, and compared their mean growth curves with those of British children. Bundi infants are breast fed for some years and then weaned onto a poor diet consisting largely of sweet potatoes. The children probably tend to be small at birth since their mothers are small. Nutritionally, socially and economically they are handicapped compared with British children, and one would expect to find that all the milestones of development were passed at a later age (Carfagna et al, 1972). The curves show that the British boys and girls grew much faster than the Bundi children and that they reached sexual maturity some years earlier; the Bundi girls in fact did not begin to menstruate till their mean age was between 18 and 19 years. The British children reached their maximum height and weight some time before the Bundi children and at that time the mean heights and weights of the Bundi were considerably below those of the British, but the Bundi went on growing for some years, the men till they were about 24, but both sexes were still below the British when growth ceased. The British reached sexual maturity about five years before the Bundi, but the Bundi females fared relatively better than the males. This is the usual result in undernourished animals, and rehabilitation does not equalise matters.

I have already mentioned the effects of undernutrition before and after the critical period of growth in early life, when the hypothalamus was being organised and co-ordinated with the size of the body at that time and that undernutrition after the critical period was always followed by 'catch up' growth, but that whether it was complete or not depended upon its timing and duration. The longer the animals are undernourished the less complete the 'catch up' becomes, in spite of an invariable vigorous start. The Bundi children were never well enough nourished to show any sign of catching up the British children before the latter were 18, but why did they go on growing after the British children had stopped and ultimately attain the same height and weight? Some of you may reply by suggesting that the Bundi may have been genetically smaller or, that, maybe they could not go on growing after their epiphyses had fused. There is much more in it than that.

Ross (1959, 1961) made some experiments with rats which may give us the answer. He worked with a highly inbred colony of pathogen free rats. One group he kept on the control diet from weaning, which had been designed to give the fastest growth attainable. At the same time another group was given a diet which was poorer in protein and calories, but was otherwise as completely satisfactory. On this diet the rats grew more slowly. They went on growing, however, after the others had stopped, but they never attained the same size although their average life span was prolonged. The controls died earlier, and it was probably because the diet that gave the fastest growth was not the right diet after maturity (Miller & Payne, 1968). The failure of the other group to attain their full genetic stature was unlikely to be due to the epiphyses undergoing fusion, for the epiphyses in rats never really fuse. All the rats, however, were very old animals when they stopped growing, and we suggest that the cessation of growth was but one of the aspects of age. There must come a time in the life of every warm blooded mammal when it can grow no more, and one must always remember two things about growth. Firstly, the rate of cell division falls off steadily from conception and ceases at a certain chronological age which is peculiar to each species, and perhaps each organ. The S shape of a growth curve itself demonstrates this and it is always the later stages of growth which fail first. One can delay the age of maturity by undernutrition but once one has allowed the animal to become mature one has set a limit to its span of life.

References

Barraclough, CA (1961) *Endocrinology, 68,* 62
Boyne, AW and Clark, JR (1959) *Human Biology, 31,* 325
Carfagna, M, Figurelli, E, Matarese, G and Matarese, S (1972) *Human Biology, 44,* 117

Coon, CS (1939) *The Races of Europe.* MacMillan, New York. Pages 10 and 233

Crisp, AH and Stonehill, E (1971) *British Medical Journal, 3,* 149

Flexner, LB (1955) In *Biochemistry of the Developing Nervous System.* (Ed) H Waelsch. Page 281

Frisch, RE (1973) *The Control of the Onset of Puberty.* (Ed) M Grumbach, G Grave and F Mayer. Wiley-Interscience Inc., New York

Frisch, RE and Revelle, R (1971a) *Human Biology, 43,* 140

Frisch, RE and Revelle, R (1971b) *Archives of Disease in Childhood, 46,* 695

Frisch, RE, Revelle, R and Cook, S (1973) *Human Biology, 45,* 469

Harris, GW (1964) *Endocrinology, 75,* 627

Harris, GW and Levine, S (1962) *Journal of Physiology, 163,* 42P

Lenz, W (1957a) *Homo, 8,* 65

Lenz, W (1957b) *Homo, 8,* 207

Lenz, W (1959) In *Akzeleration und Ernährung ettlossliche Wirkstoffe. Wissenschaftleche Veroffentlichungen der deutschen Gesellschaft fur Ernahrung 4.* Dietrich Steinkopff, Darmstadt

McCance, RA (1975) *Journal of Physiology* (In press)

McCance, RA and Widdowson, EM (1974) *Proceedings of the Royal Society B, 185,* 1

McLaren, A and Michie, D (1960) *Nature, London, 187,* 363

Malcolm, LA (1970a) *Human Biology, 42,* 293

Malcolm, LA (1970b) *Growth and Development in New Guinea – a study of the Bundi people of the Madang district. Monograph Series 1. Institute of Human Biology.* Papua, New Guinea

Miller, DS and Payne, PR (1968) *Experimental Gerontology, 3,* 231

Oppers, VM. *Analyse van de acceleratie van de menselijke lengtegroei door bepaling van het kjdstip van de groeifasen.* Thesis for the degree of Doctor of Medicine, Amsterdam

Ross, MH (1959) *Federation Proceedings, 18,* 1190

Ross, MH (1961) *Journal of Nutrition, 75,* 197

Sinclair, D (1969) *Human Growth After Birth.* Oxford University Press, London

Tanner, JM (1962) *Growth at Adolescence. 2nd Edition.* Blackwell Scientific Publications, Oxford

Walton, A and Hammond, J (1938) *Proceedings of the Royal Society B, 125,* 311

Widdowson, EM (1971) *Proceedings of the Nutrition Society, 30,* 127

Widdowson, EM and McCance, RA (1960) *Proceedings of the Royal Society B, 152,* 188

Widdowson, EM and McCance, RA (1975) *Pediatric Research, 9,* 154

Ziegler, E (1966) *Zeitschrift fur kinderheilk, 99,* 146

Energy Expenditure During the Growing Period

L E MOUNT
Institute of Animal Physiology, Agricultural Research Council, Cambridge
England

Summary

Relative to body size, heat production in the mammal is high in the period following birth, and declines progressively as the animal grows and thermal insulation increases. The cold-susceptibility of the newborn gives way to the relative heat-susceptibility of the mature animal. This trend is associated with the thermoneutral zone moving down the environmental temperature scale, an effect that is much more marked in animals that develop thick coats or layers of subcutaneous fat than it is in man. Intake of food above that required for the maintenance of energy balance leads to increased heat production and the formation of body protein and body fat in proportions depending on the animal's stage of development.

Introduction

The demands for energy expenditure by the growing homeothermic animal take several forms. The maintenance of a relatively stable deep body temperature requires the production of metabolic heat at rates that depend on the environmental temperature, body size, thermal insulation and behaviour. High food intakes are associated with increased growth rates and fat deposition and increased heat production. In addition, the characteristically high levels of muscular activity that accompany play and exploration in children and young animals lead to intermittently high metabolic rates.

In the growing animal, factors that operate to increase energy expenditure include the relatively small size and the incomplete development of thermal insulation. The young animal is susceptible to cold; this susceptibility diminishes as the animal grows, and in many species gives way to a tolerance to cold and a susceptibility to heat, although unclothed man remains cold-susceptible throughout his life. Man overcomes his susceptibility to cold through behaviour and environmental engineering, including clothes and shelter. Some animals do the same: mice can raise their young very successfuly at −3°C through the combination of building nests and making use of ample food supplies (Barnett & Mount, 1967). Energy expenditure is determined both by the nature of the animal and by its interactions with other animals and with the environment. Behavioural experiments (Baldwin, 1974) have helped in elucidating the nature of these interactions.

The interrelations between the animal's heat production and its thermal insulation, plane of nutrition and the environmental temperature, are shown in Figure 1. An important point in the relation is the critical temperature, denoted by

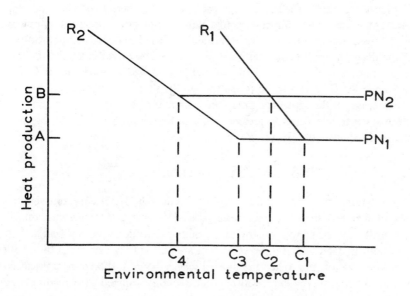

Figure 1. Generalised diagram of heat production against environmental temperature for a homeothermic animal of low (R_1) or high (R_2) thermal insulation, on a low (PN_1) or high (PN_2) plane of nutrition. C_1, C_2, C_3 and C_4 are the corresponding critical temperatures

C_1, C_2, C_3 and C_4. The critical temperature is the environmental temperature at the lower end of the zone of thermal neutrality; in this zone, heat production is constant and at a minimum. At temperatures below the critical, the animal must increase its rate of heat production if it is to maintain a constant deep body temperature. For a poorly insulated animal with thermal insulation R_1, the critical temperature is C_1 on plane of nutrition PN_1. When PN_1 is increased to PN_2, the critical temperature falls to C_2. When the animal's insulation increases from R_1 to R_2, and the animal is fed at PN_1, the critical temperature falls from C_1 to C_3. When PN_1 is increased to PN_2, the critical temperature falls still further to C_4.

The particular combination of plane of nutrition and thermal insulation thus determines the temperature at which the resting animal begins to be affected by cold. Raising the food intake from PN_1 to PN_2 gives an increment of heat production equal to AB which substitutes for what would otherwise be necessary thermoregulatory heat production if the food intake remained at PN_1 and the environmental temperature were lowered from C_1 to C_2. Similarly, heat produced by exercise substitutes for thermoregulatory heat in the cold, although exercise decreases thermal insulation through movement and consequently affects the slope R. The converse is that in a warm environment these increments in heat production must be dissipated as extra heat loss if hyperthermia is not to ensue (Ingram & Mount, 1975).

Figure 1 is a simplified and generalised diagram, where environmental temperature refers to the temperature of a standardised environment. Its implications are discussed more fully elsewhere (Mount, 1974). The actual temperature scale of the diagram varies widely with species and body size; for example, the critical temperature is about $34°C$ for the normally nourished newborn pig, $0°C$ for the calf, and $-40°C$ for the arctic fox, although the shape of the diagram is similar in each case. In the growing animal, the critical temperature and the zone of thermal neutrality move progressively down the temperature scale as body size and thermal insulation increase.

THE NEWBORN

Figure 1 refers to an animal that regulates its deep body, or core, temperature when the environmental temperature varies. However, in the newborn animal the small body size and, in many cases, lack of thermal insulation lead also to variations in deep body temperature that are particularly evident in the smallest newborn, the rodents. When the mother leaves the nest, the young animals cool and in so doing energy expenditure is considerably reduced with accompanying economy of food utilisation. The newborn cannot rewarm through their own efforts except in response to a very small drop in temperature, but on the mother's return rewarming is rapid. One of the characteristics of the newborn animal is its tolerance of deviations in body temperature from which recovery in the mature animal would be questionable; the apparent weakness of hypothermia in the newborn may be a strength when seen as an adaptation for survival (McCance & Widdowson, 1957).

Human infant Hey (1974) remarks that heat production in adult man can increase nearly three-fold in response to severe acute cold stress, and in the newborn baby the increase can be 150%. The newborn pig has a marked metabolic response to cold, and heat production in the newborn lamb increases fourfold in response to cold stress (Mount, 1968; Alexander, 1974). The newborn baby shows increased physical activity when subjected to thermal stress. In cold surroundings the increase is associated with a marked rise in heat production, but the increased movements results in a heat-dissipating rise in convective heat loss. The restlessness that occurs in a warm environment once body temperature starts to rise is also associated with an increase in heat production that adds to thermal stress.

Increased heat production in a cold environment and increased evaporative water loss in a warm environment maintain homeothermy. Increased heat production in brown adipose tissue is an extremely effective method of combating cold stress (Hull, 1966; Alexander, 1975); heat production due to muscular shivering is equally effective, but the accompanying body movement inevitably causes some increased convective heat loss. Newborn babies sweat in a warm environment when deep body temperature has risen by $0.5°C$, although babies born more than three weeks pre-term have little ability to sweat (Hey, 1974).

The provision of clothes and bedding both widens the tolerable temperature range and lowers it. The critical temperature for a naked baby in a standardised environment (that is draught-free, and with air temperature equal to mean radiant temperature) is $32.5°C$, but it is $25°C$ when the baby is well wrapped in a cot (Hey, 1975). Correspondingly, the metabolic rate is doubled in the naked baby when the temperature falls to about $27°C$, but not in the wrapped baby until the temperature falls to about $12°C$. This accords with the expected changes in heat production for a given temperature variation when thermal insulation increases from R_1 to R_2 in Figure 1.

Newborn pig This animal weighs rather more than 1 kg, and is close enough in size to the 3 kg human infant for useful comparisons to be made. In both species, the thermal insulation of an effective coat is lacking, a weakness in the face of cold which is offset by the pig huddling with its litter-mates, while the baby is clothed, and otherwise shielded. The newborn pig, with its capacity for movement over the ground from birth, is capable of greater variation of response to environment than is possible for the immobile baby. The rates of growth are quite different: whereas the piglet doubles its birth weight in one week, the baby takes six months to achieve the same relative increase. To reach mature size, however, the pig has farther to go, since at birth it is only about 1% of the mature adult size, whereas the human infant is about 5% of adult size at birth. The two factors, relative growth rate and eventual mature size, mean that the more rapid actual growth rate in the pig allows estimates to be made of the energy costs of growth in the animal, whereas in the baby this is difficult.

At birth both the pig and the baby show a fall in body temperature from which recovery takes place more rapidly in the pig. The rectal temperature in the mature pig is in the vicinity of 39°C, whereas in man it is 37°C. This complicates direct comparisons of metabolic rate in the two species, and another difficulty in the comparison arises from the different body weights: these produce different metabolic body sizes. However, expressing rates of heat production per unit of metabolic body size (see below) largely removes the effects of differing body size and using an environmental temperature scale relative to rectal temperature overcomes the complication of the different rectal temperatures. The similarity between the two species then becomes apparent (Mount, 1968).

Newborn lamb At 4 kg body weight, this animal is larger than the human infant and much larger than the newborn pig. Metabolic rate rises soon after birth, associated with the intake of milk. The type of coat influences the lamb's thermal insulation, which is in any case considerably higher than that of the pig (Alexander, 1974). The overall insulation at −10°C ambient temperature is 0.34°C.m^2.W^{-1} for lambs with fine coats, and 0.46 for lambs with hairy coats; these values may be compared with 0.23 for the newborn pig at 5°C ambient temperature, and 0.17 for the 3 kg baby at 31°C. Another way in which the lamb differs from the pig is in the lamb's higher peak metabolism, which is about 290 Wm^{-2} compared with a mean maximum in the pig of 160 Wm^{-2}. The combination of a higher metabolic capability and a higher thermal insulation confers a greater degree of cold-resistance on the lamb than on the pig, because it is the product of these two quantities that determines the core-environment temperature difference that can be maintained.

The rise in metabolic rate from the level found in the period following birth appears to be a general phenomenon (Taylor, 1960). The development of heat conservation mechanisms lags behind the increase in metabolic rate in some species, such as the dog and the pig. Although the pig shows peripheral vasoconstriction in the cold from birth, it is only after some days that its subcutaneous fat is sufficient to allow the insulative value of vasoconstriction to become effective. In this connection, Brück (1961) was the first to show that the baby has control over vasomotor tone even on the first day after birth. The calf and the lamb have by virtue of their coats an insulative advantage in the development of homeothermy over the less well insulated newborn of some other species.

METABOLIC RATE, BODY SIZE AND ENVIRONMENT

As the animal increases in size, so its heat production at thermal neutrality expressed per unit of body weight falls. This is true for all mammals once they have reached the mature level of heat production.

This relation can be typified in the pig; when comparisons are made on a weight basis (Table I), the bacon pig's rate is only about one-third that of the newborn pig. As the pig grows in size, therefore, the total metabolism increases at a slower rate than the body mass, so that metabolism is most commonly proportional to

TABLE I. Resting Rates of Oxygen Consumption (ml/kg/min) for normally fed pigs from birth to 100kg body weight, at thermal neutrality. Values of column A from Brody (1945), B from Thorbek (1967), and C from Mount (1968) [modified from Mount, 1968]

Body weight kg	Oxygen consumption ml/kg.min		
	A	B	C
1.2			15.0
5	11.1		11.3
10	10.1		
15	9.5		
20	9.4		8.7
25	9.1		
35		10.7	
50	8.5	9.2	
60			6.1
75	5.7	7.7	
100	5.1		

body weight raised to a power less than unity. In the special case of proportionality to surface area, the power is 0.67, and it is found that, on a surface area basis, levels of minimal metabolism are similar in the young and the 90 kg animal. Expressing heat production per unit of surface area rather than per unit of weight thus produces a more uniform expression of metabolism for different body sizes. This is an example of the application of the so-called 'surface law', which holds that an animal's metabolic rate is proportional to its surface area and not to its weight. This is not true for all conditions, but it tends to hold for mature animals and it provides a useful basis for comparing animals of different sizes.

From continuous 24-hour measurements of heat loss from groups of growing pigs living in a calorimeter designed as a pig pen, Holmes and Mount (1967) found that the power to which body weight must be raised to give proportionality of heat loss to body weight ranged from 0.4 to 1.0. 0.4 applies to 60 kg pigs on a constant restricted food intake, while the exponent 1.0 applies to younger 20 kg pigs receiving a food intake that rises in direct proportion to body weight. It is quite clear that no single value of the exponent can be applied over this range of conditions, and it is often most useful to calculate a specific within-experiment exponent. The resulting metabolic body size offers more versatility as a reference base than surface area.

The relation between basal metabolic rate and body weight in the human infant (Hill & Rahimtulla, 1965) shows that the rate per kg remains almost constant during the first year after birth, indicating an exponent of body weight of about unity. Later in life the exponent decreases to 0.6. Kleiber (1961) advocates the use of $W^{0.75}$ as the metabolic body size; for the inter-species comparisons of mature animals in particular this is useful, but there are many intra-species deviations, as in man.

161

GROWTH RATE AND ENERGY EXPENDITURE

An animal's intake of metabolisable energy from food is either lost as heat or retained in tissue as protein or fat:

$ME = H + ER$

where ME = metabolisable energy intake,

H = heat loss,

ER = energy retention.

At thermal neutrality

$H = H_m + H_p$

where H_m = heat production at maintenance ME intake (ME_m)

when $H_m = ME_m$, since $ER = 0$,

and H_p = additional heat production associated with food intakes above ME_m.

Below thermal neutrality, extra thermoregulatory heat is also produced.

From calorimetric experiments on pigs, these various quantities have been determined and the energy costs of deposition of protein and fat inclusive of their energy values calculated as 38.1 kJ/g for protein and 46.7 kJ/g for fat (Close et al, 1973). The measurements also allowed calculation of the partial efficiency of energy retention, as $(ER \times 100)/(ME - ME_m)$. At thermal neutrality, the partial efficiency is close to 0.7; in the cold, it approaches unity, which is to be expected as the level of heat production then tends to be independent of the plane of nutrition (Verstegen et al, 1973). Under cold conditions, the heat increment of feeding is substituted for thermoregulatory heat.

In young animals, the energy retention of protein exceeds that of fat, but in pigs above about 40 kg body weight fat energy is the larger component. For example, in the 30 kg pig receiving 13.6 MJ ME per day, 10.3 MJ was lost as heat, and of the energy retained 75% was protein and 25% fat. In the 60 kg pig receiving 27.2 MJ ME, 15.1 MJ was lost as heat, and of the energy retained 24% was protein and 76% was fat (Thorbek, 1975). In pig farming, food intake is normally restricted as the pig grows, to reduce fat deposition, and the animals are kept under equable conditions. Babies, like young farm animals, have been shown to grow faster in a thermoneutral environment (Hey, 1974).

Twenty-four-hourly measurements are essential for energy balance purposes because there is marked nycthemeral variation in metabolic rate. In the pig, the variation is about $\pm$ 20% of the mean rate, with the maximum occurring during the day. In a nocturnal mammal such as the mouse there are corresponding variations with the maximum occurring at night (Mount, 1968).

References

Alexander, G (1974) In *Heat Loss from Animals and Man.* (Ed) JL Monteith and
  LE Mount. Butterworth, London
Alexander, G (1975) *British Medical Bulletin, 31,* 62
Baldwin, BA (1974) In *Heat Loss from Animals and Man.* (EdO JL Monteith and
  LE Mount. Butterworth, London
Barnett, SA and Mount, LE (1967) In *Thermobiology.* (Ed) AH Rose.
  Academic Press, London
Brody, S (1945) *Bioenergetics and Growth.* Reinhold, New York
Brück, K (1961) *Biologia neonatorum, 3,* 65
Close, WH, Verstegen, MWA and Mount, LE (1973) *Proceedings of the Nutrition
  Society, 32,* 72A
Hey, EN (1974) In *Heat Loss from Animals and Man.* (Ed) JL Monteith and
  LE Mount. Butterworth, London
Hey, EN (1975) *British Medical Bulletin, 31,* 69
Hill, JR and Rahimtulla, KA (1965) *Journal of Physiology, 180,* 239
Holmes, CW and Mount, LE (1967) *Animal Production, 9,* 435
Hull, D (1966) *British Medical Bulletin, 22,* 92
Kleiber, M (1961) *The Fire of Life.* Wiley, New York
Ingram, DL and Mount, LE (1975) *Man and Animals in Hot Environments.*
  Springer-Verlag, New York
McCance, RA and Widdowson, EM (1957) *Lancet, ii,* 585
Mount, LE (1968) *The Climatic Physiology of the Pig.* Edward Arnold, London
Mount, LE (1974) In *Heat Loss from Animals and Man.* (Ed) JL Monteith and
  LE Mount. Butterworth, London
Taylor, PM (1960) *Journal of Physiology, 154,* 153
Thorbek, G (1967) *European Association for Animal Production.*
  Publication No 12
Thorbek, G (1975) *National Institute of Animal Science, Copenhagen.*
  Publication No 424
Verstegen, MWA, Close, WH, Start, IB and Mount, LE (1973) *British Journal of
  Nutrition, 30,* 21

Marasmus and Kwashiorkor: Detection, Treatment and Prevention

ELIZABETH M E POSKITT

The Children's Hospital, Birmingham, England

> "Severe protein calorie malnutrition (PCM) is an accident in the life of a child that can be put right through public health action. Moderate PCM is part of our society and calls for profound social change in order to achieve perhaps the most fundamental of all human rights."
>
> Bengoa, 1975

Accidents of natural or political disaster have made most people in the developed world sadly familiar, through news and television, with the severe forms of childhood malnutrition, kwashiorkor and marasmus. In the same environment as these severe cases, many children exist in states of undernutrition that place them at risk of more serious malnutrition, or more likely, death from overwhelming infection. The Inter-American Investigation of Mortality in Childhood estimated that nutritional deficiency was an associated cause of 60.9% deaths from infectious disease in children under 5, but of only 32.7% deaths from all other causes (Puffer & Serrano, 1973). Yet, of the 11,913 deaths with malnutrition as an underlying cause, 65.4% were not classifiable as kwashiorkor or marasmus. A discussion of kwashiorkor and marasmus must include consideration of the mass of children malnourished, but without the classical childhood syndromes. Unfortunately in these children, because the disturbance is less extreme, it is more difficult to diagnose, treat and prevent.

DIAGNOSIS OF MALNUTRITION

Clinical Features

The features of severe kwashiorkor and marasmus are well known (Dean, 1965). Kwashiorkor is oedematous malnutrition, with or without skin and hair changes.

Marasmus is gross wasting of fat and muscle without oedema. Classically, kwashiorkor develops when the child's energy intake is adequate, but his protein intake inadequate for growth. Marasmus occurs with overall shortage of food when protein is not more deficient than other nutrients. Certainly marasmus is common in areas of periodic food shortage, such as the dry savannah region of Northern Nigeria, where kwashiorkor is rare (Brueton, 1976). Where kwashiorkor is common, marasmus also is seen and many children show more features of both syndromes and are wasted with slight oedema, or without oedema, but showing hair and skin changes. The two classical syndromes seem to present extremes in a wide spectrum of childhood malnutrition.

Pallor and sparseness of the hair may indicate that kwashiorkor occurred some months previously, but they are not a good sign of the current nutritional state (Bradfield & Jelliffe, 1974). Reduction in the diameter and abnormalities of the hair roots are evidence of recent malnutrition, and correlate well with the loss of body weight (Bradfield & Jelliffe, 1970). Skin changes such as patchy pallor and 'peely paint' lesions are of variable significance.

There are few clinical signs in children who are moderately malnourished. Reluctance to walk and play indicate weakness and apathy perhaps associated with the need to conserve energy for basal metabolism. Their hair is often pulled out, easily pluckable even in the absence of visible changes.

Anthropometric Features

Poor nutrition results in the failure to grow in height and weight at the expected rate. Anthropometric assessment of failure of growth may be used to survey a population on one particular occasion, or to follow changes in individuals over time. Reliable simple methods are necessary so that relatively untrained staff can collect and interpret data. Striving after simplicity has led to complexity of equipment, measurements and definitions (Shakir, 1975). Ideally, measurements should clearly define the normal, and mild to moderate and severe malnutrition. Perfect definition is probably impossible on a single cross sectional survey. Measurements useful in one place may not distinguish normal from abnormal in other places where the epidemiology of malnutrition is different.

Cross Sectional Studies

Weight and Height

These are simple measurements, but they require accurate equipment and accurate age (a luxury in many developing countries) if percentage expected for age is to be determined. True weight deficit may occasionally be masked by oedema, or exaggerated by dehydration, but when these are sufficiently severe to cause confusion, they are usually obvious. Percentage weight for age, together with evidence of

165

TABLE I. Wellcome Trust International Working Party Classification of Childhood Nutrition

Weight percentage*	No oedema	Oedema
60–80%	Underweight	Kwashiorkor
Less than 60%	Marasmus	Marasmic kwashiorkor

*As percentage of 50th percentile Boston standards

oedema, is used in the Wellcome Trust International Working Party's classification of malnutrition (Table I). This remains one of the simplest and most satisfactory classifications. Height does not diminish, but only fails to increase. The degree of stunting may give some indication of how long malnutrition has lasted (Waterlow & Payne, 1975).

Weight for Height

Emphasis has been placed on this ratio as it avoids the need for accurate age. Where stuning is marked, a big weight deficit for age may not be apparent (McLaren & Read, 1975). There is also considerable overlap between the small normal and the mild to moderately malnourished child (Poskitt, 1975).

Mid Arm Circumference

Between 1 and 6 years, mid arm circumference increases by only 1.5 cm. Thus the measurement is relatively independent of age. It is also simple and repeatable

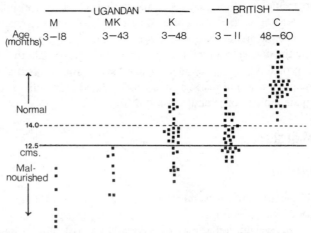

Figure 1. Mid arm circumference in Ugandan girls according to Wellcome Trust diagnosis (M=marasmus; MK=Marasmic kwashiorkor; K=kwashiorkor) compared with values for normal British infants (I) and children (C)

166

and correlates well with percentage weight for age (Shakir, 1975). As with weight, it may be falsely high where there is oedema (Figure 1).

Skinfolds

Variations between individual subjects and individual recorders make skinfold recordings not very useful in cross sectional nutritional assessment. Measurements made by the same individual in longtitudinal studies will indicate changes in subcutaneous fat.

Longtitudinal Measurements

Weight loss or poor weight gain (faltering) is evidence of deteriorating nutrition and is often associated with infection. Children in well nourished communities may lose weight with severe infection, but on a convalescent diet catch up growth is rapid. Failure of growth to accelerate after weight faltering will cause an undernourished child to depart further from expected weight for age. Longtitudinal records of weight plotted on 'Road to Health' charts illustrate the child's progress dramatically (Morley, 1973). Slow gain in height may indicate that the child is adapting his growth to suit his food intake (Waterlow &Payne, 1975).

Standards for Anthropometric Comparison

The aim of nutritional assessment is to define an 'at risk' group. Using British standards most children in an area of malnutrition may be classed as malnourished. Such classification whilst possibly correct is not particuarly helpful when medical

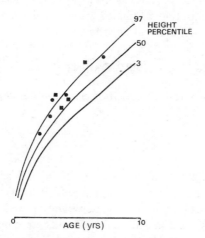

Figure 2. Height distribution of 9 obese Asian children (standards of Tanner et al, 1966). ■ = Boys; ● = Girls

167

resources are strained. Standards for well nourished local children or the Harvard standards (Vaughan, 1975) provide a suitable compromise. The difference in height and weight between well nourished pre-school children from different racial groups are less than differences between rich and poor in the same racial group (Habicht et al, 1974). Overnourished, pre-pubertal Indian children attending an obesity clinic in Birmingham, are taller than average British standards (Tanner et al, 1966), suggesting that their height potential is similar to that of British children (Figure 2). In the first few months of life, infants, even in areas of malnutrition, may grow faster than current British standards (Gopalan, 1975; Jones, 1975). Perhaps British standards for the first few months of life do not reflect ideal growth since many British babies grow faster than the standard rate. If so, is the child underweight before 3 months on British standards more poorly nourished than an older child with a similar percentage expected weight?

Biochemical Features

As with anthropometry, there is a variety of biochemical estimations that can be used to assess nutrition (Lancet, 1973). Low serum albumin is a diagnostic feature of kwashiorkor. Marasmus is not necessarily associated with abnormal serum albumin, but many patients with marasmus have serum albumin concentrations below 35 g/l. Serum albumin concentrations below 30g/l are accompanied by the biochemical and hormonal changes associated with kwashiorkor (Whitehead et al, 1973). Valine, β-lipoprotein and insulin concentrations fall and those of growth hormone and cortisol rise. Albumin may fall in infection, without weight change (Frood et al, 1971) and may be an indication of prognosis in severe kwashiorkor although in some areas transferrin levels have been shown to be more useful in this respect (McFarlane et al, 1970). Accurate estimates of serum albumin concentration, combined with clinical and anthropometric data, seems to provide the best index of nutritional state.

TREATMENT

Basic management of severe malnutrition has been described elsewhere (Staff, 1968; Ifekwunigwe, 1975).

Diet

Hospital diets for malnutrition are usually based on milk and can be administered by slow nasogastric drip to an anorexic child. Maximum growth is usually achieved with an intake in excess of 630kJ/kg body weight/day and 3—4g protein/kg body weight/day. Energy sources in addition to the milk are supplied in the form of local staple. A wholly vegetable diet, if eaten in large enough quantity, allows recovery (Rutishauser & Frood, 1973). Wharton et al (1968) have drawn attention to geographical variation in the rate of refeeding and differences in administration of vitamins, haematinics and minerals. Rapid growth will cause high demand for all nutrients.

Management of Infection

Vigorous treatment of infection is critical for the survival of the child (Staff, 1968). Investigation for infection and infestation should be part of routine treatment (Phillips & Wharton, 1968). Malnourished children may show a paradoxical response to infection with hypoglycaemia, hypothermia and low leucocyte count. Immunological responses, both humoral and cellular, are defective (Scrimshaw, 1975).

Drug Administration

Drug metabolism may be altered in malnutrition (Poskitt, 1974). Pyrexia and combinations of drugs, may affect absorption. A low serum albumin concentration may allow the rapid excretion, or alternatively, the increased activity of a drug (Koch-Weser & Seuers, 1976). Folate metabolism may be abnormal in children with malnutrition and may be further altered by drugs. The effect of some antibiotics on protein synthesis may be important in malnutrition. Tetracyclines increase the serum concentration of non-protein nitrogen and the urinary output of aminoacid. When given to adult volunteers to cure specific infections, tetracycline had little effect on nitrogen excretion compared with the effect in stopping the catabolism of infection (Beisel et al, 1967). In children on a poor diet with an infection that is not necessarily sensitive to tetracycline, increased nitrogen loss may be significant.

Iron

In kwashiorkor, transferrin levels are low and transferrin may be fully saturated with iron. Iron supplements may cause free unbound iron in the blood and encourage bacterial multiplication (McFarlane et al, 1970), but there is no direct evidence that this does happen (Suskind, 1975). Scrimshaw (1975) has suggested that functional iron deficiency associated with depression of iron transport and storage proteins may actually lower resistance to infection, since even mild iron deficiency affects the iron dependent intracellular enzyme peroxidase essential for killing phagocytosed microorganisms. Since cardiac failure in malnutrition is associated with anaemia (Wharton et al, 1967) and children may have severe iron deficiency anaemia due to hookworm, too cautious use of iron supplements may be as dangerous as over ready use.

Careful use of drugs is even more important in moderately malnourished outpatients than in in-patients. Nitrogen loss, folate deficiency or other drug effects may adversely affect nutrition when the child is only poorly supervised.

169

PREVENTION

Prevention of malnutrition involves profound social change. Better distribution of food and improved hygiene must be linked with a rise in economic standards, more education, immunisation programmes and control of high birth rates. However, much can be done at a local level to prevent severe malnutrition and to improve nutrition in a community.

We do not know exactly why some children develop kwashiorkor, some marasmus and some just remain underweight. Differences in diet give no clear indication (Gopalon, 1975) although individual variation in nutrient requirements and ability to adapt to poor food intakes may be important (Waterlow & Payne, 1975). Environmental influences such as the protein quality of a diet and the pattern of infection must have some effect, since the proportion of kwashiorkor to marasmus varies in different areas. Famine in the Sahel produced marasmus, not kwashiorkor (Greene, 1974). Whitehead and Alleyne (1972) suggest that marasmus reflects considerable adaptation to low food intake and only develops after prolonged undernutrition. Kwashiorkor may be failure to adapt adequately to a diet with relatively high carbohydrate concentration and to episodes of low food intake and increased requirement with infection. In a longtitudinal study in Uganda the 5 children who required hospital admission for serum albumin concentrations below 25g/l or profound weight loss were amongst the tallest 20% of the 60 children followed. This good height growth could indicate failure to adapt to poor food intake (Rutishauser, 1975).

If children in the developing world were as well fed as most European children, morbidity and mortality from infection would probably diminish. Similarly, if the incidence of childhood infection was at a lower level undernutrition might cease to be a problem and kwashiorkor and marasmus might disappear. Without such changes weight falters without infection and poor diet in convalescence prevent accelerated growth so the child may not recover weight loss before he is hit by further infection (Figure 3) [Mata et al, 1967; Frood et al, 1971].

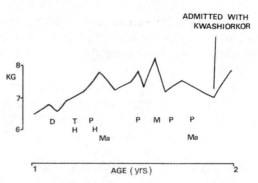

Figure 3. Weight and illness in Ugandan boy in second year of life (D=diarrhoea; T=streptococcal throat infection; P=bronchopneumonia; M=measles; H=hookworm; MA=malaria)

Improving Food Intake

Thirteen years ago a journal commented "protein deficiency is the most important nutritional disorder in the world today" (Lancet, 1963). Now there is the realisation that the most important disorder is a deficiency of food, not specifically protein. Where energy intake is inadequate, protein, often the expensive part of the diet, is being metabolised to meet energy requirements. One of the ways of getting more food into young children is to feed them more often. A small child has difficulty consuming enough bulky vegetable staple for requirements at two meals, particularly if one is at night when he is tired. Giving an extra meal, perhaps breakfast, might increase his daily intake by 50%.

If continuing deprivation and malnutrition is to be prevented, maternal nutrition must be improved. In the Dutch famine in 1944—45, babies born to mothers malnourished in the last trimester of pregnancy showed a 9% drop in mean birth weight (Stein & Susser, 1975). In the developing countries, low birth weight is combined with the potential difficulties of delivery in a mother small from lifelong malnutrition and the risks of immaturity due to poor social conditions. Many babies are born underweight and deprived. They may then be too weak or immature to feed and thrive. If they can suck, mother's milk may be inadequate because of her poor nutrition (Morley, 1973). Increasing the energy intake of pregnant women in Guatemala improved birth weight (Lechtig et al, 1975).

The worldwide decline in breast feeding has received a lot of publicity. Formula milks are liable to be administered diluted, frequently from dirty bottles. In the Inter American Investigation of Mortality in Childhood over 50% of the children who had been weaned and died between 1 and 5 months, died of diarrhoeal disease. Of those who were breast fed and not weaned at death, only 3.7% died of diarrhoeal disease (Puffer & Serrano, 1973). Malnutrition is often blamed on weaning too late. Sudden weaning in a toddler, who is then sent away to the grandmother, may produce nutritional and growth retardation due to emotional deprivation. After the body weight reached about 5kg, the requirements of the infant in a developing country are beginning to exceed the energy he is likely to be receiving from breast milk (Rutihauser et al, 1972). The gradual introduction of solids rich in energy from the age of about 4 months is probably advisable, but breast feeding should continue at least until mixed feeding is well established.

Feeding programmes for groups usually involve schoolchildren. Such programmes may improve school performance, but will not affect the children at greatest risk of malnutrition. Supplements properly administered to pre-school children in an area of malnutrition can be effective both in improving growth and decreasing morbidity from infection (Gopalan, 1975).

Treating Infection

Prevention of infection is inevitably part of the prevention of malnutrition. Better management of infection when it occurs is also important in overcoming the nutritional effect of infection.

171

Diarrhoea

Diarrhoea in young children is one of the greatest public health problems in developing countries (Martorell et al, 1975). With or without disaccharide intolerance, loss of protein and fluid in the stool contribute to malnutrition. Children managed for prolonged periods on a 'clear fluids only' regime are gradually starved. Under such circumstances marasmus may develop even in hospital in patients in developed countries. Hansen (1975) has shown loss of brush border and other degenerative changes in intestinal epithelial cells in children with severe diarrhoea. A vicious circle of poor nutrition resulting in failure of intestinal cell regeneration and further diarrhoea develops. Even when clinically dehydrated malnourished children have excess total body water and sodium (Garrow, 1968). The imbalance in sodium and water is probably related to the energy deficiency, and is unlikely to be corrected without nutrition being improved. Total parenteral nutrition is not feasible in most developing countries. It seems important therefore to continue feeding by mouth perhaps by slow nasogastric drip to malnourished children with diarrhoea (Hirschhorn et al, 1972).

Other Infections

The management of other infections is no less vital. Investigation and vigorous treatment of infection in poorly nourished children will lessen the time they are anorexic, febrile and in negative nitrogen balance. Nutritional deterioration due to measles may be inevitable once the child has become infected since little can be done to curtail the illness. But a good diet in convalescence allows rapid growth and regeneration of serum albumin and should prevent permanent nutritional deterioration.

Prevention is always better than cure, but often requires more skill. Lack of resources in developing countries means that the prevention and management of disease are undertaken almost entirely outside the confines of the hospital, but the comforting place for small sick children is in the home, not the hospital. Better management of illness in outpatients will helpt to prevent malnutrition. This is as important as any profound social changes on a national scale and the changes must come at the bottom as well as the top.

References

Beisel, WR, Sawyer, WD, Ryell, ED and Crozier, D (1967) *Annals of Internal Medicine, 67,* 744
Bengoa, JM (1975) In *Protein Calorie Malnutrition.* (Ed) RE Olson. Academic Press, New York. Page 435
Bradfield, RB and Jelliffe, DB (1970) *Nature, 225,* 283
Bradfield, RB and Jelliffe, DB (1974) *Lancet, i,* 461
Brueton (1976) Personal communication

Dean, RFA (1965) In *Recent Advances in Paediatrics. 3rd Edition.*
(Ed) D Gairdner. J & A Churchill, London. Page 234

Frood, JDL, Whitehead, RG and Coward, WA (1971) *Lancet, ii,* 1047

Garrow, JS (1968) *Electrolyte Metabolism in Severe Infantile Malnutrition.*
Pergamon Press, Oxford. Page 131

Gopalan, C (1975) In *Protein Calorie Malnutrition.* (Ed) RE Olson. Academic
Press, New York. Page 330

Greene, MH (1974) *Lancet, i,* 1093

Habicht, JP, Martorell, R, Yarbrough, C, Malina, RM and Klein, RE (1974)
Lancet, i, 611

Hansen, JDL (1975) In *Protein Calorie Malnutrition.* (Ed) RE Olson. Academic
Press, New York. Page 413

Hirschhorn, N, Cash, RA, Woodward, WE and Pivey, GH (1972) *Lancet, ii,* 15

Ifekwunigwe, AE (1975) In *Protein Calorie Malnutrition.* (Ed) RE Olson.
Academic Press, New York. Page 390

Jones, MD (1975) *Journal of Tropical Pediatrics and Environmental Child Health,*
21, 26

Koch-Weser, J and Sellers, EM (1976) *New England Journal of Medicine, 294,*
526

Lancet (1963) *ii,* 1320

Lancet (1973) *i,* 1041

Lechtig, A, Habicht, JP, Delgado, H, Klein, RE, Yarbrough, C and Martorell, R
(1975) *Pediatrics, 56,* 508

McFarlane, H, Reddy, S, Adcock, KJ, Adeshina, H, Cooke, AR and Akene, J
(1970) *British Medical Journal, 4,* 268

McLaren, DS and Read, WWC (1975) *Lancet, ii,* 219

Martorell, R, Habicht, JP, Yarbrough, C, Lechtig, A, Klein, RE and Western, KA
(1975) *American Journal of Diseases in Children, 129,* 1296

Mata, LJ, Urrutia, JJ and Garcia, B (1967) In *Nutrition and Infection. CIBA*
Foundation Study Group No.31. (Ed) GEW Wolstenholme and M O'Connor.
J & A Churchill, London. Page 112

Morley, D (1973) *Paediatric Priorities in the Developing World.* Butterworth,
London.

Phillips, I and Wharton, BA (1968) *British Medical Journal, 1,* 407

Poskitt, EME (1974) *Proceedings of the Nutrition Society, 33,* 203

Poskitt, EME (1975) *Lancet, ii,* 367

Puffer, RR and Serrano, CV (1973) *Patterns of Mortality in Childhood. Scientific*
Publication No 262 Pan American Health Organisation. WHO, Washington

Rutishauser, IHE (1974) *East African Medical Journal, 51,* 659

Rutishauser, IHE, Burgess, AP, Jones, PRM, Krueger, RH and Geber, M (1972)
In *Medicine in a Tropical Environment.* (Ed) AG Shaper, JW Kibukamusoke
and MSR Hutt. British Medical Association, London. Page 227

Rutishauser, IHE and Frood, JDL (1973) *British Journal of Nutrition, 29,* 261

Scrimshaw, NS (1975) In *Protein Calorie Malnutrition.* (Ed) RE Olson. Academic
Press, New York. Page 353

Shakir, A (1975) *Journal of Tropical Pediatrics and Environmental Child Health,*
21, 69

Staff, THE (1968) *East African Medical Journal, 45,* 399

Stein, Z and Susser, M (1975) *Pediatric Research, 9,* 70

Suskind, R (1975) In *Protein Calorie Malnutrition.* (Ed) RE Olson. Academic
Press, New York. Page 385

Tanner, JM, Whitehouse, RH and Takaishi, M (1966) *Archives of Disease in Childhood, 41,* 454

Vaughan, VC (1975) In *Nelson Textbook of Pediatrics.* (Ed) VC Vaughan, RJ McKay and WE Nelson. WB Saunders, Philadelphia. Page 13

Waterlow, JC and Payne, PR (1975) *Nature, 258,* 113

Wharton, BA, Howells, GR and McCance, RA (1967) *Lancet, ii,* 384

Wharton, BA, Jelliffe, DB and Stanfield, JP (1968) *Journal of Pediatrics, 72,* 721

Whitehead, RG and Alleyne, GAO (1972) *British Medical Bulletin, 28,* 72

Whitehead, RG, Coward, WA and Lunn, PG (1973) *Lancet, i,* 63

Energy Costs and Protein Requirements for Catch-up Growth in Children

J C WATERLOW, ANN ASHWORTH HILL and D W SPADY
London School of Hygiene and Tropical Medicine, London, England

An immense amount of work has been done on the nutrient requirements for growth in farm animals because of their economic importance. There is also a great deal of information from experiments on laboratory animals. Until fairly recently, however, there have been few direct observations in man. The discussion on this subject in the report of the Princeton Conference on Human Protein Requirements (1957) illustrates how confused and fragmentary our knowledge was at that time.

This paper is based on results obtained in children at the Tropical Metabolism Research Unit (TMRU), Jamaica, which represent our own experience. It was in 1960 that we first began to consider seriously the protein and energy needs of children recovering from malnutrition. At that time the late RFA Dean, working at the Child Nutrition Unit in Uganda, was advocating very high protein intakes, of the order of 5 or even 7 g kg^{-1} d^{-1}. Very little attention had been paid to the energy requirements of these children.

In what follows, for the sake of simplicity, the protein and energy requirements for catch-up growth will be considered separately. Of course it is understood that no diet is effective which does not supply both together. It will also be convenient

TABLE I. Characteristics of a 'Reference' Child Aged 1 Year

Weight	kg	10
Height	cm	75
Rate of weight gain	g/kg/d	1.0
N content of body	g/kg	23.1*
N retention for growth	mg/kg/d	16†

*from Fomon (1967)   †from FAO/WHO (1973)

175

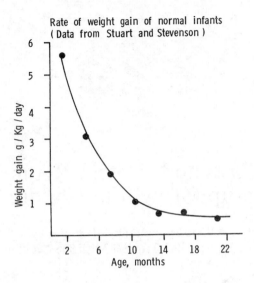

Figure 1. Rate of weight gain (g/kg/d) in the normal child. 50th centile Harvard Standards (Stuart & Stevenson, 1959)

to compare the malnourished child with a 'normal' or reference child whose characteristics are shown in Table I and Figure 1. There may well be some difference of opinion about the body composition and nitrogen content of a normal child at 1 year, because we do not have adequate analytical data. The values given in Table I are based on those used in the FAO/WHO Report of 1973, and will serve as well as any others for the purpose of developing the argument.

The Protein Requirement for Catch-up Growth

The protein intake has to cover the needs for maintenance and for the formation of new tissue. Even during rapid catch-up growth, the component representing maintenance is still a large proportion of the total.

Maintenance Fomon and co-workers (1965) found that infants aged 4–6 months on a virtually protein-free diet excreted about 60 mg N kg^{-1} d^{-1}. Chan and Waterlow (1966) and Arroyave et al (1969) estimated the maintenance requirement of infants from the regression of N retention at different levels of intake. Our results are shown in Figure 2. From this study the average maintenance requirement, in terms of milk protein, was taken to be 100 mg N kg^{-1} d^{-1}. The Guatemalan workers obtained a similar figure. This is a little higher than the most recent estimates of the maintenance requirements of adults (FAO/WHO, 1973), partly because the faecal loss is higher in infants. Perhaps the reason for this is that the surface area of the gut is larger in relation to the body weight.

176

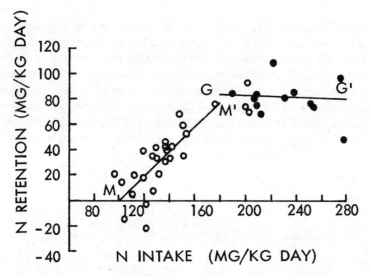

Figure 2. Relation between nitrogen intake and retention in children aged about 1 year (Chan & Waterlow, 1966, reproduced by permission of the British Journal of Nutrition)

Growth The word 'growth' is used here to indicate weight gain produced by the deposition of new tissue of normal composition. An increase in weight caused by the laying down of fat, i.e. the development of obesity, could hardly be called growth.

Provided that the energy intake is adequate, the amount of protein needed for maximum weight gain will depend on the child's capacity for growth and on the efficiency with which protein is utilised. One would expect these two variables

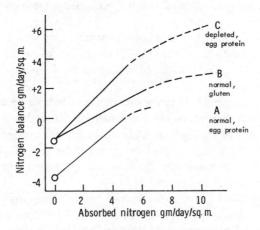

Figure 3. Nitrogen balance vs absorbed nitrogen in dogs: the effect of the quality of the protein and of the state of protein nutrition (Allison, 1950, by permission of CC Thomas, Springfield, Illinois)

to be related: the more depleted the child, the greater his growth potential and the greater the efficiency of protein utilisation. These relationships are well shown in the classical studies of Allison (1950) on dogs. Figure 3 shows that the depleted animal retains more N at a given protein intake. The dotted line at C suggests that retention continues to increase at higher intakes. What is not clear is whether it increases linearly until the organism is 'saturated', so that up to that point the slope (i.e. the efficiency of utilisation) is constant; or whether efficiency gradually falls off with increasing intake. These two possibilities are shown hypothetically

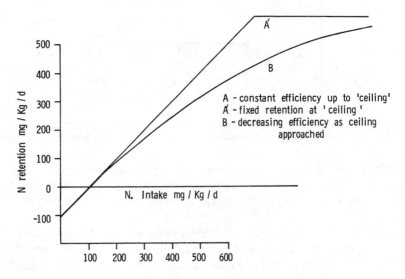

Figure 4. Hypothetical relationship between nitrogen intake and retention

in Figure 4. To distinguish between them experimentally would be very difficult, as pointed out by Said and Hegsted (1970) and to our knowledge has not been attempted in children. The work done in Jamaica does, however, provide some relevant information.

1. In Figure 2 the line M—M represents results of balance measurements made in children who were recovering from malnutrition. At intakes below 190 mg N kg⁻¹ d⁻¹ the slope of the regression line shows that the efficiency of utilisation of protein (NPU) was 97%. Here we have optimum conditions for efficiency — depleted children and a low intake. What we do not know is whether the slope would have continued at higher intakes.

2. The line G—G in Figure 2 was obtained from children who had essentially recovered from malnutrition; on average they were 97% expected weight for height, although still below normal height for their age. In these children there was no increase in N retention with increasing intake. Retention was constant at about 80 mg N kg⁻¹ d⁻¹, which presumably represents their growth potential.

178

Obviously in this group, the higher the intake the lower the NPU.

3. Table II shows N retention in two groups of children in the rapid growth phase during recovery from malnutrition. Even at the higher level of intake the efficiency of retention was 74%. This N retention was accompanied by a weight gain of nearly 13 g kg⁻¹ d⁻¹, which is about fifteen times the normal rate of gain

TABLE II. Efficiency of Nitrogen Utilisation in Children During Catch-up Growth (Jamaica)

		Series I (1961)	Series II (1968)
No of children		11	4
Weight gain	g/kg/d	6.4	12.85
Energy intake	kcal/kg/d	173	179
Protein intake	g/kg/d	2.25	4.1
N intake	mg/kg/d	360	655
N retained	mg/kg/d	172	386
N utilised*	%	73	74

* calculated as $\dfrac{\text{N retained} + \text{N for maintenance}}{\text{N intake}}$

maintenance N taken as 100 mg/kg/d

at 1 year (Figure 1). It is quite possible that in these children weight gain was limited by energy intake. Rutishauser and McCance (1968) found weight gains of 15 g kg⁻¹ d⁻¹ (and in one case even 20 g kg⁻¹ d⁻¹) on a daily protein intake of 4 g kg⁻¹ d⁻¹, provided that enough energy was supplied. It is very interesting that there was no benefit when the protein intake was increased to 6–8 g kg⁻¹ d⁻¹.

From these data, although incomplete, we could perhaps assume that during catch-up growth milk protein can be utilised with an efficiency of at least 75%, provided, of course, that enough energy is available.

TABLE III. Nitrogen Content of Weight Gain During Catch-up Growth

Author	Weight gain g/kg/d	N retained mg/g wt gain
1. Waterlow, 1961	9.1	25
2. Chan and Waterlow, 1966	2.9	29
3. Ashworth et al, 1968	12.8	31
4. Spady, 1976 (in press)	8.4	22

The N content of weight gained, as measured by N balance, is shown in Table III. The results of these four studies are similar, and agree well with accepted values for the N concentration of the body after maturation is complete.

TABLE IV. Calculation of the Protein Requirement for Catch-up Growth

	mg N/kg/d	g protein/kg/d
Maintenance requirement	100	
Growth requirement		
weight gain: 20 g/kg/d		
N content of weight gained 25 mg N/g		
∴ N retained	500	
Total	600	3.75
Required intake if NPU = 75%	800	5.0

The protein intake needed for any given rate of catch-up growth can then be calculated, on the basis that (i) tissue laid down contains 25 mg N per g; (ii) the NPU is 75%. Table IV is a sample of such a calculation. It may well err on the side of caution, since Rutishauser and McCance (1968) obtained comparable rates of gain with lower intakes.

The Energy Requirement for Growth

It is convenient to consider this problem in chronological order of the studies done on it.

The gross energy cost of growth   The first estimates which we obtained of the gross energy cost of growth were derived from a simple regression analysis of weight gain against energy intake in malnourished children during recovery (Waterlow, 1961; Ashworth et al, 1968). The slope which we obtained represented a requirement of 12.8 kcal (53.5 kJ) per g weight gain. Such a figure gave some kind of indication of the large amounts of energy needed to promote catch-up growth in children and made it clear that in order to achieve rapid growth it was necessary to add extra energy to the food in the form of oil. The composition of

TABLE V. Composition of High Energy Feed

		per litre
Dried skim milk	g	90
Sugar	g	65
Oil	g	80 (100 ml)
kcal		1340
Protein	g	32 (approx)
P/E ratio		9.4

180

a typical mixture used at the TMRU is shown in Table V (Picou et al, 1975). However, this value was not an accurate estimate of the true energy cost of growth for several reasons: no allowance was made for faecal loss, which in later work was found to average 8% of the intake. It was also subsequently found that the fat content of the milk mixture was less than had been thought, because some of the added oil adhered to the cylinder from which it was poured into the mixture. As a result energy intakes were overestimated.

Table VI shows the results of later studies of the same kind in Jamaica and Uganda. The growth requirement (energy per g weight gain) was in all cases

TABLE VI. Regressions of Weight Gain on Energy Intake

	Maintenance* requirement kcal/kg/d	Growth requirement kcal/g
Ashworth et al, 1968	42	12.8
Rutishauser and McCance, 1968	~ 120	~ 7.5
Kerr et al, 1973	100	6.9
Spady, 1976 (in press)	81	4.4

*Intake at zero weight gain

lower than in the original Jamaica study. It is not clear why this should be: all that can be said is that the more careful the measurements, the greater the efficiency that has been found.

Another approach has to be used when all the observations fall within a narrow range. The equation for the partition of energy can be written:

$$E_I = E_M + E_A + E_G$$

where E_I is intake, E_M maintenance expenditure, E_A activity expenditure and E_G the energy used for growth. E_G includes, of course, both the energy content of the tissue laid down and the energy cost of its formation. From this equation, E_G / g weight gain = $\dfrac{E_I - E_M - E_A}{\text{weight gain}}$.

The maintenance requirement, E_M, is the energy intake needed to maintain energy balance. In addition to the basal expenditure it must cover the extra energy output provoked by food (so-called specific dynamic action) and that needed for a minimal level of physical activity. The concept is not very clearly defined; nevertheless, data collected from the literature by Payne (1975, unpublished) and summarised in Table VII suggest that in a wide range of animals E_M is about 1.5 x the basal metabolic rate. Numerous measurements have been made in Jamaica by open circuit calorimetry of the metabolic rates of babies while asleep 4 hours after the last meal. These conditions are as close to basal as can reasonably be achieved. The results show a fairly wide range (Brooke et al,

181

TABLE VII. Maintenance Energy Requirement of Different Species in Relation to Metabolic Mass

Species	Maintenance requirement kcal/kg$^{0.75}$/d	Maintenance BMR
Young rat	107	1.53
Hens	110	1.57
Young pigs	101	1.45
Lambs	105	1.50
Calves	106	1.53
Bullocks	107	1.53
Cows	109	1.56
Horses	104	1.47
Human infant	124	1.51
Human adult	80	1.38

(Data collected by Payne, 1975, unpublished)

1974; Ashworth, 1969a): an average value for the BMR would be about 55 kcal (230 kJ) kg^{-1} d^{-1}. From this the estimate of E_M would be 82 kcal (345 kJ) kg^{-1} d^{-1}.

Until measurements became available (see below) of the actual energy expenditure of children during catch-up growth, all we could do was to make the limiting assumption that during catch-up no energy is expended on physical activity, over and above that included in maintenance. Table VIII shows results of Ashworth (1969b) recalculated on this assumption. The energy 'available' for growth is

TABLE VIII. Energy Requirement for Growth. 'Available' energy calculated as [intake − 8% for faecal losses − maintenance requirement (82 kcal/kg)]. Mean of 8 cases (Data of Ashworth, 1969b)

'Available' energy for growth	kcal/kg/d	55.5 ± 3.0 (SD)
Weight gain	g/kg/d	10.0 ± 1.27
kcal/g weight gain		5.5 ± 0.8

taken as intake, corrected for faecal loss at 8%, minus 82 kcal (345 kJ) kg^{-1} d^{-1} representing the maintenance requirement. The value of 5.5 kcal (23 kJ) per g weight gain must be an overestimate, because physical activity is neglected. Moreover, for the reason given above, the intakes were probably overestimated.

Energy expenditure and energy retention No further progress could be made in estimating the energy cost of growth without direct measurements of energy expenditure. The difference between intake and expenditure is the energy retained

182

or stored in new tissue. This study was undertaken by Spady (in press), who determined energy expenditure with the SAMI, a device which integrates the number of heart beats over a period of 24 hours or more, without interfering with the child's activity. It is, of course, necessary to calibrate heart rate against oxygen consumption at various levels of activity, not only in each child individually but also in the same child in different nutritional states. It is very interesting, although

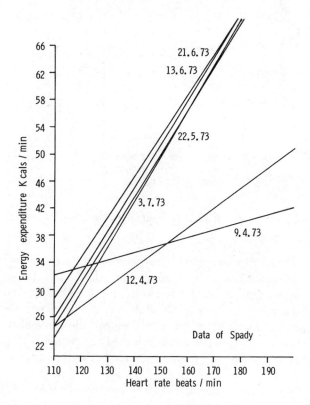

Figure 5. Relation between energy expenditure and heart rate in a child in the malnourished state and at different stages of recovery from malnutrition

not strictly relevant to the present discussion, that the relationship varies with the state of nutrition. For a given rate of oxygen consumption the heart rate is much faster in the malnourished than in the recovered child (Figure 5).

The results of these measurements during catch-up growth are shown in Figure 6. The line A—A is the regression of energy intake on weight gain. The maintenance requirement, that is, energy intake at zero weight gain, comes out at 81 kcal (340 kJ) kg^{-1} d^{-1}, which agrees well with Payne's theoretical figure of 1.5 x BMR. The slope of A—A, which gives the energy cost of growth, is 4.4 kcal (18.4 kJ)

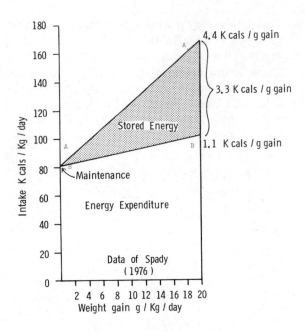

Figure 6. Partition of energy intake at different rates of weight gain. Data of Spady, 1976 (in press)

per g. This is lower than any of the other previous estimates and is probably more accurate, because faecal losses were allowed for and the actual energy content of the food was measured by bomb calorimetry instead of being calculated from the supposed composition. The line B–B shows the relation between energy expenditure measured with the SAMI and weight gain during rapid growth. Two questions arise from this figure. The first is the composition of the tissue laid down. The second is the energy cost of the synthetic processes.

TABLE IX. Calculation of Composition of Tissue Laid Down from Amount of Energy Retained

Let χ = proportion of lean) in tissue laid down
$1-\chi$ = proportion of fat)
y = energy cost of growth (kcal/g)

If protein = 20% of lean tissue

heat of combustion of protein = 5.7 kcal/g

heat of combustion of fat = 9.0 kcal/g

Then y = $(5.7 \times 0.2\chi) + 9.0 (1-\chi)$ [neglecting energy cost of synthesis]

If y = 3.3 kcal/g [see Figure 6]

Then lean = 72.5%

fat = 27.5%

protein = 14.5%

184

The slope of the line B—B is 1.1 kcal (4.6 kJ) per g. The difference between the slopes A—A and B—B is 3.3. kcal (13.8 kJ) per g, and represents the average amount of energy stored per g tissue laid down. We can calculate, as shown in Table IX, that this figure of 3.3 kcal per g should correspond to a tissue containing 27.5% fat and 14.5% protein, i.e. 23 mg N per g. These are very reasonable estimates which agree well with those obtained by balance measurements (see Table III) and with those derived by Ashworth (1969b) from the increase of total body K during rapid growth.

The results quoted so far are averages. There are naturally individual variations between children in the values obtained for the energy cost of growth. One explanation for this comes from recent work of Jackson et al (1976), who measured muscle mass with ^{15}N-creatine in five children before and after recovery. They took the ratio   increase in muscle mass

increase in body weight

as a measure of the protein content of the tissue laid down. It is apparent from the calculation in Table IX that in theory there should be an inverse linear relation between protein content and energy cost of weight gain, so that the greater the protein content, the lower the energy cost. Figure 7 shows that the results of

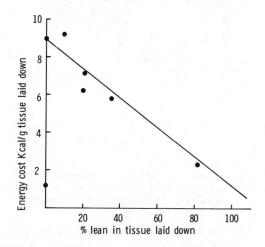

Figure 7. Relation between energy cost of weight gain and proportion of lean to fat in tissue laid down. The points are experimental observations of change in muscle mass (Jackson et al, 1976). The line is the theoretical relationship

Jackson et al fit the theoretical line rather well. Thus a major cause of variability in the energy cost of growth is the composition of the tissue laid down.

The energy cost of synthesis The energy cost of synthesis is the total energy cost of growth, less the stored energy. The slope of the regression line B—B in

185

Figure 6, which relates energy expenditure to rate of weight gain, might be taken to represent the cost of synthesis. The slope is 1.1 kcal (4.6 kJ) per g weight gain. However, the deduction is not valid for two reasons. First, it assumes that physical activity is in no way related to the rate of growth — an assumption which is obviously unjustified because, as far as we know, the SAMI cannot distinguish between energy expended on synthesis and energy expended on activity. Second, the slope of B—B has a coefficient of variation of 50%. However much the methods are refined, it seems unlikely that it will ever be possible to get an accurate estimate of the energy cost of tissue deposition by this approach.

Another way of attacking this problem arises from the work of Brooke and Ashworth (1972) on the increased oxygen consumption of children after a meal.

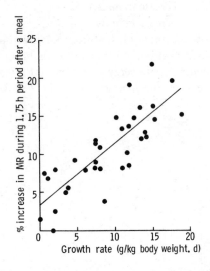

Figure 8. Relation between growth rate and increase in metabolic rate after a standard test meal containing 27 kcal (113 kJ) and 0.7 g protein/kg. Data of Brooke and Ashworth (1972) reproduced by permission of the British Journal of Nutrition

Figure 8 shows that the post-prandial increase was greater, the more rapid the rate of growth. It is therefore reasonable to suppose that the extra energy expenditure represents the cost of forming new tissue. The children in this study were receiving six identical feeds a day. If the same increase occurs after each feed, then from the slope of the regression in Figure 8 the total post-prandial increase in 24 hours comes to 0.266 kcal (1.11 kJ) per g weight gain. This is a much lower figure than that derived by the previous method, and is probably more realistic. From it we can obtain a maximum value for the energy cost of protein synthesis, on the assumption that the cost of fat synthesis is negligible, particularly when the food contains a considerable amount of pre-formed tri-

186

glyceride. If 1 g weight gained contains 0.145 g protein (see above), then the energy cost of synthesising that protein would be 1.85 kcal (7.7 kJ) per g.

This, as stated earlier, must be a maximum value since the post-prandial increase in energy expenditure must cover other processes such as active absorption and transport as well as protein synthesis. However, it agrees quite well with another estimate obtained in a completely different way. Sender et al (1975) compared the fall in BMR with the fall in protein synthesis in obese subjects after transfer from a normal to a low energy intake. If the two changes are causally related, then the saving in energy expenditure caused by the reduction in protein synthesis amounts to 1.5 kcal (6.3 kJ) per g.

It has always been difficult to reconcile estimates of the energy cost of protein synthesis derived from measurements on the whole animal with those based on the biochemistry of peptide bond formation. Even when account is taken of associated processes such as synthesis of messenger RNA, it seems likely that the energy cost of protein synthesis is less than 1 kcal (4.2 kJ) per g (Buttery & Annison, 1973). On the other hand, extensive studies in farm animals have led to much higher estimates. For example, Kielanowski (1972), from studies on growing pigs, concluded that the metabolisable energy cost of deposition of 1 g protein in the body of the baby pig is 10.0−11.5 kcal. If the calorific value of protein (5.7 kcal g^{-1}) is subtracted, this gives an energy cost of synthesis of about 5 kcal (22 kJ) per g. The results of Brooke and Ashworth (1972) and of Sender et al (1975) lead to estimates which are lower than any others obtained in the whole animal, and closer to those expected on biochemical grounds. However, they depend on a hypothesis which remains to be proven − that the observed changes in the rate of energy expenditure do in fact reflect changes in the rate of protein synthesis.

Finally, although there is no space to consider in detail the mechanisms which

TABLE X. Hormone Response During Catch-up Growth: Comparison of Slowly and Rapidly Growing Children

		Slow growing	Fast growing	
Number		7	12	
Weight gain	g/kg/d	5.4	12.3	
Energy intake	kcal/kg/d	148	178	
Cost of growth	kcal/g*	10.0	6.7	
Insulin response†		267	433	P<0.025
Growth hormone response		169	279	P<0.01

*calculated as intake − 8% for faecal loss − 82 kcal/kg/d for maintenance
†response to a standard high energy test meal. Arbitrary units calculated from the area under the curve from 0−120 minutes.
Data of Robinson et al (1976)

187

control catch-up growth, to round off this account of work in Jamaica it is appropriate to mention some recent studies by Robinson et al (1976). They have shown that rapid catch-up is associated with increased secretion of insulin and of growth hormone in response to a test meal. These results are summarised in Table X.

Conclusion

Much of this discussion has been theoretical. From the practical point of view what matters is the demonstration by the group in Jamaica and by Whitehead and co-workers in Uganda, that, contrary to earlier belief, catch-up growth in malnourished children is more likely to be limited by the supply of energy than by that of protein. The children themselves, once they have begun to recover, show a remarkable capacity for growth, in the sense of the formation of new tissue. Although measurements of N balance and of increase in total body K suggest that there is a rapid deposition of new protein, we do not know how far the process is going on harmoniously in all organs and tissues. This is a problem for future research.

In the meantime we have tried to examine the quantitative relationships. To summarise, if 100 kcal (420 kJ) kg^{-1} d^{-1} are allowed for maintenance plus normal physical activity an additional 100 kcal (420 kJ) should promote growth at 10–20 times the normal rate. The protein intake needed to secure this maximum rate of growth is 4–5 g kg^{-1} d^{-1}, on the assumption that the efficiency of utilisation is about 75%. The composition of the diets and the amount and frequency of feeds needed to produce this rapid catch-up have been described in detail by Picou et al (1975) and by Hay and Whitehead (1973).

Some may question whether it may not be harmful to 'rev up' the synthesising machinery to this extent. To our knowledge no ill effects have been demonstrated, provided that the high energy regime is not instituted too early and that it provides adequate amounts of vitamins and minerals. On the other hand, there are certain benefits. We believe, although it is difficult to document, that if a child is fully rehabilitated, in the sense of reaching his expected weight for height, he is much less likely to relapse when he returns to the environment in which he became malnourished. If the child is being treated in hospital, the economic and psychological advantages of achieving full catch-up growth rapidly are obvious.

References

Allison, JB (1950) In *Symposia on Nutrition, Volume II. Plasma Proteins.* CC Thomas, Springfield, Illinois. Page 123

Arroyave, G, Viteri, F, Alvarado, J and Behar, M (1969) *Proceedings 8th International Congress of Nutrition, Prague.* Page A19

Ashworth, A (1969a) *Nature, 223,* 407

Ashworth, A (1969b) *British Journal of Nutrition, 23,* 835

Ashworth, A, Bell, R, James, WPT and Waterlow, JC (1968) *Lancet, ii,* 600
Brooke, OG and Ashworth, A (1972) *British Journal of Nutrition, 27,* 407
Brooke, OG, Cocks, T and March, Y (1974) *Acta Paediatrica Stockholm, 63,* 817
Buttery, PJ and Annison, EF (1973) In *The Biological Efficiency of Protein Production.* (Ed) JWG Jones. Cambridge University Press, Cambridge
Chan, H and Waterlow, JC (1966) *British Journal of Nutrition, 20,* 775
FAO/WHO (1973) *World Health Organisation Technical Report Series No 522.* Geneva
FAO/WHO/Josiah Macy Jr Foundation (1957) *Human Protein Requirements and their fulfilment in Practice. Proceedings of a Conference in Princeton, United States 1955*
Fomon, SJ (1967) *Pediatrics, 40,* 863
Fomon, SJ, DeMaeyer, EM and Owen, GM (1965) *Journal of Nutrition, 85,* 235
Hay, RW and Whitehead, RG (1973) *The Therapy of the Severely Malnourished Child.* National Food and Nutrition Council of Uganda and MRC Child Nutrition Unit
Jackson, AA, Picou, D and Reeds, PJ (1976) *Proceedings of the 21st Scientific Meeting.* Commonwealth Caribbean Medical Research Council, Tropical Metabolism Research Unit, University of the West Indies
Kerr, D, Ashworth, A, Picou, D, Poulter, N, Seakins, A, Spady, D and Wheeler, E (1973) In *Endocrine Aspects of Malnutrition.* Kroc Foundation Symposia No 1. (Ed) LI Gardner and P Amacher. Kroc Foundation, Sta Inez, California. Page 476
Kielanowski, J (1972) *Pig Production.* (Ed) DJA Cole. Butterworth, London
Payne, PR (1975) Unpublished
Picou, D, Alleyne, GAO, Kerr, DS, Miller, C, Jackson, A, Hill, A, Bogues, J and Patrick, J (1975) *Malnutrition and Gastroenteritis in Children. A Manual for Hospital Treatment and Management.* Caribbean Food and Nutrition Institute, Kingston, Jamaica
Robinson, H, Cocks, T, Alexander, A, Kerr, D and Picou, D (1976) *Proceedings of the 21st Scientific Meeting.* Commonwealth Caribbean Medical Research Council, Tropical Metabolism Research Unit, University of the West Indied
Rutishauser, IHE and McCance, RA (1968) *Archives of Disease in Childhood, 43,* 252
Said, AK and Hegsted, DM (1970) *Journal of Nutrition, 100,* 1363
Sender, PM, James, WPT and Garlick, PJ (1975) In *Regulation of Energy Balance in Man.* (Ed) E Jequier. Editions Medecine et Hygiene, Geneva
Spady, DW (1976) In press
Stuart, HC and Stevenson, SS (1959) In *Textbook of Pediatrics.* (Ed) W Nelson. 7th Edition. Saunders, Philadelphia. Page 12
Waterlow, JC (1961) *Journal of Tropical Paediatrics and African Child Health, 7,* 16

Adolescent Development

W A MARSHALL
Institute of Child Health, University of London, England

There is very little information about either the nutritional needs of adolescents or the nutritional status of normal adolescents at the present time. This lack of information is due partly to the fact that in most relevant studies the nutritional data have been related only to the age of the subjects and have not made allowance for the fact that children of a given age may differ widely in their sexual development and their progress towards, or through, the adolescent growth spurt. As a result of these differences, it is impossible to decide whether or not a child is going through the changes of puberty by reference only to his or her age. A knowledge of the extent of variation which occurs in the manifestations of normal puberty amongst healthy children is an essential basis for further nutritional investigations. These variations are therefore discussed in some detail below.

The Secondary Sex Characters in Boys

Enlargement of the testes is usually the first sign of puberty in boys. Testicular size may be measured with sufficient accuracy for clinical purposes by means of the Prader Orchidometer (Zachmann et al, 1974). Testes with volumes of 1, 2 or 3 cm^3 are found in prepubertal boys, but a greater volume nearly always indicates that puberty has begun. The volume of the adult testis varies between 12 and 25 cm^3.

The development of the penis and scrotum may be described according to five stages (Tanner, 1962). The first of these is the infantile state. In stage 2, which represents early puberty, the scrotum has begun to enlarge and there is some change in the texture of the scrotal skin. In stage 3, the penis and the scrotum are further enlarged and in stage 4 the glans has developed. Stage 5 is reached when the genitalia have attained their adult size and shape. In healthy European boys, the genitalia may attain stage 2 at any time after the ninth birthday (Figure 1) but, at the other extreme, some quite normal 14 or 15 year old boys have genitalia in stage 5 before their 13th birthday, but other boys may

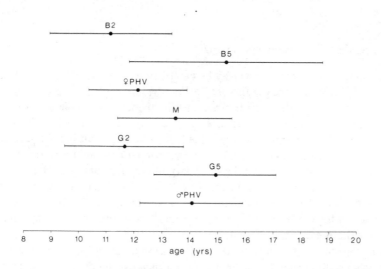

Figure 1. Range of ages within which 95 per cent of girls reach breast stage (B2), breast stage 5 (B5), peak height velocity (PHV), and menarche (M). Also, range of ages within which boys reach genital stages 2 and 5 (G2 and G5) and peak height velocity (PHV). The point at the centre of each line represents the mean age at which the corresponding stage is reached. (Based on data from Marshall & Tanner, 1969 and 1970)

be 18 years old before they reach this stage of development. Thus a representative sample of 13 year old boys, for example, will contain a few individuals who have completed their adolescence, a few who are still sexually infantile and the remainder will be in various stages of sexual development.

Pubic hair growth is also usually described in five stages (Tanner, 1962) with stage 1 being the infantile stage in which there is no pubic hair and stage 5, in both sexes, being a distribution of hair in an inverse triangle, as in the adult female. The range of ages within which pubic hair growth may begin (stage 2) or reach stage 5 is similar to that for the genitalia.

Axillary hair begins to appear, on the average, about 1.3 years later than pubic hair (Neyzi et al, 1975), and in a sample of Turkish boys facial hair began to appear at the corner of the upper lip at a mean age of 14.7 years. The spread of the hair to the whole of the upper lip with some on the cheeks and chin was not seen before the age of 16.5 years.

The age at which the changes of puberty begin in a given boy is not a reliable indication of the age at which we may expect him to reach maturity. Some boys pass through the whole process of genital development in less than two years, while others may take about five years to do so (Marshall & Tanner, 1970). Thus a boy who begins to develop a year or so before another may not be the first of the two to reach maturity. There is no clear relationship between the rate at which the genitalia develop at puberty and the age at which this development begins.

The Secondary Sex Characters in Girls

The development of the breasts may be described in five stages (Tanner, 1962). Stage 2, the 'bud' stage is the first indication of adolescent development in the breast. In this stage, the areola has increased in diameter and is elevated on a small mound of underlying tissue. In stage 3, the breast and areola are further enlarged and the appearance is rather like that of a small adult breast. In stage 4, the areola is further enlarged and forms a secondary mound projecting above the corpus of the breast. When the secondary mound has disappeared, and a continuous rounded contour is restored, we refer to the breast as being in stage 5.

In some girls, the secondary mound typical of stage 4 persists until the first pregnancy or beyond while a few girls apparently pass directly from stage 3 to stage 5 without exhibiting stage 4.

In European girls the breasts may begin to develop at any age from about 8 years onwards (Marshall & Tanner, 1969) and they usually do so before the 13th birthday (Figure 1). Some 12 year old girls have fully mature breasts but others do not reach maturity in this respect until they are 19 or even older. A typical group of 12 year old girls may include some who are fully mature and others whose breasts have not yet begun to develop.

The five stages used to describe pubic hair growth in girls are the same as those used for boys, but the first growth of hair may appear on either the labia or the mons pubis. Pubic hair begins to appear within a range of ages similar to that in which the breasts begin to develop and an adult distribution of hair is usually acquired between the ages of 12 and 17.

The Adolescent Growth Spurt

The adolescent spurt is a sharp increase in growth velocity which rises to a maximum but begins to decrease again almost immediately. The maximum speed attained is usually called peak height velocity or PHV. From the growth velocity curve of any individual who has been measured repeatedly throughout puberty we can clearly recognise the age at which peak height velocity was reached and identify its actual value in cm/yr. Because the age at PHV can be identified reasonably accurately it is a useful landmark in the growth process. The mean value of PHV in 49 boys studied by Marshall and Tanner (1970) was 10.3 cm/yr

192

with a variation between subjects of about 3 cm/yr on either side of this. The average for 41 girls in the same study was 9.0 cm/yr (Marshall & Tanner, 1969). These values are based on estimates of the true peak velocity in each of the children studied. In practice this velocity is not maintained for a whole year and the actual rate of growth over the year extending from six months before to six months after the peak is, on average, 9.5 cm/yr for boys and 8.4 cm/yr for girls. As the average rate of growth just before the adolescent spurt is 5 cm/yr in both sexes, the growth rate is very nearly doubled during the adolescent spurt. The actual gain in stature during the year in which peak height velocity occurs varies between 7 and 12 cm in boys and between 6 and 11 cm in girls.

Children who reach their peak velocity at an early age usually attain a higher speed of growth at this stage than those who reach the peak later. According to Marshall and Tanner (1969;1970) the mean age at peak height velocity was 12.14 ± 0.1 years for girls and 14.06 ± 0.1 years for boys. The standard deviation was 0.9 years in both sexes. Thus the age at peak height velocity varies approximately between 10 and 14 years in girls as compared with between 12 and 16 years in boys.

The lower limbs reach their maximum rate of growth in length slightly before the trunk. However, the spurt in sitting height is greater than that in the length of the lower limbs so that the proportion of the total stature which is due to the trunk increases.

Interrelationship of Secondary Sex Characters

In boys, the genitialia and pubic hair do not always develop concurrently. Also, different individuals may not be at the same stages of either genital or pubic hair development when they attain peak height velocity. The great majority of boys are in genital stages 3 or 4 when pubic hair growth begins, so that pubic hair growth without genital development is unusual, while it is entirely normal for a boy whose genitalia are in stages 3 or 4 not to have any pubic hair. Thus the appearance of pubic hair does not represent the beginning of puberty.

In most girls the breasts begin to develop before there is any growth of pubic hair and a girl without pubic hair, whose breasts are in stage 4, is not necessarily abnormal. However, in some normal girls the reverse situation arises and pubic hair may reach stage 3 or 4 before the breasts begin to develop. Axillary hair also may appear before the breast buds but in most girls the breasts are in stage 3 or 4 when the first axillary hair is seen.

Menarche usually occurs when the breasts are in stage 4 and is therefore rather late in the sequence of events at puberty. However, some 25 per cent of girls experience their first menses while the breasts are in stage 3 and about 10 per cent do not do so until their breasts are mature in appearance.

Girls, unlike boys, usually reach peak height velocity while their secondary sex characters are in early stages of development. Some 30 or 40 per cent do so when their breasts are in stage 2 and this implies that their growth is slowing down rather than accelerating throughout the remainder of the time in which their secondary sex characters are developing. Apparently, peak height velocity is always attained before menarche and there are no well-documented exceptions to this. Thus it is safe for practical purposes to assume that the growth of post-menarcheal girls is slowing down and will continue to do so until it stops.

Sex Difference in Age at Puberty

A 12 year old girl who has experienced her adolescent growth spurt at the average age will be growing at or near her maximum speed (PHV) whereas the majority of boys at this age are still growing at a preadolescent rate or just beginning to accelerate. A very small number, about 5 per cent, will have reached PHV. Those girls who mature later may not reach PHV until they are 14, that is at about the average age for boys.

The difference of two years between the sexes in the average age at peak height velocity does not accurately reflect the difference in age at which the secondary sex characters begin to appear. The boy's genitalia begin to develop on average only a few months later than the girl's breasts and the secondary sex characters reach their adult state at about the same age in the two sexes.

These clinical observations are at variance with the impression obtained in the normal course of life. Girls appear to reach puberty much earlier than boys because their growth spurt and breast development radically change their appearance, even when they are fully clothed, while the development of the genitalia in boys, although occurring at very nearly the same time, is not apparent when they are clothed. The more obvious signs in boys, the growth spurt, the appearance of facial hair and the breaking of the voice occur later.

Nutrition During Adolescence

An increased intake of nutrients is necessary to sustain the greatly accelerated growth which occurs during the adolescent spurt. The effect of undernutrition on the spurt is not known. One might envisage either that the total gain in stature would be reduced or, that the maximum growth rate achieved (PHV) would be less but that the continuation of somewhat accelerated growth for a longer period might compensate for this. Only detailed studies of undernourished adolescents with a well matched control sample of the same ethnic and cultural group would yield reliable information about this.

Evidence of undernutrition in adolescent populations is difficult to interpret. The rapid increase in haemoglobin levels which occurs during adolescence makes haemoglobin estimations, in relation to age, useless as a measure of the prevalence of anaemia in adolescent populations. A detailed study of the haemoglobin level at different stages of progress through adolescence, rather than age, might be more fruitful.

194

The same problem arises in interpreting measures of free protoporphyrin in circulating red blood cells as an index of iron deficient erythropoiesis. However, in the 12—16 year age group approximately 15 per cent of boys living in poverty have iron deficient erythropoiesis, which is found only in 3 per cent of boys in high income families (Smith, 1975). In girls of the same age group, some 20 per cent have iron deficient erythropoiesis with no difference between the rich and the poor groups. It must be remembered, however, that in terms of adolescence, this age group does not have the same meaning in the two sexes. Fifty per cent of the girls would probably have passed the peak of their growth spurts by the age of 12, begun to menstruate by 13 and stopped growing by about 16. In contrast, virtually all the boys would reach PHV within this range and very few would stop growing.

Overnutrition at adolescence, as at any other time of life, causes a tendency to accumulate fat. In boys, however, there is a tendency to lose fat from the limbs during the adolescent spurt (Tanner, 1965). This is due to the action of androgen and should not be taken as evidence of undernutrition.

Effects on Adolescence of Undernutrition in Childhood

Malnourished children apparently reach puberty at a later age than normal. However, information about population differences in the age at which changes of puberty, other than menarche, occur is confined almost entirely to developed European and American groups which show only slight differences from each other.

The age at menarche varies widely amongst different populations and socio-economic classes. Nutrition throughout childhood may be one of the factors leading to this variation. de Wijn (1966) observed a mean age at menarche of 13.8 years amongst Dutch girls whose fathers were in the lower and middle socio-economic groups as compared with 13.5 for the daughters of wealthier parents. A variation of up to six months is found in different parts of the United Kingdom and this seems to be largely associated with socio-economic conditions. In North-East England the number of children in the family is related to age at menarche, which is later in girls from large families and, once allowance is made for this, the difference between social classes is no longer apparent (Roberts et al, 1971). Wide differences between social classes are found in some countries and this may reflect more extreme differences between the richer and poorer classes in variables such as hygiene and nutrition. For example, in North-East Slovenia, poor girls menstruate almost a year later (14.2 years) than those described as of good social standing (13.3 years) [Kralj-Cercek, 1956]. In Turkish girls not only menarche but all stages of breast development are earlier in the higher than in the lower socio-economic groups (Neyzi et al, 1975). In India there is an average difference in age at menarche of about two years between the rich (12.8 years) and the poor (14.4 years) [Madhavan, 1965].

The effect of social status and family size on the age at menarche is generally thought to be due largely to nutrition although it is difficult to isolate the effects of undernutrition from other factors such as poor hygiene, or endemic disease which often accompany it.

Between modern European populations there are only slight differences in the average age at menarche, varying between about 12.9 years in Sweden (Ljung et al, 1974) and 13.4 years for the Netherlands (van Wieringen et al, 1968). The Italians are the exception to the general rule, being much earlier. A mean value of 12.5 years has been quoted for a poor rural population near Naples (Carfagna et al, 1972).

Some racial factors appear to have greater effect on menarcheal age than social conditions. For example, well-off Chinese girls in Hong Kong have menarche at a median age of 12.5 years (Chang, 1969) but in this population even poor girls begin to menstruate as early as Europeans in more favourable economic circumstances (Lee et al, 1963).

In Africa menarche is usually late, e.g. 13.4 years in Uganda and 14.1 in the Nigerian Ibo (Burgess & Burgess, 1964; Tanner & O'Keefe, 1962). However, no data are yet available concerning well-off Africans living in Africa.

The Melanesians of New Guinea exhibit the latest recorded median ages of menarche, different studies giving values ranging from 15.5 to 18.4 years (Malcolm, 1970; Wark & Malcolm, 1969).

There is evidence that menarche tends to be earlier in countries with higher temperatures (Roberts, 1969) and this is another factor which complicates any attempt to isolate the effects of nutrition from those of other variables.

The Trend Towards Earlier Menarche

During the last 100 years or so the age at menarche has become progressively earlier in North America, Europe and other parts of the world. Although some of the data are not entirely reliable, there appears to be little doubt that menarche has been getting earlier at an average rate of four months per decade in most developed populations. There is also some evidence that the adolescent spurt is becoming progressively earlier. The trend towards earlier menarche is apparently continuing in many parts of the world, although there is evidence that it may be stopping in London (Tanner, 1973) and Oslo (Bruntland & Wallφ, 1973). It is generally believed that this trend is due to improved health and nutrition and that it will stop when these reach optimal levels and the genetic potential of the population is achieved.

References

Bruntland, GH and Wallφ, L (1973) *Nature, 241,* 478
Burgess, AP and Burgess, HJL (1964) *Human Biology, 36,* 177

Carfagna, M, Figurelli, E, Matarese, G and Matarese, S (1972) *Human Biology, 44,* 117

Chang, KSF (1967) *Growth and Development of Chinese Children and Youth in Hong Kong.* University of Hong Kong

de Wijn, JF (1966) In *Somatic Growth of the Child.* (Ed) JJ van der Werff ten Bosch and A Haak. Stenfert Kroese, Leiden. Page 16

Kralj-Cercek, L (1956) *Human Biology, 28,* 398

Lee, MC, Chang, KSF and Chan, MMC (1963) *Paediatrics, 42,* 389

Ljung, B, Bergsten-Brucefors, A and Lindgren, G (1974) *Annals of Human Biology, 1,* 245

Madhavan, S (1965) *Indian Journal of Medical Research, 53,* 669

Malcolm, LA (1970) *Human Biology, 42,* 293

Marshall, WA and Tanner, JM (1969) *Archives of Disease in Childhood, 44,* 291

Marshall, WA and Tanner, JM (1970) *Archives of Disease in Childhood, 45,* 13

Neyzi, O, Alp, H and Orhon, A (1975) *Annals of Human Biology, 2,* 49

Neyzi, O, Alp, H, Yalcindag, A, Yakacikli, S and Orhon, A (1975) *Annals of Human Biology, 2,* 251

Roberts, DF (1969) *Journal of the Biosocial Society, Suppl. 1,* 43

Roberts, DF, Rozner, LM and Swan, AV (1971) *Acta Paediatrica Scandinavica, 60,* 158

Smith, NJ (1975) In *Puberty.* (Ed) SR Berenberg. Stenfert Kroese, Leiden

Tanner, JM (1962) *Growth at Adolescence, 2nd Edition.* Blackwell Scientific, Oxford

Tanner, JM (1965) In *Body Composition. Symposia of the Society for the Study of Human Biology, Vol.6.* (Ed) GA Harrison. Pergamon Press, Oxford

Tanner, JM (1973) *Nature, 243,* 95

Tanner, JM and O'Keefe, B (1962) *Human Biology, 34,* 187

van Wieringen, JC, Wafelbakker, F, Vebrugge, HP and de Haas, JH (1968) *Groeidiagrammen nederland 1965.* Wolters-Noordhoff n.v., Groningen

Wark, ML and Malcolm, MA (1969) *Medical Journal of Australia, 2,* 129

Sachmann, M, Prader, A, Kind, HP, Haflinger, H and Budlinger, H (1974) *Helvetica Paediatrica Acta, 29,* 61

Hormonal Aspects of Growth and Composition of the Body

D LISTER
ARC Meat Research Institute, Bristol, England

"Man is not a rat"; neither, one might add to Edholm's (1971) aphorism is he a pig. There are, nevertheless, striking comparisons that can be drawn between men, pigs and rats which help us in the search for a better understanding of the mechanisms controlling growth, energy balance, or, the partition of dietary constituents between somatic tissues.

Human beings differ in stature, corpulence, activity and so forth which, apart from some familial tendencies, appear to be spread randomly within populations. Attempts to interfere with this pattern have, happily, had little success. Animal breeding, on the other hand, progresses by the identification of particular physiological and metabolic characteristics in populations of animals and the juggling of such criteria to improve growth rates, leanness or the efficiency with which food is converted to bodily tissues. The chicken has been most affected by genetic selection, but I would be reluctant to offer it as a complete model for human growth and development. The pig has also been similarly manipulated and offers more scope for anthropomorphism, but I shall leave that aspect to others. In this paper I shall try to collate some of our, and others', observations on hormonal and metabolic features which are, for the most part, genetically determined characteristics of pigs differing widely in body type and growth.

A major concern in animal production is the efficiency with which feed energy is used for growth. This depends on the animal's ability to consume food, to partition it between the tissues of the body and on the so-called maintenance requirement of the animal (for review see Webster, 1976). In practical terms efficiency of feed use will be reflected by an animal's appetite and by the extent and composition of the bodily gain. There are indications that reproductive efficiency can be similarly characterised (Frisch, 1976). In our work we have

198

limited the scope of investigations to consider the hormonal control of energy balance and energy-protein interactions, thus to provide an endocrinological framework on which the specific actions of other hormones may depend or impinge.

BODY COMPOSITION

Over the last 100-150 years the domestic pig has been modified both by breeding and improved nutrition. Originally its job was to store as body tissue, mainly fat, summer surpluses of perishable food against winter scarcity (hence lard and larder). The typical 'lard' pig is not now represented in pig production in the western world which requires pigs to have a minimum capacity to retain fat in their carcases. It is possible, however, to identify genotypes within a population which possess distinct physiological propensities. In our work we have used fatter strains of the Large White breed of pig and compared them with exceptionally lean strains of the Belgian Pietrain breed which at the same body weight may contain 10% more muscle than the Large Whites. In human terms these might represent extremes of endo- and mesomorphism.

There is no doubt that the carcases of pigs reared today contain proportionately more lean tissue than those of earlier generations. It is also evident that the age of slaughter has been reduced although of late the reduction has not been so marked. Less clear, however, are the ways in which these changes have been achieved, i.e. whether by improved nutrition, housing or breeding. The physiological mechanisms responsible for the genetic changes are only now being fortified.

The question which still has not been answered satisfactorily is whether the apparent leanness of today's carcases results from an increased ability of animals to deposit lean tissue, or from a reduced ability to deposit fat. Our recent work and that of others suggests that it may be this latter which differs most between genotypes and accounts for the differences in body composition (Perry et al, 1973; Wood, 1973; Fuller et al, 1974).

In our experiments Large White pigs were pair fed with Pietrains to the latter's lower voluntary food intake from the same starting weight (20 kg) for a fixed period of time when each animal had consumed the same total amount of food. At slaughter at about 45 kg, the Large Whites were heavier than the Pietrains by an amount equivalent to the extra fat which they had deposited even though they had consumed the same amount of food as their Pietrain mates. Over the same period of time, both breeds had deposited identical amounts of muscle. The practical consequences of this pattern of tissue deposition can be seen in Figure 1 which is based on unpublished information from recent experiments conducted in our laboratory in which Pietrain and Large White pigs were fed ad libitum. In this case allowing the Large Whites to satisfy their larger appetite served only to increase further the greater amount of fat they deposited. The

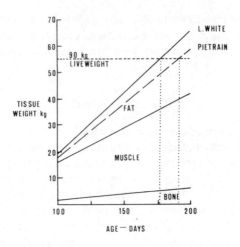

Figure 1. Age related changes in tissue growth — pigs

apparent leanness of Pietrain pigs at 90 kg liveweight is thus attributable to their reduced fat deposition which requires them to take a longer period of time to reach the usual slaughter weight. During the extra 10 days required to attain this they deposited more muscle, but only that amount which Large Whites would have deposited in the same period. This comparison illustrates that between breeds that are as obviously different in carcase composition as Pietrains and Large Whites there may be an easily measurable difference in the rate at which fat is deposited but no obvious difference in the rate of lean tissue deposition.

The realisation that differences in fat were more important than differences in protein metabolism in determining the body forms of the two pig breeds caused us to look more closely at other aspects of the lipogenesis and fat deposition. It had been recognised that the backfat of lean breeds of pig was inclined to be soft at room temperature, a property related to the proportions of saturated and unsaturated fatty acids it contained (Lea et al, 1970). This was firmly established for Pietrain pigs (Wood, 1973) but its cause was not entirely clear for both the amount of food consumed and its composition are known to influence the composition of body fat. Wood (1973), however, was able to show that these did not account entirely for the compositional differences between the fat of Pietrains and Large Whites fed identical amounts of the same diet; Pietrains still deposited relatively more unsaturated fat than Large Whites.

Other investigations have shown that the utilisation of free or nonesterified, fatty acids (FFA) is greater in both fed and fasting Pietrains (Wood, unpublished observations), and that fatty acids are more readily mobilised from the adipose tissue of these animals has recently been confirmed using infusions of noradrenaline into pigs fitted with in-dwelling venous cannulas (Wood et al, 1976, but see also Lister, 1976).

200

HORMONAL MECHANISMS

The results of these experiments taken together suggest that the higher heat production of Pietrains is supported to a greater extent by fatty acid metabolism than by carbohydrate metabolism which appears to predominate in Large Whites. This is borne out still further by measurements of fasting plasma levels of FFA and insulin which are higher and lower respectively in Pietrains compared with Large Whites. Furthermore insulin levels in blood are stimulated by tolbutamide to a lesser degree in Pietrains than they are in Large Whites.

In view of the major lipogenic and antilipolytic effects of insulin we were interested to know whether fasting insulin concentrations in plasma might profitably be used to predict the amounts of body fat in the two breeds of pig. The work of Bagdade et al (1967) in human beings showed a significant correlation between the percentage of ideal body weight and the levels of circulating insulin and, of course, it has been well established that obese people have higher blood insulin concentrations. In our work (Gregory et al, 1976; Gregory, 1976) we used pigs of the two breeds kept in metabolic crates and fed identically. Blood samples were taken at standard times via in-dwelling cannulas and analysed in various ways. At the end of the experiments the animals were slaughtered and the amounts of the fat, muscle and bone in the body measured. In general plasma insulin correlated poorly with absolute tissue weights but rather well ($P < 0.05$) – both within and between breeds – with the proportion of muscle and fat or some index of it. This would seem to add support to the notion that in addition to any effect it might have on lipogenesis, insulin also affects protein deposition, apparently by enhancing the uptake of certain amino acids, by stimulating the protein-synthetic machinery inside the muscle cell and by inhibiting proteolysis (Cahill et al, 1972).

Given the same amount of food, Large White pigs retain more of it as body mass than Pietrains, and far more in energetic terms. On this basis Pietrains appear to have a higher heat production. By the same token and on clinical observation one might expect to find the Pietrain to be hyperthyroid relative to the Large White. Measurements of some index of the circulating levels of free biologically active thyroid hormone, for example the free thyroxine index (FTI), however, suggest the contrary (Lister, 1972). Close investigation revealed that both the secretion and utilisation, of thyroid hormones is raised in Pietrains (Moss, 1975; Lister, 1976) and that the lowered values for FTI in the serum of pigs reflected a higher rate of utilisation of hormone which momentarily was raised even further and was not matched by an increased secretion rate when the animals were retrained for blood sampling. The rate of peripheral utilisation of thyroid hormone is increased by a variety of stimuli apart from excitement including cold, exercise and fatigue. Recent work from our laboratory suggests that α-adrenergic stimulation may be responsible. When anaesthetised Pietrains are given the depolarising muscle relaxant suxamethonium they develop a massive acidosis and hyperthermia and eventually they may die. The extreme stimulation of muscle induced by such a treatment is associated with a fall in the serum FTI. This fall, and the fatal hyperthermia may be prevented by the administration of large doses of α-adrenergic blocking agents such as phentolamine, prior to the administration of suxamethonium. The usual substantial (> 30–50 fold) rise in catecholamines, predominantly noradrenaline, still occurs but its metabolic effects are suppressed (Lister et al, 1974). α-blockade similarly reduces the fall in FTI which occurs during blood sampling of the conscious animal. These observations compare with those of Melander (1971) who showed that α-adrenergic stimulation was involved in the TSH-induced release of thyroid hormones and provide the evidence for a distinct contribution of the sympathetic nervous system in the control of thyroid function. Our latest results have confirmed that resting TSH levels are significantly higher in Pietrains (5.1 $\pm$ 0.4 μU/ml) than in Large White pigs (3.2 $\pm$ 0.5 μU/ml).

IMPLICATIONS

Although this work is at a relatively early stage, a number of issues have emerged which identify possible practical contributions of neuro-endocrine responses to the control of energy balance and the composition of the body of normal, healthy individuals. The question remains of whether the Pietrain/Large White model is relevant to pigs generally such that the animal breeder simply alters the physiological type 'Large White' to 'Pietrain', when he selects and breeds animals to become leaner. There are two series of experiments which suggest that this may well be the case. They also indicate how variations in the growth of the lean body mass arise for, although it was convenient for the interpretation of the experimental findings that our Pietrains and Large Whites accumulated lean body at similar rates, this result must have been fortuitous for all genotypes of pigs do not possess the same ability for lean deposition.

Standal and his colleagues in Norway (Standal et al, 1973) found that when animals were selected to produce less backfat there was also an associated increase in the rate of deposition of lean tissue. Nevertheless, the physiology of these pigs measured in terms of lipid mobilisation from fatty tissue in vitro, the fatty acid composition of the depot fats (Vold, 1974) and the fasting levels of plasma FFA (Bakke, 1975) became increasingly 'Pietrain'. Hetzer and his coworkers in the United States showed that selection for less backfat also promoted lean deposition in the relatively fat Duroc breed, but only curtailed even further the limited deposition of fat in the Yorkshire breed in a manner reminiscent of the Pietrain (Hetzer & Miller, 1973).

It seems, therefore, that a physiology which allows animals to restrict the deposition of fat may well also limit the ability to deposit protein. There is evidence also (Davey & Morgan, 1969; Davey et al, 1969) that fatter animals deposit more protein with additional dietary protein whereas the leanest animals respond only to increased dietary energy. Thus excessive leanness is not only liable to prove energetically inefficient but it may also prejudice the efficiency with which protein is deposited. For maximum efficiency in the use of food it appears necessary for the deposition of protein to be combined with a fixed proportion of fat.

The role of the mechanisms controlling energy balance is obviously critical in this discussion and it is from this point of view that we have tried to elucidate the role of hormones. Catecholamines and the sympathetic nervous system are of major importance in the more bizarre metabolic responses of Pietrain pigs (Lister et al, 1974; Lucke et al, 1976). It may well be that such sensitivity to stress is not simply a feature associated with mesomorphism, but a direct cause of it and a regulatory mechanism for body form generally. Insulin, catecholamines and thyroid hormones have well established roles in the control of lipolysis and lipogenesis but there are other associations of importance in the present context which have been described in recent reviews (Turner & Munday, 1976). The control of food intake via the hypothalamus is one such consideration. Catecholamines have profound effects on eating and satiety (Bray, 1974). and tend to be anorexic (Porte & Robertson, 1973). The reduced voluntary food intake of the Pietrain may result from this and the suppression of insulin which has additional effects on protein and fat deposition. These ideas provide only the starting hypothesis for investigation.

The animal physiologist is at a considerable advantage over his counterpart in human medicine in investigations of this nature. We can always kill and dissect the carcase of experimental animals to validate our findings. The opportunity to do this in studies on human beings is becoming increasingly rare! However, I have recently been attempting to provide, for farm animal species, diagnostic criteria which do not necessarily require the slaughter of an animal to relate hormonal status in the terms described above to body composition or form. 'Pietrain like' individuals deposit relatively more of their fat internally, i.e. intra abdominally and intermuscularly and less subcutaneously than 'Large White like' animals. The identification of this pattern of deposition or some index of it can be accomplished by indirect means. The same pattern of fat partition is to be found in cattle and sheep (Lister, 1973 and in preparation). It would be surprising indeed if the same characteristics were not to be found in human beings. Indeed, the pattern can be identified quite clearly from mice to elephants and might offer a basis for the linking of anatomy and physiology of growth.

Acknowledgment

My colleagues Drs JD Wood, BN Perry and NG Gregory have contributed substantially to the development of the philosophy expressed in this paper, which is based on a contribution to a NATO advanced Study Institute, the proceedings

203

of which are published in *Meat Animals: Growth and Productivity.* (Ed) D Lister, DN Rhodes, VR Fowler and MF Fuller. Plenum Press, London and New York (1976)

References

Bagdade, JD, Bierman, EL and Porte, D (1967) *Journal of Clinical Investigation, 46,* 1549

Bakke, H (1975) *Acta Agriculturae Scandinavica, 25,* 113

Bray, GA (1974) *Federation Proceedings, 33,* 1140

Cahill, GF, Aoki, TT and Marliss, EG (1972) In *Handbook of Physiology, Section 7, Volume 1 – Endocrine Pancreas.* Williams & Wilkins, Baltimore. Page 563

Davey, RJ and Morgan, DP (1969) *Journal of Animal Science, 28,* 831

Davey, RJ, Morgan, DP and Kincaid, CM (1969) *Journal of Animal Science, 28,* 197

Edholm, OG (1971) quoted by Garrow, JS (1974) *Energy Balance and Obesity in Man.* North Holland Publishing Company, Amsterdam and London

Frisch, RE (1976) In *Meat Animals: Growth and Productivity.* (Ed) D Lister, DN Rhodes, VR Fowler and MF Fuller. Plenum Press, London and New York. Page 327

Fuller, MF, Yen, HT and Lin, HS (1974) *Proceedings of the British Society of Animal Production, 3,* 86

Gregory, NG (1976) PhD Thesis, University of Bristol (in preparation)

Gregory, NG, Wood, JD and Lister, D (1976) *Proceedings of the British Society of Animal Production* (in press)

Hetzer, HO and Miller, RH (1973) *Journal of Animal Science, 35,* 730, 743

Lea, CH, Swoboda, PAT and Gatherum, DP (1970) *Journal of Agricultural Science, Cambridge, 74,* 279

Lister, D (1972) In *Proceedings of the European Association for Animal Production Pigs Commission, Verona, Italy*

Lister, D (1973) *Proceedings of the British Society of Animal Production, 2,* 88

Lister, D (1974) *Proceedings of the British Society of Animal Production, 3,* 87

Lister, D (1976) In *Meat Animals: Growth and Productivity.* (Ed) D Lister, DN Rhodes, VR Fowler and MF Fuller. Plenum Press, London and New York. Page 355

Lister, D, Hall, GM and Lucke, JN (1974) *British Journal of Anaesthesia, 46,* 803

Lister, D, Hall, GM and Lucke, JN (1975) *Lancet, i,* 519

Lucke, JN, Hall, GM and Lister, D (1976) *British Journal of Anaesthesia, 48,* 297

Moss, BW (1975) PhD Thesis, University of Bristol

Melander, A (1971) *Acta Endocrinologica, 66,* 151

Perry, BN, Wood, JD and Lister, D (1973) *Proceedings of the British Society of Animal Production, 2,* 88

Porte, D and Robertson, RP (1973) *Federation Proceedings, 32,* 1792

Standal, N, Vold, E, Trygstad, O and Foss, I (1973) *Animal Production, 16,* 37

Turner, MJ and Munday, KA (1976) In *Meat Animals: Growth and Productivity.* (Ed) D Lister, DN Rhodes, VR Fowler and MF Fuller. Plenum Press, London and New York. Page 197

Vold, E (1974) In *Proceedings of the 20th European Meeting of Meat Research Workers, Dublin.* Page 176

Wood, JD (1973) *Animal Production, 17,* 281

Wood, JD (1974) *Proceedings of the Nutrition Society, 33,* 61A

Wood, JD, Gregory, NG, Hall, GM and Lister, D (1976) *British Journal of Nutrition* (submitted for publication)

Webster, AJF (1976) In *Meat Animals: Growth and Productivity.* (Ed) D Lister, DN Rhodes, VR Fowler and MF Fuller. Plenum Press, London and New York. Page 89.

Interactions of Nutrition, Food and Drugs

A S TRUSWELL
Queen Elizabeth College, London, England

In the broadest sense there are as many as six ways in which drugs, food and nutrition can interact, using the term 'drugs' in the wider meaning of the English word.

1. Some foods interfere with the absorption of particular drugs.
2. Nutritional status may affect the distribution or metabolism of some drugs and hence lead to toxicity or ineffectiveness unless the dose is adjusted.
3. Drugs can affect nutritional status, leading to altered biochemical tests or even clinical under-, mal- or over-nutrition.
4. Some drugs make normally harmless minor substances in foods become toxic, e.g. cheese becomes dangerous in patients taking monoamine oxidase inhibitors.
5. Some components of ordinary meals are consumed for their drug effects, e.g. alcoholic beverages, tea and coffee.
6. The essential nutrients are all obtainable in pure form.

With one or two exceptions they are now relatively inexpensive and several are used for pharmacological actions, usually in doses much larger than their recommended daily intakes as nutrients.

These six different groups of interaction and interchange are somewhat confusing so I have put them in shorthand form in Table I.

TABLE I

1. Foods can affect drugs	4. Drugs can affect foods
2. Nutrition can affect drugs	5. Drugs are used as food
3. Drugs can affect nutrition	6. Nutrients are used as drugs

FOODS CAN AFFECT DRUGS

In general foods tend to delay absorption of drugs taken at the same time both because access to the gastro-intestinal wall is impeded and because of delayed gastric emptying. We know most about this in the case of oral antibiotics. For many other drugs there is less information. Prior ingestion of food is associated with lower blood levels of many oral penicillins, erythromycin salts and linco-mycin but penicillin V (phenoxymethyl penicillin) and clinimycin are not affected (Krondl, 1970). This effect of food on penicillins is probably due to stimulation of gastric HC1; it does not occur in patients with achlorhydria.

Blood levels of demethyl-chlortetracycline are reduced when it is taken orally at the same time as milk, buttermilk or cottage cheese. Other types of meal did not have this effect (Scheiner & Altemeier, 1962) which may be due to chelation of demethylchlortetracycline by calcium caseinate. A preceding fatty meal increases serum levels of griseofulvin; the more fat in the meal the greater the effect (Crounse, 1961; Beare, 1968). This is due to differential solubility, griseofulvin being more soluble in fat than water.

A third way in which food can interfere with drug absorption is from precipitation of insoluble salts. Phytic acid in unrefined cereals and some other plant foods precipitates copper, zinc, iron and calcium. Large intakes of 'dietary fibre' than the cellulose seem to have the major activity (Ershoff, 1974). Possibly diets high in fibre could interfere with absorption and require larger doses of some drugs in man. The effect of foods on drug absorption is not always negative. One example of a synergistic effect is the enhanced absorption of iron when it is taken with fruit, fruit juice (sources of ascorbic acid) as well as meat (IAEA/USAID/WHO, 1975).

NUTRITION CAN AFFECT DRUGS

Most of the small number of experiments in laboratory animals have been concerned with protein-calorie malnutrition and with drug metabolism by the liver microsomal system. There is very little information about drug metabolism in other organs, by other enzyme systems and in deficiencies of minerals or vitamins. Activity of the hepatic microsomal drug metabolising system varies with age and sex. It can be induced by a number of relatively non-polar foreign compounds, including insecticides and drugs like barbiturates. When microsomal enzyme activity is induced, drugs are metabolised more rapidly. A few toxic agents and severe liver disease can, on the other hand inhibit liver microsomes. There are genetic differences in microsomal activity. In all these different circumstances there are differences in the rates of metabolism of individual drugs but they tend to show group behaviour, depending partly on the way in which they become bound to cytochrome P-450 and alter its spectral absorption characteristics. Ethylmorphine and phenobarbital are examples of type I substrates while aniline and aminopyrine are type II substrate. Azo and nitro-reduction occur in microsomes and require NADPH but not oxygen, unlike other compounds. The synthetic conjugation reactions are chemically different, e.g. glucuronide formation.

Starvation for 36 hours decreased the ability of male mice to metabolise, in vivo and in vitro, hexobarbital (aliphatic oxidation), chlorpromazine (sulphur oxidation), aminopyrine (N-dealkylation) and acetanilid (aromatic hydroxyla-tion) but nitro- and azo-reductions were not impaired (Dixon et al, 1960). In rats the effect depends on the sex of the animals. Hexobarbital and aminopyrine metabolism are normally three times greater in male livers than female. Starvation for 72 hours reduced the metabolism of these drugs in male rats but increased it in females: metabolism of aniline, which shows no sex-dependence, was enhanced in male rats. The differences between male and female rats were abolished by castration and restored with testosterone (Kato & Gillette, 1965). Glucuronide conjugation is reduced in vivo (Parke, 1968). One of the enzymes involved, UDP glucose dehydrogenase in the cytoplasm, is increased in activity (Miettinen & Leskinen, 1963) but glucuronide formation depends on adequate liver glycogen stores, which are depleted in starvation.

In rats *undernourished* during the first 3 weeks after birth, the activity of drug-metabolising enzymes has not been found to be changed when expressed *per g. of liver* (Basu & Dickerson, 1974). Total liver activity is reduced because the livers are smaller. However there is a good response to inducing agents, in which animals with early undernutrition resemble immature animals.

Low protein diets in male and female rats are associated with reduced cyto-chrome P-450 per unit of liver weight. Increased toxicities of pentobarbital, strychnine and zoxazolamine, aniline and aminopyrine (Kato et al, 1968) and paracetamol(McLean & Day, 1975) and dieldrin (Lee et al, 1964; Krishnamurthy et al, 1965) have been reported. On the other hand, the toxicity of carbon tetrachloride (Campbell and Kosterlitz, 1948; McLean & McLean, 1966) and the lethal effect of dimethylnitrosamine (McLean & Verschuuren, 1969) are *reduced* in rats given low protein diets, apparently because each gives rise to a metabolite which is more toxic than the parent substrate.

When an inducing substance, phenobarbitone was given to rats on 3% casein diets, hepatic concentration of cytochrome P-450 increased from 23 to 81 nmoles/g compared with 40 nmoles on a normal diet unstimulated and 142 nmoles/g after phenobarbitone (McLean & Day, 1975) Dickerson et al, (1976) measured the metabolism of 3 substrates in liver homogenates from immature rats fed either a 7% protein diet ad libitum or a control diet or the control diet fed to provide protein equal to that consumed by the low protein group. Glucuronyl transferase was depressed more by the low energy than the low protein diet; cytochrome P-450 concentration was reduced more by the low protein diet. Aromatic hydroxylation (with biphenyl as substrate) was reduced in activity per g. liver at first but after 2 weeks this *increased* in the low protein group, enough to compensate for the smaller liver weight. Activity per liver was now the same as in controls. Nitroreductase (with p-nitrobenzoate as substrate) concentration was reduced more by protein than energy deficiency and activity per liver remained half that in the controls. Dickerson suggests that the late adaptive changes can be explained by the synchronous increase in endogenous corticosteroids (Basu et al, 1975a).

Other components of the diet can affect liver microsomal activity under rather extreme conditions. Dietary fats are needed for full activity and inducibility. This does not appear to be related to EFA: fish and linseed oils have more effect than sunflower or corn oil (Century, 1973; Marshall & McLean, 1971 a and b) the antioxidant BHA reduced the effect of polyunsaturated oil (McLean & Marshall, 1971) which might therefore be due to fatty acid hydroperoxides (McLean, 1974). In weanling rats fed 60% sucrose but otherwise adequate diets Basu et al (1975b) found lower aromatic hydroxylation activity per g. of liver and prolonged sleeping time after hexobarbital, but in adult rats Bender et al, (1973) find a shortened sleeping time after pentobarbitone possibly because the liver is enlarged.

It would be unwise to extrapolate from these animal experiments to patients. Men who fasted 7 days (but for obesity) showed no change in metabolic clearance of antipyrine or tolbutamide (Reidenberg & Vesell, 1975). Starvation is usually dealt with quickly, if necessary by intravenous infusion, once a malnourished child comes into hospital. Dosages are usually worked out per kg body weight, which may allow for reduced metabolising activity for many drugs. But other drugs are metabolised in different ways, e.g. glycine or sulphate conjugation or methylation by 5-adenosylmethionine might all be affected by protein deficiency. Absorption of drugs given by mouth may be impaired in malnourished children with diminished gastrointestinal enzymes and atrophic intestinal mucosa. A low plasma albumin concentration, on the other hand, may potentiate the effect of drugs which are carried in plasma mostly bound to protein, by increasing the free/bound drug ratio.

There have been few reports about sensitivity (or resistance) to drugs or studies of drug metabolism *in children with protein-calorie malnutrition.* What is known of the subject has been reviewed by Poskitt (1974) and Truswell, (1975a).

It might be expected that oral antibiotic syrups, which are usually in the form of an ester, would not be digested because of the diminished pancreatic lipase in untreated PCM (Barbezat & Hansen, 1968) but the blood level of chloramphenicol is adequate when it is given orally as the palmitate (Wittman et al, unpublished).

In Uganda metabolic studies were made with three useful drugs in the former MRC Child Nutrition Unit. Urinary metabolites of chloroquine did not appear to be grossly different in kwashiorkor from the considerable range in controls (Wharton & McChesney, 1970). Tetrachlorethylene in a standard single dose

209

(0.1mg/kg) was associated with transient possible side effects in only 2 out of 43 children with kwashiorkor; biochemical liver function tests did not change and hookworm counts were greatly reduced (Balmer et al, 1970). The antibacterial agent trimethoprim was associated with increased urinary FIG1u after 10 days in kwashiorkor, compared with control children (Poskitt & Parkin, 1972).

This last example raises the question that several of the antibiotics and chemotherapeutic agents, used so commonly in malnourished children, act by interfering with nutrition at the cellular level. Trimethoprim and pyrimethamine are folate antagonists in micro-organisms, and potentially so in human cells (Waxman & Herbert, 1969). Tetracycline causes a negative nitrogen balance in normal people (Shils, 1963) and chloramphenicol interferes with mitochondrial protein synthesis (Weinstein, 1970).

Buchanan, in Johannesburg, has started some new lines of investigation of drug metabolism in children with kwashiorkor. Intramuscular benzylpenicillin gave good peak levels in the blood and they fell off more slowly in untreated children, possibly because of impaired renal function (Buchanan et al, 1976). In an in vitro dialysis system, the binding of sodium salicylate by serum from children with kwashiorkor was less than half that in normals (Eyberg et al, 1974) Salicylate is normally more than 80% bound to plasma albumin (Koch-Weser & Sellers, 1976).

Other common drugs that are strongly bound include cloxacillin (95%), sulphisoxazole ('Gantrisin') (94%), indomethacin (97%), diazepam ('valium') (99%), phenytoin (91%), frusemide (97%) and thiopentone ('Pentothal') (87%) (Koch-Weser & Sellers, 1976). Patients with low plasma albumin (mostly not from primary malnutrition) have been reported to show increased sensitivity to phenytoin (Porter & Layzer, 1975), diazepam and prednisone (Greenblatt & Koch-Weser, 1974) and to have an increase of unbound frusemide (Prandota & Pruit, 1975). I have never read or heard of direct experience with thiopentone in malnourished children but Quimby (1972) states that thiopentone will diffuse more rapidly into the brain in patients with lowered plasma proteins, so the dose for induction of anaesthesia must be smaller and it should be given in small increments, waiting about a minute between each and observing consciousness and vital signs.

As well as protein and energy there may well be other micronutrients whose levels in the body can affect drug metabolism. An obvious example is that potassium depletion or hypercalcaemia predispose to digitalis toxicity. There is at present, however, very little systematic information.

DRUGS CAN AFFECT NUTRITIONAL STATUS

The following is a selection of effects that may be encountered in paediatric practice.

Appetite   Apart from the anorectic agents like diethylpropion ('Tenuate') and fenfluramine ('Ponderax') many other drugs can reduce appetite and some do so often. If appetite is suppressed for weeks there can be much loss of weight. Almost every drug data sheet metnions nausea and vomiting as possible adverse reactions. If they occur anorexia accompanies them. Some drugs that commonly cause anorexia include digitalis, oral antibiotics, opiates, biguanides, indomethacin, glucagon, mustine and cyclophosphamide. Any experienced practitioner can add to this list from his own experience. A smaller number of drugs are liable to increase appetite and so produce a weight gain (Editorial, 1974) such as sulphonylureas, cyptroheptidine ('Periactin'), chlorpromazine, amitriptyline, lithium carbonate, corticosteroids, anabolic agents, oral contraceptives and insulin.

Malabsorption (Longstreth & Newcomer, 1975; Roe, 1974; Douglas, 1974; Dobbins, 1968). Several drugs are liable to produce some degree of malabsorption. The first group usually have multiple effects: neomycin, and to a lesser extent kanamycin, colchicine, methotrexate, fluorouracil, laxatives, cholestyramine and ethanol. Other drugs usually affect only a single or small number of functions. PAS, biguanides (vitamin B_{12}) potassium chloride (vitamin B_{12}), mineral oil (fat-soluble vitamins), sulphasalazine ('Salazophyrin') (folate).

Carbohydrate Tolerance is imparied by corticosteroids, thiazide diuretics, diazoxide, some oral contraceptives, glucagon and phenytoin (Malherbe et al, 1972), nicotinic acid in large doses, and, catecholamines. Drugs which tend to lower blood sugar, include as well as insulin, sulphonylureas and biguanides, β-adrenergic blockers (e.g. propranol), alcohol and salicylates.

The effects of drugs on carbohydrate metabolism have been reviewed by Marks (1974) and on *lipid metabolism* by Truswell, (1974).

Protein Metabolism Adrenal corticosteroids, thyroid hormones, vaccines (Gandra & Scrimshaw, 1961) and tetracyclines (Shils, 1973; Korkeila, 1971) except doxycycline ('Vibramycin') (Editorial, 1972a) cause increased nitrogen excretion in the urine and negative nitrogen balance.

A few drugs are known to affect fasting plasma amino acid patterns and there may be more. Oral contraceptives (Craft & Wise, 1969) and insulin (Cahill et al, 1972) lower and tranylcypromine ('Parnate') elevates (Davis, 1972) the plasma concentrations of several amino acids. Co-trimoxazole and methotrexate interfere with phenylalamine metabolism (England and Coles, 1972).

Folate Alcohol (Halsted et al, 1967), cycloserine (Klipstein et al, 1967) and oral contraceptives (Streiff, 1970) may all antagonise folate. Folate-responsive megaloblastic anaemia is a well-known side effect of long-term treatment with anticonvulsants (Reynolds, 1973), usually combinations of phenytoin with phenobarbital or primidone. Administration of folic acid to epileptics with low red cell folate, however, tends to lower blood phenytoin levels and can precipitate fits (Bayliss et al, 1971). The most likely explanation is that anticonvulsant drugs induce hepatic microsomal drug oxidising enzymes, which are known to require folate as co-factor (Maxwell et al, 1972). Some workers report that folate absorption is impaired by phenytoin (Gerson et al, 1972) but others have not found this (Fehling et al, 1973). Methotrexate is a structural analogue of folate; it owes its cytotoxic action to competitive inhibition of folate reductase. Pyrimethamine ('Daraprim') and trimethoprim-sulphamethoxazole (co-trimoxazole, 'Bactrim') are inhibitors of dihydrofolate reductase in plasmodia and bacteria, but in special circumstances they can occasionally precipitate megaloblastic anaemia in man (Waxman & Herbert, 1969; Chanarin & England, 1972, El Tamtamy, 1974).

Vitamin D Epileptics on long-term anticonvulsants have a greatly increased risk of rickets or osteomalacia. This side effect was first reported by Kruse (1968) and Dent et al (1970) and has since been found in several temperate countires. In such patients raised alkaline phospatase and low serum calcium are common (Tolman et al, 1975) and bone mineral is subnormal (Christiansen et al, 1972). Plasma 25-hydroxy vitamin D is reduced and vitamin D metabolism is accelerated (Editorial, 1972b) probably because of hepatic microsomal induction by the drugs and is shown by an increase in the urinary output of D-glucaric acid (Hunter et al, 1971). The disease responds to vitamin D treatment, usually in ordinary therapeutic doses (Silver, 1974; Peterson et al, 1976). A report from Nigeria suggests that anticonvulsant osteomalacia may not occur in sunny tropical countries (Apantaku et al, 1975). This type of vitamin D deficiency is not confined to epileptics. It has been reported in association with signs of hepatic microsomal induction in a woman who took the hypnotic glutethimide ('Doriden') every night for 10 years (Greenwood et al, 1973).

Potassium Deficiency may be induced by drugs. This is important and well-known. Long term purgatives can produce faecal loss and diuretics like the thiazides, frusemide ('Lasix') and ethacrynic acid can produce renal loss of potassium. After measuring total body potassium, Dargie et al (1974) question whether potassium supplementation is necessary in uncomplicated hypertensives taking frusemide.

Calcium Aluminium hydroxide and cholestyramine (Briscoe & Ragan, 1963) increase calcium absorption. Adrenal corticosteroids reduce it, possibly by antagonising vitamin D (Kimberg, 1969). Thiazide diuretics decrease the urinary output of calcium (Parfitt, 1969). Serum calcium is reduced by phosphates (Thalassinos & Joplin, 1968) and by mithramycin (Singer et al, 1970).

Iron Allopurinol (Hoenig et al, 1967), fructose (Davis & Deller, 1967) and ascorbic acid (Callender & Warner, 1969) increase iron absorption. Phosphates, antacids (Herbert, 1970) tetracycline (Greenberger et al, 1966) and cholestyramine (Greenberger, 1973) can reduce absorption. Plasma iron concentration is increased by oral contraceptives, as is total iron-binding capacity (Mardell & Zilva, 1967). The most important way in which drugs produce iron depletion is indirectly by gastro-intestinal bleeding following the consumption of aspirins and related analgesics.

Iodine Sulphonylureas, phenylbutazone, cobalt (Blacow & Wade, 1972),

PAS (Torikai & Kumaska, 1956) and lithium (Temple et al, 1972) interfere with ^{131}I uptake or release and can cause goitre. Plasma protein-bound iodine is reduced by phenytoin (Drug and Therapeutics Bulletin, 1972) and increased by oral contraceptives (thyroxine-binding globulin) (Catt, 1971), X-ray contrast media and cough medicines containing potassium iodide.

The above is only a selection. I have reviewed elsewhere the effects of drugs on some 18 nutrients (Truswell, 1973). The list continues to grow and very little is known about many of the more recently discovered nutrients.

DRUGS CAN AFFECT FOODS

Some drugs make normally harmless minor substances in foods toxic. The outstanding examples are the MAO inhibitors (Table II), used as second-line drugs for depression. Tyramine and related amines (Asatoor et al, 1963) in certain foods are not quickly metabolised as normally happens and they elevate the blood pressure and a severe reaction may occur. Foods to avoid include cheese (especially strong cheddar, Camembert and Stilton), game, yogurt, stored liver, 'Marmite', 'Bovril', pickled herrings, broad beans, Chianti wine and chocolate.

TABLE II MAO inhibitors that have been reported to cause the 'Cheese Reaction'

> Phenelzine ('Nardil')
> Tranylcypromine ('Parnate', 'Parstelin')
> Iproniazid ('Masilid')
> Isocarboxizid ('Marplan')
> Nialamide ('Niamid')
> Mebanazine ('Actomol')
> [Pargyline ('Eutonyl')]

SOME DRUGS ARE PART OF THE DIET

Some components of ordinary meals are consumed for their drug effects. The big three are alcohol, coffee and tea. Alcohol is both a psychotropic agent and a source of dietary energy. Coffee and tea differ considerably. I used to be puzzled because older textbooks of nutrition estimated that the average cup of tea contains about the same amount of caffeine as a cup of coffee. (Davidson et al, 1972; Sinclair & Hollingsworth, 1969) while pharmacologists have emphasised that tea contains theophylline in addition (Ritchie, 1970). We measured the methylxanthines in cups of coffee and tea as people actually made them by a modern specific thin-layer chromatographic method. We found that a cup of coffee usually contains about 95mg caffeine whereas tea contains 43 to 92mg caffeine and negligible amounts of theophylline (Al-Samarrae et al, 1975).

SOME NUTRIENTS ARE USED AS DRUGS

Several of the essential nutrients are used in doses larger than the recommended dietary intake for their pharmacological action. Calcium, magnesium and iodine are obvious examples. Nicotinic acid is effective too in some types of hyperlipid-aemia (the dose is 100 times the nutrient requirement or more) and pyridoxine is used as an anti-emetic. Tryptophan has been shown in controlled trails to be effective as an antidepressant (Jensen et al, 1975).

There is a hazy borderline between therapeutics and nutrition and between scientifically established use and crankiness. There is no scientific reason why ordinary people should take vitamin E tablets for vitality or vitamin A to prevent sunburn (Drug & Therapeutic Bulletin 1975).

It is more difficult to be dogmatic about megavitamin therapy for mental disease – orthomolecular psychiatry (Pauling, 1968) and vitamin C to prevent colds. We now know there are inborn errors of vitamin metabolism (Davidson et al, 1975) and that several nutrients have effects on brain function. The idea that vitamin C may protect against respiratory infections is not new. In the 1930s it was said to prevent and to help in the treatment of pneumonia, tuber-culosis, whooping cough, tonsillitis, influenza and the common cold (Bicknell & Prescott, 1942). However, then as now there were difficulties with obtaining adequate controls. Korbsch (1938) produced shortening of symptoms with 1g of ascorbic acid but subsequently found results were as good with dummy tablets containing citric acid. Glazebrook & Thomson (1942) found no significant prophylactic effect in a controlled trial. I have records of 18 published trials; they differ in many ways – in numbers, ages and sex of subjects, duration of trial, doses of ascorbic acid, recording of symptoms and whether double blind or not. In just over half the authors concluded there was no significant difference but how can one compare a trial in 60 subjects and one with 2349 (Anderson et al, 1974)? The authors of the two best recent trials both conclude that their results (Anderson et al, 1974) and those of the best controlled trials together (Karlowski et al, 1975) are 'compatible with an effect of small magnitude from both the prophylactic and therapeutic regimes'. There may be more effects in females (Wilson & Loh, 1973: Coulehan et al, 1974). As the British Medical Journal put it 'Perhaps the most valuable outcome of the recent interest in ascorbic acid has been that it has stimulated research into the role of this vitamin in tissue healing and our defence mechanisms against disease' (Editorial, 1976). To some extent this means going back to where a lot of research in this area came to a stop with the Second World War and the beginning of the antibiotic era.

214

References

Al-Samarrae, W, Ma, M.C.F. & Truswell, A S (1975) *Proceedings of the Nutrition Society, 34,* 18A
Anderson, T W, Suranyi, G & Beaton, G H (1974) *Canadian Medical Association Journal, 111,* 31
Apantaku, J B, Afonja, O A & Boyo, A E (1975) *Tropical and Geographical Medicine, 27,* 418
Asatoor, A M, Levi, A J & Milne, M D (1963) *Lancet, 2,* 733
Balmer, S, Howells, G & Wharton, B (1970) *Journal of Tropical Pediatrics, 16,* 20
Barbezat, G & Hansen, J D L (1968) *Pediatrics, 42,* 77
Basu, T K & Dickerson, J W T (1974) *Chemico-Biological Interactions, 8,* 193
Basu, T K, Dickerson, J W T & Parke, D V (1975a) *Nutrition and Metabolism, 18,* 49
Basu, T K, Dickerson, J W T & Parke, D V (1975b) *Nutrition and Metabolism, 18,* 302
Bayliss, E M, Crowley, J M, Preece, J M, Sylvester, P E & Marks, V (1971) *Lancet, 1,* 62
Beare, J M (1968) *Prescribers' Journal, 8,* 30
Bender, A E, Damji, K B & Ismail, K S (1973) *Proceedings of the Nutrition Society, 32,* 73A
Bicknell, F & Prescott, F (1942) *The Vitamins in Medicine, pp 382-390.* London, Heinemann
Blacow, N W, & Wade, A (1972) *Martindale. The Extra Pharmacopoeia.* London, The Pharmaceutical Press
Briscoe, A M & Ragan, C (1963) *American Journal of Clinical Nutrition, 13,* 277
Buchanan, N, Robinson, R & Koornhof, H J (1976) *South African Medical Journal, 50* p.
Cahill, G F et al, (1972) *Proceedings of the Nutrition Society, 31,* 233
Callender, S T & Warner, G T (1969) *British Medical Journal, 4,* 532
Campbell, R H & Kosterlitz, H W (1948) *British Journal of Experimental Pathology, 29,* 149
Catt, K J (1971) *An ABC of Endocrinology.* London, Lancet
Century, B (1973) *Journal of Pharmacology and Experimental Therapeutics, 185,* 185
Chanarin, I & England, J M (1972) *British Medical Journal, 1,* 651
Christiansen, C Rodbro, P & Lund, M (1973) *British Medical Journal, 4,* 695
Coulehan, J L, Reisinger, K S, Rogers, K D & Bradley, D W (1974) *New England Journal of Medicine, 290,* 6
Craft, I L & Wise, I (1969) *Lancet, 2,* 1139
Crounse, R G (1961) *Journal of Investigative Dermatology, 37,* 529
Dargie, H J, Boddy, K, Kennedy, A C, King, P C, Read, P R & Ward, D M (1974) *British Medical Journal, 4,* 316
Davidson, S, Passmore, R & Brock, J F (1972) *Human Nutrition and Dietetics, 5th Ed.,* p.205. Edinburgh and London, Churchill Livingstone
Davidson, S, Passmore, R, Brock, J F & Truswell, A S (1975) *Human Nutrition and Dietetics, 6th Ed.,* pp 376 and 377. Edinburgh and London, Churchill Livingstone
Davis, J M (1972) *American Journal of Clinical Nutrition, 25,* 302
Davis, P S & Deller, D J (1967) *Gut, 8,* 198
Dent, C E, Richens, A & Rowe, D J F & Stamp, T C B (1970) *British Medical Journal, 4,* 69

Dickerson, J W T, Basu, T K, & Parke, D V (1976) *Journal of Nutrition, 106*, 258
Dixon, R L, Schultice, R W & Fouts, J R (1960) *Proceedings of the Society for Experimental Biology and Medicine, 103*, 333
Dobbins, W O, III (1968) *Gastroenterology, 54*, 1193
Douglas, A P (1974) *Adverse Drug Reaction Bulletin, No.48*, p.160
Drug and Therapeutics Bulletin, 1972, 10, 69
Drug and Therapeutics Bulletin, 1975, 13, 64
Editorial (1972a). *British Medical Journal, 3*, 370
Editorial (1972b) *Lancet, 2*, 805
Editorial (1974). *British Medical Journal, 1*, 168
Editorial (1976). *British Medical Journal, 1*, 606
Ershoff, B H (1974) *American Journal of Clinical Nutrition, 27*, 1395
El Tamtamy, S (1974) *Lancet, 1*, 929
England, J M & Coles, M (1972) *Lancet, 2*, 1341
Eyberg, C, Moodley, G P & Buchanan, N (1974) *South African Medical Journal, 48*, 2564
Fehling, C, Jägerstad, M, Lindstrand, K & Westesson, A-K (1973) *Clinical Science, 44*, 595
Gandra, Y R & Scrimshaw, N S (1961) *American Journal of Clinical Nutrition, 9*, 159
Gerson, C D, Hepner, G W, Brown, N, Cohen, N, Herbert, V & Janowitz, H D (1972) *Gastroenterology, 63*, 246
Glazebrook, A J & Thomson, S (1942) *Journal of Hygiene (Cambridge), 42*, 1
Greenberger, N J, Ruppert, R D & Cuppage, F E (1966) *Gastroenterology, 53*, 590
Greenberger, N J (1973) *American Journal of Clinical Nutrition, 26*, 104
Greenblatt, D J & Koch-Weser, J (1974) *European Journal of Clinical Pharmacology, 7*, 259
Greenwood, R H, Prunty, F T G & Silver, J (1973) *British Medical Journal, 1*, 643
Halsted, C H, Robles, E A & Mezey, E (1973) *Gastroenterology, 64*, 526
Herbert, V (1970) in Goodman, L S & Gilman, A (eds) *The Pharmacological Basis of Therapeutics, 4th Ed*, p.1399 London, Collier-Macmillan
Hoenig, V, Brodanova, M, Strejček, J & Kordač, V (1967) *Lancet, 1*, 387
Hunter, J, Maxwell, J D, Stewart, D A, Parsons V & Williams, R (1971) *British Medical Journal, 4*, 202
IAEA/USAID/WHO Joint Meeting (1975) *Control of Nutritional Anaemia with special reference to Iron Deficiency. WHO Technical Report series No.580.* Geneva, WHO
Jensen, K, Freunsgaard, K, Ahlfors, U-G, Pihkanen, T A, Tuomikoski, S, Ose, E, Dencker, S J, Lindberg, D & Nagy, A (1975) *Lancet, 2*, 920
Karlowsi, T R, Chalmers, T C, Frenkel, L D, Kapikian, A Z, Lewis, T L & Lynch, J M (1975) *Journal of the American Medical Association, 231*, 1038
Kato, R, Oshima, T & Tomizawa, S (1968) *Japanese Journal of Pharmacology, 18*, 356
Kato, R & Gillette, J R (1965) *Journal of Pharmacology and Experimental Therapeutics, 150*, 279 and 285
Kimberg, D V (1969) *New England Journal of Medicine, 280*, 1396
Klipstein, F A, Berlinger, F G & Reed, L J (1967) *Blood, 29*, 697
Koch-Weser, J & Sellers, E M (1976) *New England Journal of Medicine, 294*, 311 & 526

Korbsch, R (1938) *Medizinische Klinik, 45,* 1500
Korkeila, J (1971) *Lancet, 1,* 974
Krishnamurthy, K, Subramanya, T S & Jayaraj, P (1965) *Indian Journal of Experimental Biology, 3,* 168
Krondl, A (1970) *Canadian Medical Association Journal, 103,* 360
Kruse, R (1968) *Monatsschrift für Kinderheilkunde, 116,* 378
Lee, M, Harris, K & Trowbridge, H (1964) *Journal of Nutrition, 84,* 136
Longstreth, G F & Newcomer, A D (1975) *Mayo Clinic Proceedings, 50,* 284
McLean, A E M (1974) *Proceedings of the Nutrition Society, 33,* 197
McLean, A E M & Day, P A (1975) *Biochemical Pharmacology, 24,* 37
McLean, A E M & McLean, E K (1966) *Biochemical Journal, 100,* 564
McLean, A E M & Marshall, W J (1971) *Chemico-Biological Interactions, 3,* 294
McLean, A E M & Verschuuren, H G (1969) *British Journal of Experimental Pathology, 50,* 22
Malherbe, C, Burrill, K C, Levin, S R, Karam, J H & Forsham, P H (1972) *New England Journal of Medicine, 286,* 339
Mardell, M & Zilva, J F (1967) *Lancet, 2,* 1323
Marks, V (1974) *Proceedings of the Nutrition Society, 33,* 209
Marshall, W J & McLean, A E M (1971a) *Proceedings of the Nutrition Society, 30,* 66A
Marshall, W J & McLean, A E M (1971b) *Biochemical Journal, 122,* 569
Maxwell, J D, Hunter, J, Stewart, D A, Ardeman, S & Williams, R (1972) *British Medical Journal, 1,* 297
Miettinen, T A & Leskinen, E (1963) *Biochemical Pharmacology, 12,* 565
Parfitt, A M (1969) *New England Journal of Medicine, 281,* 55
Parke, D V (1968) *The Biochemistry of Foreign Compounds.* Oxford: Pergamon
Pauling, L (1968) *Science, 160,* 265
Peterson, P, Gray, P & Tolman, K G (1976) *Clinical Pharmacology and Therapeutics, 19,* 63
Porter, R J & Layzer, R B (1975) *Archives of Neurology, 32,* 298
Poskitt, E M E (1974) *Proceedings of the Nutrition Society, 33,* 203
Poskitt, E M E & Parkin, J M (1972) *Archives of Disease in Childhood, 47,* 626
Prandota, J & Pruitt, A W (1975) *Clinical Pharmacology and Therapeutics, 17,* 159
Quimby, C W, Jr (1972) *Anaesthesiology. A Manual of Concept and Management* p.172. London, Butterworths.
Reidenberg, M M & Vesell, E S (1975) *Clinical Pharmacology and Therapeutics, 17,* 650
Reynolds, E H (1973) *Lancet, 1,* 1376
Ritchie, J M (1970) in Goodman, L S & Gilman, A (eds) *The Pharmacological Basis of Therapeutics.* 4th Ed., p. 358. London, Collier-Macmillan
Roe, D A (1974) *Life Sciences, 15,* 1219
Scheiner, J & Altemeier, W A (1962) *Surgery, Gynaecology and Obstetrics, 114,* 9
Shils, M E (1963) *Annals of Internal Medicine, 58,* 389
Silver, J (1974) *Getting the Most out of Food, No.9,* p.69. London, Van den Berghs and Jurgens
Sinclair, H M & Hollingsworth, D F (1969) *Hutchinson's Food and the Principles of Nutrition, 12th Ed.,* p.468. London, Arnold
Singer, F R, Neer, R M, Murray, T M, Kentman, H T, Deftos, L J & Potts, J T, Jr. (1970) *New England Journal of Medicine, 283,* 634

Streiff, R R (1970) *Nournal of the American Medical Association 214*, 105
Temple, R, Berman, M, Carlson, H E, Robbins, J & Wolff, J (1972) *Mayo Clinic Proceedings, 47,* 872
Thalassinos, N & Joplin, G F (1968) *British Medical Journal, 3,* 14
Tolman, K G, Jubiz, W, Sannella, J J, Madsen, J A, Belsey, R E, Goldsmith, R S & Freston, J W (1975) *Pediatrics, 56,* 45
Torikai, T & Kumaoka, S (1956) *Lancet, 1,* 84
Truswell, A S (1973) *Update, 7,* 179
Truswell, A S (1974) *Proceedings of the Nutrition Society, 33,* 215
Truswell, A S (1975) in Olson, R E (ed) *Protein-Calorie Malnutrition,* p.412 New York & London: Academic Press
Waxman, S & Herbert, V (1969) *New England, Journal of Medicine, 280,* 1316
Wharton, B A & McChesney, E W (1970) *Journal of Tropical Pediatrics, 16,* 130
Wilson, C W M & Loh, H S (1973) *Lancet, 1,* 538

Weinstein, L (1970) in Goodman, L S & Gilman, A (eds) *The Pharmacological Basis of Therapeutics, 4th Ed.* p. 1270. New York: Collier-Macmillan

Upbringing, Appetite and Adult Obesity

J S GARROW
Clinical Research Centre, Watford, England

A young man who passes a routine medical inspection, but who is 10 kg over-weight, is much more likely to die before normal retiring age than a similar man who is of normal weight. It is of importance to life assurance companies to quantitate the extra risk associated with overweight, since if the person they insure is likely to die before the policy matures they must charge higher pre-miums to make a profit on the transaction. The data in Table I are taken from Haines and Blair (1966): the mortality ratio is expressed to a base of 100.

TABLE I. Analysis of Mortality Ratios by Weight, Age at Issue and Duration of Policy: where there were less than 25 deaths in an age/weight/policy year group, no value is shown. Data from Blair and Haines, 1966

Age at issue 15–34 years

Deviation from standard weight	Policy years: 16-20	21-25	26-30	31-34
−23 lb or more	102	78	80	95
−22 to −8 lb	77	76	91	98
−7 to + 7 lb	82	107	108	108
+8 to + 22 lb	166	131	115	94
+ 23 lb or more	137	184	143	−

The effect of excess weight on mortality in women is less marked than in men, but here too there is an increasing mortality with increasing excess weight. Obesity in adults is therefore a matter for concern, and it is important to know to what extent obesity in adults caused by early nutrition?

Several studies have shown that babies who grow rapidly in the first 6 months of life are more likely to be overweight at school entry than those who gain weight more slowly in the first few months. For example Eid (1970) found that 28 out of 138 infants with rapid weight gain were at least 10% overweight at the age of 6–8 years, but only 6 out of 86 infants who did not gain weight so rapidly were subsequently overweight. Statistical tests show that these differences are unlikely to have arisen by chance, but it should be noted that 110 of the 138 infants with early rapid weight gain were *not* subsequently overweight by 10%. Thus the fat baby is more likely to become a fat schoolchild, but this fate is by no means certain. Also, this study does not tell us if the adiposity of the babies was due to genetic trait or early feeding. A valuable investigation is that of Johnson et al (1973), who were able to investigate the relative contribution of genetic endowment and early nutrition in determining the subsequent obesity of the Zucker rat. The homozygote (fafa) is genetically obese, while the heterozygote (Fafa) is not. For the first three weeks of life baby rats were fed more, or less, than normal, and during this period weight gain was dictated by the diet. When the rats were offered stock diet ad libitum, the genotype expressed itself in the weight curve, so that by the age of 12 weeks the genetically obese were heavier than the heterozygotes, but within each genetic class there was a distinction according to the plane of early nutrition. These results may be interpreted to mean that the propensity to adult obesity depends on an interaction between genetic endowment and early nutrition. Since in clinical medicine we can do little about the genetic factors, I will concentrate on the effects of infant feeding, which we may hope to influence. Since obesity in adults is so difficult to cure, we should do whatever we can to prevent it (Editorial, 1974).

There are many hypotheses, but few indisputable facts, about the cause of adult obesity. One thing is certain: obesity results from a failure of energy balance. The adult who carries 10 kg of excess adipose tissue, which has an energy value of about 70,000 kcal, must at some time have ingested 70,000 more kcal than he expended. We also know that within groups of normal individuals, matched for age and sex, there is at least a two-fold range of energy intake (Widdowson, 1947), and the big eaters are not generally the more obese. Rose and Williams (1961) compared the metabolism of selected large and small eaters to see if they could account for the differences in energy requirements, and had some difficulty in matching the two groups for body weight, since the big eaters tended to be lighter than the small eaters. Similarly Ries (1973) compared the food intake of 123 men of normal weight with that of 221 overweight men, and found that 7 men who were more than 60% overweight had higher intakes than the average normal men, but the men with lesser degrees of overweight tended on average to eat less than normal. Among 130 women of normal weight and 552 overweight women the differences in intake on average were even less than among the men. The mystery which no-one has yet explained is how energy balance is usually controlled accurately in the face of these wide variations of intake between indi-

220

viduals, or from time to time in an individual. Edholm et al (1955) made meticulous measurements of the energy intake and expenditure of 12 military cadets over a period of 14 days, and showed that there was a very wide range within and between individuals, and only two of the 12 cadets balanced average daily intake and output within 150 kcal over the 14 day experiment.

However it is evident that almost everyone does balance intake and output of energy with an accuracy better than 150 kcal per day in the long run. Dr FW Fox is a distinguished nutritionist, and may well be a better energy regulator than most of us. He reported (Fox, 1973) that between 1953 and 1972 his weight had not strayed from the range 70.9 to 77.3 kg. If we assume that the difference between maximum and minimum weight is attributable to adipose tissue with an energy value of 7000 kcal per kg, this means a maximum error in balance of 44800 kcal. Over a span of 19 years this is an average difference between intake and output of less than 6.5 kcal per day.

At the opposite extreme is William Campbell, the British record holder for obesity, who died in 1878 in Newcastle at the age of 22 years. He weighed 340 kg, and was 191 cm tall, so making reasonable assumptions about his death, he seems to have acquired an excess of intake over output of about 1,750,000 kcal during his short life, an average daily excess of 218 kcal. To find the cause of adult obesity, therefore, we need to understand how energy balance is regulated to within about 1% of daily intake, since in the case of William Campbell an error of about 8% won him a place in the book of records, but brought him to an early death.

It is orthodox teaching that energy balance is controlled by two centres in the hypothalamus: a lateral 'hunger' centre and a ventomedial 'Satiety' centre. This dual centre theory is undergoing revision in the light of recent neurophysiological research. If the lateral nucleus in an experimental animal is damaged this will inhibit feeding, but it affects many other types of behaviour also. Amphetamine is a stimulant drug which is anorectic in the normal animal, but it will enhance feeding in an animal with a lateral hypothalamic lesion. The same effect may be achieved by pinching the animal's tail. It appears, therefore, that the lateral hypothalamic syndrome relates more to the state of arousal of the animal than to a true change in hunger. The ventromedial nucleus is also losing status as a satiety centre. Gold (1973) has shown by precise knifecut lesions that the damage to the nucleus did not contribute to the production of hypothalamic obesity, but that the effects which had been attributed to these lesions really involved the nearby ventral noradrenergic nerve tracts. Liebling et al (1975) have shown in rats that satiety is closely related to the contents of the duodenum, and the gut hormone cholecystokinin is probably the mediator of this response.

Recent research on the neurophysiology of hunger seems to indicate that the hypothalamus integrates a large amount of information from many different sources to determine food intake. For a recent review see Russek (1976) who has described an equation by which food intake can be modelled. The variables include the concentration in the blood of glucose, glucagon, insulin and adrenalin, the osmolarity and glycogen content of the body, the rate of glucose utilisation by the lateral hypothalamus, air temperature and body weight. All these factors can be shown experimentally to affect feeding in animals.

Hervy (1971) pointed out that most physiological control systems, and indeed many man-made control systems also, have a capacity to respond rapidly to a set of open-loop influences, but that long-term stability must depend on a closed-loop feedback which may operate quite slowly. The variables in Russek's equation indicate known short term influences, since if early nutrition does have an influence on adult obesity, it must be through the slow, closed-loop part of the control system. Specifically, it seems useful to examine two hypotheses about the nature of this closed loop which are independent but not contradictory: either or both might be true. One is succinctly stated by Hirsch (1975) "…. the hypothesis that obesity may be accompanied by an excessive number of adipocytes, possibly brought about by excess feeding in infancy and childhood, and that the excessive number of adipocytes remains constant and in some way causes a drive for maintaining the obese state." Another hypothesis was offered by Garrow (1974) "Energy intake is normally determined during infancy and childhood by the amount needed to satisfy hunger and support an acceptable growth rate. In adult life intake continues generally to follow the pattern established earlier in life, modified in the short term by the sensations of hunger and satiety. When energy imbalance occurs during adult life it is corrected by more or less conscious effort at a stage when the change in body weight is no longer acceptable."

Hypotheses can never be proved, but the more robustly they stand up to critical assault the more likely they are to be true. Hirsch's hypothesis has much supporting evidence. Excellent studies by Salans et al (1973) and Brook et al (1972) showed that in spontaneous obesity the earlier the onset the greater the number of fat cells, and Sims et al (1968) found that men rendered obese by experimental overfeeding did not have a measurable increase in fat cell number, but stored the excess fat by enlarging existing fat cells. However there is also some evidence against the hypothesis. Widdowson and Shaw (1973) pointed out that if piglets are undernourished from the age of 10 days and provided with plentiful food later, they become very fat: the longer the period of deprivation the fatter they tend to become. This is not consistent with the view that early nutrition determines fat cell number, and fat cell number determines later obesity.

We tried to test the hypothesis in several ways. Some obese patients give a clear history of the onset in adult life of obesity of massive degree: for example a woman who had certainly gained 40 kg in weight in the 6 years following her marriage at the age of 19 years. Her adipose tissue showed large cells, but not nearly large enough to accommodate all the extra fat she had acquired since the age of 19 unless there had also been an increase in cell number. However, this is not conclusive evidence of fat cell replication in an adult, since we cannot be sure that she was not fat as an infant, and that she had not replicated her adipocytes at that stage. A more direct test was to take fat biopsies from a normal adult, cause a gain in weight by overfeeding, and then to take further biopsies from the sites where fat had been laid down to see if we could detect new small fat cells. We reported this experiment (Ashwell & Garrow, 1973) and thought that we had shown development of new fat cells, but again the evidence was not conclusive, since with the techniques which we then used the small cells in the second biopsy might have been due to artefact. The critical test of the ability of an adult to make new fat cells would be to go on overfeeding a lean adult, with normal fat cell number, for a very long time. The time would come when all available fat cells would be as full as possible, and at that stage further overfeeding would result either in recruitment of new fat cells (which would disprove the hypothesis) or else in some other reaction which would prevent the further deposition of lipid. It is difficult to imagine what that reaction might be, but more difficult still to mount so heroic an experiment. The constancy of fat cell number in the adult is thus very difficult to prove or disprove, since everything hinges on the correct identification of an adipocyte when it does not contain fat (Widdowson & Shaw, 1973).

It is technically easier to test the proposition that the excessive number of fat cells causes a drive which maintains the obese state. The mechanism by which adipose hypercellularity might act to perpetuate the obese state is unknown (Salans, 1974), but it presumably involves a greater drive to eat. Whatever the mechanism, one would expect that hypercellular obese patients would be more resistant to treatment than those with a normal complement of fat cells. So far we have not found this to be so. Among 2333 women who answered a questionnaire about their efforts to lose weight, those who dated the onset of their obesity from childhood fared no worse than those of adult onset (Ashwell, 1975). This result might be influenced by the response rate of different types of obese women to postal questionnaires, but our observations on patients in hospital point in the same direction. The loss of weight of obese women on a known reducing diet under controlled conditions showed no advantage to those with fewer fat cells: on average the better losers had slightly more cells (Ashwell et al, 1975).

These observations do not disprove the hypothesis that excess feeding in infancy and childhood causes replication of extra adipocytes. The observation that fat children have many fat cells may mean that some children are genetically programmed to have many fat cells, and are hungry, and tend to get fat, or alternatively that the replication of the fat cells is a consequence of overfeeding rather than a cause of it. In practice it does not much matter which explanation is correct, since either way it is prudent to try to stop such children gaining weight excessively. The practical aspect is involved, however, in the second part of the hypothesis, since if the increased cell number perpetuates the obese state the clinician may despair of treating early onset obesity. If the doctor thinks the child with early onset obesity is doomed by his hyperplastic adipocytes this prophecy will become self-fulfilling. In the light of the present evidence such fatalism is unjustified.

The alternative hypothesis is the reverse of fatalistic: put in its most extreme form it says "You are as fat as you want to be." The main point on which it differs from the Hirsch hypothesis, and from the Russek equation, is that these postulate a 'set point' for body weight, which is defended with reference to some internal standard, as for example body temperature, or the concentration of most components of the blood are regulated. Obviously the constancy of plasma calcium concentration in normal people has nothing to do with voluntary effort: we do not know what our calcium concentration is, and could not alter it voluntarily if we wanted to. This is an example of true 'set point' physiological regulation, with no conscious component. In the case of body temperature the situation is less clear cut. There is certainly a 'set point' at about 37°C, and although some mystics may be able to move this set point by deep meditation, most of us cannot, and do not want to. However there is a conscious component in maintaining the set point temperature. We know when we are too hot or too cold, and act to correct the situation. Part of the response to cold is involuntary, like shivering and the erection of hair in fur-bearing mammals, and part of the response is voluntary, like seeking shelter or huddling together. The human species relies rather heavily on voluntary responses like putting on more clothing or turning up the central heating: if we are forced to rely on shivering and gooseflesh to defend outselves against cold we fare worse than most other animals. Our success as a species depends on the substitution of strategems for physiological responses, but now we rely on these strategems to preserve our homeostasis in situations where the physiological responses (such as shivering) would be inadequate.

Let us return now to the regulation of body weight, and the particular cases of Dr Fox and William Campbell. Dr Fox evidently has a set point around 74 kg, and has not deviated more than 4 kg from that for many years. It is hard to say where William Campbell's set point was: it might be argued that it was even higher than 340 kg, and he was still trying to reach it when he died. This illustrates the difficulty of testing the set point hypothesis, namely that you can only recognise someone's set point by the fact that their weight has been there for some time, without conscious effort. For example I thought my own set point was around 75 kg, since that has been my spontaneous weight for many years. In the experiment reported by Ashwell and Garrow (1973) I overate to increase my weight by 6 kg, to see if we could detect new fat cells, and it was quite hard work to get up to 81 kg, at which the second set of fat biopsies were taken. Although it had not been part of the original experimental design, it seemed interesting to see what would happen to my acquired adiposity: would my setpoint reassert itself and steer my weight back to 75 kg or so? I waited for 200 days, and this did not seem to be happening, so an alternative hypothesis arose. Had I now reset my set-point to 80 kg? Would it now be impossible to get back to 75 kg? Again the answer was no, and the results of this rather anecdotal experiment were reported by Garrow and Stalley (1975). Among the comments which I received was one from Dr Otto Edholm, one of the great contributors to the study of energy balance in man. He would bet, he said, that if I pushed my weight down by a similar amount it would spontaneously come up again.

At first I had little enthusiasm for this plan, but it happened that work with Dr David Halliday had shown that we could measure the rate of muscle protein turnover (Halliday & McKeran, 1975), and I was interested to see if we could establish a link between the fall in resting metabolic rate which occurs with rapid weight loss and a decrease in muscle protein turnover rate. Obviously we could do two experiments in one, so I lost weight by undereating, as Edholm had suggested, and when the second set of protein turnover measurements had been made I ate entirely according to inclincation, and was careful not to pay attention to any clue to weight change. Over the next year my weight was

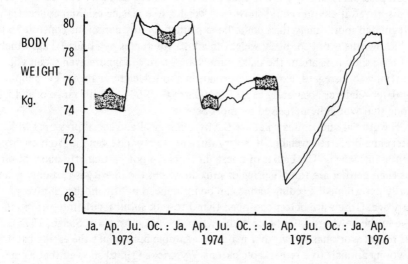

Figure 1. Fluctuations in the author's body weight over three years. The rapid changes were achieved by deliberate over- or under-eating. The stippled areas show the range of weight when the subject knew his weight but was not trying to alter it. The unshaded areas show the range when he was not trying to alter his weight, but was weighed 'blind'

recorded by Susan Stalley using a zero-muddler weighing machine, with the result shown in Figure 1. My weight drifted gradually upwards until it reached about 79 kg, at which stage I could not help noticing that clothing was tight, as it had been during the previous over-eating experiment in the latter part of 1973 and early 1974. Although I was not trying to stop a further increase, a little introspection showed that I was no longer eating as freely as before, and indeed weight

225

increase stopped at this point. The experiment in spontaneous regulation finished in March 1976, and the decrease in weight since then has been deliberate.

One should not found general theories on the experiences of individuals, but the following information emerges from the data in Figure 1. It seems that I have two preferred weights, one at about 75 kg which I have maintained for many years without conscious effort, and another some 5 kg higher at which I tend to stick even if I do not know my weight, since at that stage clothes become uncomfortably tight. Furthermore, having pushed my weight down by 69 kg by deliberate undereating, it spontaneously increased by 10 kg in the next 10 months. This is a level of energy imbalance of the same order as that calculated for William Campbell. An important difference between us is that I stopped at 79 kg and he did not.

I will now stop autobiographical reminiscence, and return to the influence of early nutrition on adult obesity. I am suggesting that adults regulate their body weight in relation to a set-point which is determined more by psychological and social pressures than by genetic endowment or fat cell number. This theory would be disproved if anyone could show that weight, like plasma calcium concentration, is regulated more finely than could be explained by any conscious control. So far as I know this is not so: body weight in adults fluctuates by about 10 kg, which, as I have shown, is about the maximum change you can ignore even when you are trying to disregard external information about weight change. Few people regulate weight as accurately as Dr Fox (Garrow, 1964), and his range of 6.4 kg is one that would be perceived by most people.

The crucial question is what are the psychological and social pressures which determine preferred weight? It is very difficult to separate genetic from environmental influence. The babies of obese mothers are not particularly obese at birth, but then neither are the offspring of mice in whom the obesity is certainly genetically determined. Feeding habits can be influenced by the mother at a very early age. Others are better equipped than I to talk about regulation of food intake in the newborn infant (see Widdowson, 1971; Ounstead & Sleigh, 1975), but recent work has shown that maternal example determines the eating habits of young animals to a remarkable extent. Wyrwicka (1976) showed that a cat could be induced to eat banana in preference to meat pellets by electrical stimulation of the brain, and that this behaviour was followed by her 2-month old kittens, even though the kittens had already acquired a natural preference for meat before they were put in the same cage as the mother cat whose choice had been perverted. Wyrwicka cites other examples to show that the mother's behaviour strongly influences the choice of food of the young. Hilda Bruch (1940) has been saying for many years that anxious, overprotective parents thrust food on their children at the least sign of distress, so they never learn to interpret the sensation of hunger in an appropriate manner, but equate food with consolation in any stressful situation. If babies are bottle fed it is easier to force food upon them, and it may be, as Hall (1975) suggests, that the changing composition of breast milk educates the appetite of the suckled infant, but not the bottle fed infant.

This is not intended to be a balanced review but as a basis for discussion. Elsewhere I have written (Garrow, 1974) about the metabolic adaptation to changes in energy intake, but which I still believe to be important. My proposition about the relationship of upbringing, appetite and adult obesity is this: long-term control of body weight in man depends on voluntary effort to maintain it within a desirable range, and short-term control of energy balance permits imbalances of 200 kcal per day, which in the long term would be disastrous. It is likely that one of the important effects of feeding patterns in infancy and childhood is to influence appetite and the psychological 'set point' for body weight which will ultimately determine whether the adult finds it easy or difficult to remain within the 'desirable range' of weights defined by life assurance companies.

References

Ashwell, MA (1975) *British Journal of Nutrition, 34,* 201

Ashwell, M and Garrow, JS (1973) *Lancet, i,* 1021

Ashwell, MA, Priest, P, Bondoux, M and Garrow, JS (1975) *Proceedings of the Nutrition Society, 34,* 85A

Blair, BF and Haines, LW (1966) *Transactions Actuarial Society of America, 18,* 35

Brook, CGD, Lloyd, JK and Wolf, OH (1972) *British Medical Journal, 2,* 25

Bruch, H (1940) *American Journal of Diseases in Childhood, 59,* 739

Edholm, OG, Fletcher, JG, Widdowson, EM and McCance, RA (1955) *British Journal of Nutrition, 9,* 286

Eid, EE (1970) *British Medical Journal, 2,* 74

Editorial (1974) *Lancet, i,* 17

Fox, FW (1973) *Lancet, ii,* 1487

Garrow, JS (1974) *Energy Balance and Obesity in Man.* North Holland Publishing Co, Amsterdam. Page 25

Garrow, JS and Stalley, SF (1975) *Proceedings of the Nutrition Society, 34,* 84A

Gold, RM (1973) *Science, 182,* 488

Hall, B (1975) *Lancet, i,* 779

Halliday, D and McKeran, RO (1975) *Clinical Science and Molecular Medicine, 49,* 581

Hervey, GR (1971) *Proceedings of the Nutrition Society, 30,* 109

Hirsch, J (1975) In *Childhood Obesity.* (Ed) M Winick. John Wiley, New York. Page 15.

Johnson, PR, Stern, JS, Greenwood, MRC, Zucker, LM and Hirsch, J (1973) *Journal of Nutrition, 103,* 738

Leibling, DS, Eisner, JD, Gibbs, J and Smith, GP (1975) *Journal of Comparative and Physiological Psychology, 89,* 955

Ounstead, M and Sleigh, G (1975) *Lancet, i,* 1393

Reis, W (1973) *Proceedings of the Nutrition Society, 32,* 187

Rose, GA and Williams, RT (1961) *British Journal of Nutrition, 15,* 1

Russek, M (1976) In *Hunger: Basic Mechanisms and Clinical Implications.*

(Ed) D Novin, W Wyrwicka and G Bray. Raven Press, New York. Page 327
Salans, LB (1974) In *Treatment and Management of Obesity.* (Ed) GA Bray and
JE Bethune. Harper and Row, Hagerstown. Page 17
Salans, LB, Cushman, SW and Weissman, RE (1973) *Journal of Clinical
Investigation, 52,* 929
Sims, EAH, Goldman, RF, Gluck, CM, Horton, ES, Kelleher, PC and Rowe, DW
(1968) *Transactions of the Association of American Physicians, 81,* 153
Widdowson, EM (1947) *Special Report Series of the Medical Research, No 257.*
HMSO, London
Widdowson, EM (1971) *Proceedings of the Nutrition Society, 30,* 127
Widdowson, EM and Shaw, WT (1973) *Lancet, ii,* 905
Wrywicka, W (1976) In *Hunger: Basic Mechanisms and Clinical Implications.*
(Ed) D Novin, W Wyrwicka and G Bray. Raven Press, New York. Page 203

Can the Choice Foods During Childhood Affect the Time of Onset of Degenerative Diseases in Later Life?

A S TRUSWELL
Queen Elizabeth College, London, England

The main purpose of this paper is to consider how the food given to and selected by babies and children may influence their development of degenerative disease later in life. I propose to concentrate on the problem of whether paediatricians are responsible for preventing atherosclerotic diseases or not. I shall then discuss the possible role of nutrition as one factor determining longevity.

ATHEROSCLEROSIS AS A PAEDIATRIC PROBLEM

At What Age Does Atherosclerosis Start?

A large proportion (77%) of a sample of American soldiers killed in battle in the Korean war had some degree of atherosclerosis in their coronary arteries and 15% of the sample had considerable narrowing as assessed by conventional post-mortem examination (Enos et al, 1953). If these findings are representative of the whole population in the USA and not the result of the stress of war, they suggest that atherosclerosis is well established by the early twenties in western industrial men. However this is not a new phenomenon; Monckeberg (1915) looked for atherosclerosis at post-mortem examination in 65 combatants (mostly German) in the First World War: he reported "nearly 9 out of 20 men in the prime of life show atherosclerosis of the aorta or the coronary arteries or of both vessels". This was before the modern epidemic of coronary heart disease (CHD). American battle victims in the Vietnam war were examined by McNamara et al (1971). Although 45% showed some degree of coronary atherosclerosis, post-mortem angiography demonstrated functional stenosis in only one of 105 autopsies and this was not severe. It is not enough to talk about atherosclerosis; it must be des-

TABLE I. Fatty Streaks at Autopsy in Males from 6 Different Countries or Ethnic Groups. Aorta and Coronary Arteries*

Location and ethnic group	10–14 years		15–19 years		20–24 years		25–29 years		30–34 years		35–39 years	
	aorta	coronary	aorta	coronary	aorta	coronary	aorta	coronary	aorta	coronary	aorta	coronary
New Orleans white	100	40	100	78	100	95	100	100	100	98	100	100
New Orleans negro	94	67	100	83	100	94	100	99	100	100	100	100
Santiago	100	34	100	89	100	81	100	91	100	96	100	96
Costa Rica	100	32	100	66	100	72	100	92	100	88	100	96
Guatemala	100	18	100	47	100	64	100	79	100	86	100	91
Durban Bantu	95	25	100	65	100	81	100	91	100	95	100	97

*Source Strong and McGill, 1969

TABLE II. Raised Atherosclerotic Lesions at Autopsy in Males. Coronary Arteries by Age from 6 Countries/Ethnic Groups. Cases = percent of all cases of this age with any such lesion. Area = average percent of intima = affect by these lesions

Location and ethnic group	10–14 years		15–19 years		20–24 years		25–29 years		30–34 years		35–39 years	
	cases	area	cases	area	cases	area	cases	area	cases	area	cases	area
New Orleans white	0	0	7	1	44	3	71	11	78	16	86	24
New Orleans negro	22	0	22	0	34	2	44	4	54	6	81	13
Santiago	0	0	10	0	18	0	29	1	53	3	57	6
Costa Rica	0	0	7	0	15	1	21	1	43	3	60	4
Guatemala	0	0	7	0	23	1	21	1	35	2	38	4
Durban Bantu	5	0	12	0	17	0	31	2	54	3	45	4

cribed and graded by quantitative and reproducible techniques.

Coronary and cerebral lesions must be considered separately from those in the aorta, and raised lesions of atherosclerosis from fatty streaks. The International Atherosclerosis Project examined 23,000 sets of coronary arteries and aortas from post-mortems in 14 different countries by standardised methods (Guzman et al, 1968). This study showed that almost everyone has aortic fatty streaks by age 10 and most people have some fatty streaks in the coronary arteries by age 20 (Strong & McGill, 1969 — Table I). Raised atherosclerotic lesions start to appear in the coronary arteries after the age of 15 but their frequency and extent in different populations do not correspond with the relative rates of coronary *disease* until the early twenties in men (Table II) and the late twenties in women. It appeared that coronary fatty streaks sometimes develop into raised atherosclerotic lesions but this does not always happen and occurred more frequently in New Orleans Whites than in the Negroes. Unlike the aorta (Schwartz & Mitchell, 1962) the distributions of coronary fatty streaks and raised lesions are similar in the arteries (McGill, 1968).

In the aorta there are histological and chemical differences between fatty streaks and raised atherosclerotic lesions. In fatty streaks the lipid is mostly intracellular (Smith et al, 1967), consists predominantly of cholesterol esters rich in oleic acid, low in linoleic acid, with a raised C20:3 (Smith et al, 1968) and is not associated with low density lipoprotein (Smith & Slater, 1972). These features contrast with those of mature atherosclerosis and it is thought that the lipids in fatty streaks are synthesised in situ. A histological study showed more frequent leucocytic infiltration of aortic fatty streaks in populations that develop extensive raised lesions (Restrepo & Tracy, 1975) and incidentally that mural thrombosis is very rarely associated with fatty streaks. When it becomes possible to make studies like these in coronary arteries it will be easier to state the frequency distribution of onset of atherosclerosis. On present evidence it starts at about the age of 20 years in western males but appears to be labile and reversible for some years after this.

The situation is different in young people with familial hypercholesterolaemia. Atherosclerosis appears prematurely (Roberts et al, 1973) and this is greatly exaggerated in homozygotes (Starzl et al, 1973).

Coronary Disease Risk Factors in Childhood

The major risk factors, established in several prospective studies (all with adults) are hypercholesterolaemia, hypertension, cigarette smoking, lack of exercise, obesity, diabetes mellitus and possibly hypertriglyceridaemia.

Surveys of plasma cholesterol in school children have been reported from Evans County, Georgia, USA (Hames & Greenberg, 1961), Brusselton, South Africa (du Plessis et al, 1967), Australia (Godfrey et al, 1972), Tucson, Arizona, USA (Friedman & Goldberg, 1973) and from the Netherlands (Hautvast et al,

1975). In Brusselton the median value at 6 years was 160 mg and at 17 years was 183 mg per 100 ml. (the latter corresponds to our own experience — Truswell & Mann, 1972). Of nearly 1,300 children, 13% had cholesterols above 200mg, 2.5% above 238 mg and 0.5% above 270 mg/100 ml. Friedman and Goldberg (1973) note that the frequency distribution was skewed towards the upper end in their children. In some studies higher values can be seen in girls than boys early in puberty (De Lange & Theron, 1960; Lund et al, 1961; Johnson, 1965). In the Netherlands, Hautvast et al (1975) have found higher values in one town (Roermond) in the south than another (Heerenven) in the north. The town with higher cholesterols has a higher CHD mortality.

In infants plasma cholesterol is higher in breast fed babies than in bottle fed; the difference between breast fed babies and those on filled milks high in polyunsaturated fats is striking (Darmady et al, 1972; Fomon, 1971). Potter and Nestel (1976) however, changed the plasma cholesterols in a small group of infants from a mean of 185 to 157 mg/100 ml by changing their mothers from diets high in meat and dairy produce to polyunsaturated oils.

By far the most important type of hyperlipidaemia in childhood is familial hypercholesterolaemia (type II). Screening by cord blood total cholesterol proposed by Glueck et al (1971) or cord blood LDL (Kwiterovich et al, 1973) have not been found reliable by others (Darmady et al, 1972; Ose, 1975). Type II can usually be recognised by one year of age and the prevalence is about 1 to 2% of the population in western countries (Drash, 1972).

Hypertriglyceridaemia is uncommon in childhood (Fredrickson et al, 1967) though Fallat et al (1974) report that a minority of the offspring of adults with type IV have some degree of hypertriglyceridaemia. The proportion increased from 10% in the first decade, to about 20% in the second and to over 50% in the fourth decade of life. Most children with hypertriglyceridaemia are obese. Familial hypertriglyceridaemia cannot be diagnosed in cord blood (Truswell, 1973): the hyperlipaemia which may occur at this time reflects intrauterine nutrition (Fosbrooke & Wharton, 1973) and intra-partum and intra-uterine hypoxia and stress (Tsang & Glueck, 1974).

Those with experience report that the plasma cholesterol in patients with heterozygous type II hyperlipidaemia can be reduced by from 12% (Fallat et al, 1974) to 20% (Lloyd et al, 1975) on appropriate diets. The latter group reported that addition of polyunsaturated oil to a low fat diet had no additional cholesterol-lowering effect in these children (Segall et al, 1970). Adequate treatment of homozygous type II is very difficult even with diet and multiple drugs (Ahrens, 1974). In normal teenage boarding school children, workers at Harvard and in the Netherlands have shown that it is quite feasible to lower plasma cholesterol by 15% (Ford et al, 1972) or more (Vergroesen, 1972) mainly by reducing the intake of saturated fats and replacing them partially (Ford et al, 1972) or completely (Vergroesen, 1972) with polyunsaturated fats.

Family studies by Zinner et al (1971) suggest that the process of hypertension in adult life could possibly be predicted from the blood pressure pattern in youth. Most prospective studies of hypertension in adults also reveal that, despite its high prevalence, few entirely new cases evolve among normotensive patients after age 30 (Kannel & Dawber, 1972). Hypertension is one of the three major risk factors for CHD but treatment of established hypertension appears to have little effect on CHD, though it does reduce strokes (Veterans Administrative Cooperative Study Group, 1970). This indicates the importance of prevention or early treatment of hypertension.

Between communities and with repeated measurements in individuals there appears to be a relationship between salt intake and blood pressure (Dahl, 1972; Truswell et al, 1972; Joossens, 1973). The salt in baby foods should be strictly limited (Working Party on the Panel on Child Nutrition, 1974) and paediatricians should discourage the common habit of adding salt to childhood diets (Kannel & Dawber, 1972).

The number of children who do not get regular vigorous exercise has recently increased and so has the number of smokers *in* school.

What Action Should be Taken in Childhood to Reduce or Delay CHD

There are, broadly, four possible strategies.

1. Case finding by routinely examining the children of patients with early CHD, with hypertension or hyperlipidaemia. This approach was recommended by the subcommittee on Atherosclerosis of the Council of Rheumatic Fever and Congenital Heart Disease of the American Heart Association (Mitchell et al, 1972) and is now recommended by the Joint Working Party of the Royal College of Physicians of London and the British Cardiac Society (RCP + BCS, 1976).

2. Routine screening of plasma cholesterol and blood pressure in children. Since cord blood is unreliable this strategy is not generally considered practical at present. It is not recommended by the RCP + BCS (1976).

3. Health education in childhood. The principal components of this should be advised to avoid high consumption of saturated fat and to limit salt, to take regular exercise, to avoid obesity and not start smoking. This is recommended by the RCP + BCS (1976).

4. Either going easy on the advice above (3) during childhood and then introducing it or intensifying it for school leavers. This is the age when food is no longer needed for growth but dairy food consumption is often very high (McGandy,1971; Atkinson et al, 1972), when facilities and time for exercise are not routinely provided, when people start to smoke, plasma cholesterol increases in man and the pace of development of atherosclerosis speeds up. At the same time people in their early twenties are probably less interested in advice from an older generation about their health than at any other age in life. The NIH/MIT conference on nutrient requirement in adolescence thought that "the most appropriate time to apply preventive measures and to provide nutritional education is during adolescence. The two problems of atherosclerosis and obesity raise the question whether there should be a recommended dietary maximum as well as a recommended dietary allowance for some nutrients" (McKigney & Munro, 1975).

Diet and Longevity

McCay et al (1943) first showed that rats fed on restricted rations throughout life live for longer than animals eating ad libitum. However the rats were under-weight, small in size and sexual maturity was delayed or suppressed. Subsequently there have been further instructive results in this field of work. Ross (1972) has shown that if rats are fed a restricted ration (6g food/day) from 21 to 70 days and then fed ad lib they live 19% longer. If they are fed ad lib until 70 days and then restricted they live 65% longer. Both these groups of restricted rats ended up weighing 200g. When food restriction was started after 300 days, mortality increased unless the restriction was less severe (8g food/day), which permitted an increased life span. Berg & Simms (1961) were able to extend the life span in rats from 800 to 1000 days by restricting their food to 54% of ad libitum. The diets were started at 4 weeks and were qualitatively normal (e.g. 24% protein). Restricted males weighed about 250g and their length was 22 cm as against 350g or more and 25 cm in males fed ad libitum. The restricted rats were healthy and active and had a high rate of fertility; they had lower incidences of all degenerative diseases, including tumours. To carry out such experiments in man would take 60—80 years and this doesn't fit the career structure or funding arrangements for medical research. Dr Alex Comfort (1972) proposed that useful human results could probably now be obtained in 5 to 10 years given sufficient funds, by using a battery of biochemical and physiological tests that reflect the process of ageing.

Meanwhile there appear to be some experiments of nature. In three different parts of the world centenarians are much more common than their rate of about 3 in 100,000 in the USA. The places are the Hunza Province of Pakistan, parts of Georgia and Azerbaijan in southern USSR and Vilcabamba in the highlands of Ecuador. Leaf (1973), a Harvard physician, has visited all three places. The ages seem most secure in Vilcabamba because baptisms are recorded in the local church but this is a very small pocket of longevity. Diets are frugal and predominantly vegetarian in Hunza and Vilcabamba. Estimated averages for Hunza are 1923 kcal, 50g protein, 36g fat (largely apricot seed oil), with only 1% meat and dairy products per day in adult men (Leaf, 1973); and in Vilcabamba corresponding figures (apparently for men *and* women) are 1200 kcal, 37g protein, 17g fat (mostly vegetable) per day. The people do hard physical work in the fields all their lives and there is no obesity in Hunza or Vilcabamba. Things are somewhat different in Georgia. The people eat well, enjoy occasional banquets, milk is the main source of protein, and wine is plentiful. Some of the old people are obese and many of them smoked. It is hard to understand how a way of life like this can be associated with unusual longevity. Food was not always so plentiful during these people's lifetime and Medvedev (1974) thinks the ages have become exaggerated in the SS Republic of Georgia. He suggests that there is a cult of old people in Georgia, which has become incorporated into state propaganda. Medvedev is a gerontologist who used to work in Russia.

Considering the animal experiments and at least two of these apparently long-lived human communities we must seriously wonder whether maximal growth rates throughout childhood, achievement of the full genetic potential for height and widespread mild obesity in adult life are not having an adverse influence on the life expectancy of our western industrial populations. But the animals lived in pathogen-free environments and the long-living human groups live in rural mountainous areas away from tropical infections and industrial pollution. So this idea is based on much less evidence and is far more speculative than the conclusions about coronary heart disease.

References

Ahrens, EH Jr (1974) *Lancet, ii,* 449
Atkinson, SJ, Nicholas, P and Wyn-Jones, C (1972) *Proceedings of the Nutrition Society, 31,* 82A
Berg, BN and Simms, HS (1961) *Journal of Nutrition, 74,* 23
Comfort, A (1972) *New Scientist, 30 March,* 689
Dahl, LK (1972) *American Journal of Clinical Nutrition, 25,* 231
Darmady, JM, Fosbrooke, AS and Lloyd, JK (1972) *Lancet, ii,* 685
De Lange, DJ and Theron, JJ (1968) *Proceedings of the Nutrition Society of South Africa, 1,* 71
Drash, A (1972) *Journal of Pediatrics, 80,* 693
du Plessis, JP, Vivier, FR and De Lange, DJ (1967) *South African Medical Journal, 41,* 1216
Enos, WF, Holmes, RH and Beyer, J (1953) *Journal of the American Medical Association, 152,* 1090
Fallat, RW, Tsang, RC and Glueck, CJ (1974) *Preventive Medicine, 3,* 390
Fomon, SJ (1971) *Bulletin of the New York Academy of Medicine, 47,* 569
Ford, CH, McGandy, RB and Stare, FJ (1972) *Preventive Medicine, 1,* 426
Fosbrooke, AS and Wharton, BA (1973) *Biology of the Neonate, 23,* 330
Fredrickson, DS, Levy, RI and Lees, RS (1967) *New England Journal of Medicine, 276,* 32, 94, 148, 215, 273
Friedman, G and Goldberg, SJ (1973) *Journal of the American Medical Association, 225,* 610
Godfrey, RC, Stenhouse, NS, Cullen, KJ and Blackman, V (1972) *Australian Paediatric Journal, 8,* 72
Greten, H, Wengler, H and Wagner, H (1973) *Nutrition and Metabolism, 15,* 128
Guzman, MA, McMahan, CA, McGill, HC Jr, Strong, JP, Tejada, C, Restrepo, C, Eggen, DA, Robertson, WB and Solberg, LA (1968) *Laboratory Investigation, 18,* 19
Hames, CG and Greenberg, BG (1961) *American Journal of Public Health, 51,* 374
Hautvast, JGAJ, van der Haar, F and Kromhout, D (1975) *Paper presented at X International Congress of Nutrition, Kyoto*

Johnson, BC, Epstein, FH and Kjelsberg, MO (1965) *Journal of Chronic Diseases, 18,* 147

Joint Working Party of the Royal College of Physicians of London and the British Cardiac Society (1976) *Journal of the Royal College of Physicians, 10,* 260

Joosens, JV (1973) *Triangle, 12,* 9

Kannel, WB and Dawber, TR (1972) *Journal of Pediatrics, 80,* 544

Kwiterovich, PO Jr, Levy, RI and Fredrickson, DS (1973) *Lancet, i,* 118

Leaf, A (1973) *Nutrition Today, 8,* 4

Lloyd, JK, Fosbrooke, AS, West, R and Wolff, OH (1975) *British Medical Journal, 1,* 35

Lund, E, Geill, T and Andresen, PH (1961) *Lancet, ii,* 1383

McCay, CM, Sperling, G and Barnes, LL (1943) *Archives of Biochemistry, 2,* 469

McGandy, RB (1971) *Bulletin of the New York Academy of Medicine, 47,* 590

McGill, HC Jr (1968) *Laboratory Investigation, 18,* 100

McKigney, JI and Munro, HN (1975) *Nöringsforskning, 19,* 121

McNamara, JJ, Molot, MA, Stremple, JF and Cutting, RT (1971) *Journal of the American Medical Association, 216,* 1185

Medvedev, ZA (1974) *The Gerontologist, 14,* 381

Mitchell, S, Blount, SG Jr, Blumenthal, S, Jesse, MJ and Weidman, WH (1972) *Pediatrics, 49,* 165

Monckeberg, JG (1915) *Zentralblatt für Herz und Gefasskrankheiten, 7,* 7

Ose, L (1975) *Lancet, ii,* 615

Potter, JM and Nestel, PJ (1976) *American Journal of Clinical Nutrition, 29,* 34

Roberts, WC, Ferrans, VJ, Levy, RI and Fredrickson, DS (1973) *American Journal of Cardiology, 31,* 557

Ross, MH (1972) *American Journal of Clinical Nutrition, 25,* 834

Restrepo, C and Tracy, RE (1975) *Atherosclerosis, 21,* 179

Segall, MM, Fosbrooke, AS, Lloyd, JK and Wolff, OH (1970) *Lancet, i,* 641

Schwartz, CJ and Mitchell, JRA (1962) *Circulation Research, 11,* 63

Smith, EB and Slater, RS (1972) *Lancet, i,* 463

Smith, EB, Evans, PH and Downham, MD (1967) *Journal of Atherosclerosis Research, 7,* 171

Smith, EB, Slater, RS and Chu, PK (1968) *Journal of Atherosclerosis Research, 8,* 399

Starzl, TE, Chase, HP, Putnam, CW and Porter, KA (1973) *Lancet, ii,* 940

Strong, JP and McGill, HP Jr (1969) *Journal of Atherosclerosis Research, 9,* 251

Truswell, AS (1973) *British Medical Journal, 4,* 490

Truswell, As, Kennelly, BM, Hansen, JDL and Lee, RB (1972) *American Heart Journal, 84,* 5

Truswell, AS and Mann, JI (1972) *Atherosclerosis, 16,* 15

Tsang, R and Glueck, CJ (1974) *American Journal of Diseases of Children, 127,* 78

Vergroesen, AJ (1972) *Proceedings of the Nutrition Society, 31,* 323

Veterans Administration Cooperative Study Group (1970) *Journal of the American Medical Association, 213,* 1152

Working Party of the Panel on Child Nutrition, Committee on Medical Aspects of Food Policy (1974) *Present day Practice in Infant Feeding. Department of Health and Social Security Report on Health and Social Subjects No 9.* HMSO, London

Zinner, SH, Levy, PS and Kass, EH (1971) *New England Journal of Medicine, 284,* 401